INTERNATIONAL LAW
Second Edition

By

Sherri L. Burr
Professor of Law
University of New Mexico

Mat #40603411

Sum & Substance Quick Review of International Law is a publication of West

© West, a Thomson business, 2006
© 2008 Thomson/West
     610 Opperman Drive
     St. Paul, MN 55123
     1-800-313-9378
Printed in the United States of America

ISBN: 978-0-314-18086-5

TEXT IS PRINTED ON 10% POST CONSUMER RECYCLED PAPER

TABLE OF CONTENTS

DEDICATION

DEDICATION —

I dedicate this book to my brothers who have served in the United States military, and to my public international law teachers W. Michael Reisman and Richard Falk. Thank you for all that you taught me over the years.

Sherri Burr

PREFACE

Students should be aware of the distinction between public international law, the focus of this book, and private international law. Public international law governs relations between and among states. It is state-centered. Private international law governs relations between individuals, between and among corporations, and between corporations and states in their international transactions. The relationship is private in nature.

Thus, if the Coca-Cola Bottling Company, a U.S. based company, decides to set up a factory in Colombia, it engages in international business transactions. Private international law and the state law of Colombia and the United States would regulate this transaction, as it concerns commercial entities. If on the other hand, the U.S. government provides assistance to the government of Colombia in an effort to combat cocaine trafficking, public international law governs this interaction between two states.

The two types of law may overlap when a public entity, like the government of Nigeria, contracts with a private company to import cement for constructing government businesses. In one well known case, *Texas Trading & Milling Corp. v. Fed. Republic of Nigeria*, 647 F.2d 300 (2d Cir. 1981), **cert. denied**, 454 U.S. 1148 (1982), a U.S. company sued Nigeria after it canceled cement contracts and refused to pay. Nigeria claimed sovereign immunity, the prerogative of states not to be sued against their wishes. The Second Circuit said, however, that when Nigeria entered into the contracts, it was engaging in a commercial activity. Because Nigeria acted more like a private company than a public entity in its relationship with the Texas Trading & Milling Corp., the state could not claim sovereign immunity to shield its actions from legal liability.

Sovereign immunity issues are addressed herein and they also crop up in books related to private international law or international business transactions. This book reviews a number of issues related to states as public entities. It will cover state relationships with each other, with individuals (usually their citizens or the nationals of other states), and with international organizations.

Sherri Burr

ACKNOWLEDGEMENTS

Professor Burr thanks former Princeton Professor Richard Falk and former University of New Mexico School of Law Dean Ted Parnall for reading chapters and providing expert commentary. She also thanks University of New Mexico law students Alberto Casas and Michael Lane for their research assistance.

Professor Burr expresses gratitude to the following students who read a draft of the 2006 edition while studying International Law during the fall of 2005 at the University of New Mexico: Edward Burch, Douglas Carver, Sol Davis, Christopher Frey, Kaili Gordon, Courtney Jakowatz, Edward Kelley, Anna Lehnert, Ramona Martinez, David Meilleur, Christa Okon, Rae Ann Red Owl, Renee Ruybal, Noel Schaefer, Rebecca Shreve, Pam Stokes, Niki Tantalou, and Stephen Vigil. These students' questions and comments led to many revisions of the 2006 edition.

Professor Burr also expresses appreciation to University of New Mexico secretaries Barbara Jacques and Nancy Huffstutler, and word processing assistant Joseph Blecha. The following students and staff provided some cite-checking assistance through the University of New Mexico Library research pool: Tyler Atkins, Eileen Cohen, Lisa Collins, Lorraine Lester, Elaine Lujan, Marcos Perales, Renee Ruybal, Rebecca Shreve, and Ron Wheeler. Many thanks to law librarian Sherri Thomas who researched new international law cases for the 2008 edition, and to third-year law student Amy Williams who assisted with proofreading the 2008 edition.

ABOUT THE AUTHOR —

Professor Sherri Burr has taught International Law at the University of New Mexico School of Law since 1988. She has also taught International Business Transactions, International Entertainment & Sports Law, and International Entertainment Law as a visiting professor during summer programs in Barcelona, Spain; Guanajuato, Mexico; Innsbruck, Austria; and Honolulu, Hawaii.

xvii

In addition, Professor Burr has lectured in countries as diverse as Barbados, Japan, Canada, Greece, Chile, France, Mexico, South Africa and Spain. Her public service includes serving as a president of the International Law Section of the Association of American Law Schools and as a member of the Executive Council of both the American Society of International Law and the International Law Society (American Branch).

Professor Burr is a graduate of Yale Law School, Mount Holyoke College, and Princeton's Woodrow Wilson School of Public and International Affairs. From the latter, she obtained a masters degree in public affairs with a concentration in international relations.

She is the author or co-author of the following books: *Sum & Substance* Audio Book on *International Law* (Thomson West 2006); *Entertainment Law: Cases and Materials in Film, Television and Music* (with Henslee) (Thomson West 2004); Teacher's Manual for *Entertainment Law* (with Henslee) (Thomson West 2004); *Entertainment Law in a Nutshell* (Thomson West 2004); *Entertainment Law in a Nutshell* 2nd Edition (Thomson West 2007), *Art Law: Cases and Materials* (with DuBoff and Murray) (William S. Hein & Co. 2004); *Wills and Trusts in a Nutshell 3rd Edition* (with Mennell) (Thomson West 2007); and *Sum & Substance* Audio Book on *Entertainment Law* (Thomson West 2008). She has also published numerous law journal articles and has been a columnist for four different publications. The 2006 edition of the *Quick Review of International Law* won first place in the 2007 New Mexico Press Women contest and second place in the 2007 National Press Women contest for best nonfiction instructional book.

Professor Burr is a photographer who has exhibited her work in an art gallery and published in magazines and newspapers.

CHAPTER I

I. What is International Law?

A. International Law Covers Three Broad Areas [§1]

This body of law is sometimes referred to as the law of nations. It governs the relations between and among states; the relations between states and individuals, addressing issues related to nationality, international crimes, and human rights; and the relations between states and international organizations. All of these relations take place on a global scale, requiring international rules.

This book first introduces the historic foundations of international law, which grew out of wars between and among European states, and between European states and the indigenous peoples they discovered on other continents. This book then examines the role of states in the international arena, which includes state formation, state succession, and governmental changes.

Next, this book outlines the sources of international law, and how international law is made. The Statute of the International Court of Justice, 59 Stat. 1055, T.S. 993, 3 Bevans 1179 (hereinafter "Statute of the I.C.J."), permits the I.C.J. to apply four major sources of law to resolve disputes in contentious cases between two or more states, or to issue advisory opinions at the request of an organ of the United Nations. International conventions or treaties may be considered as contracts between two or more states or between states and international organizations, which establish rules to govern general or specific relationships between them. International customary law developed through the general practice among states, which they accept as law. General principles of law are those recognized and applied by civilized nations and can be found in varied legal systems throughout the world. Judicial decisions and the teachings of qualified publicists or scholars can also inform the I.C.J.'s opinions. There is no *stare*

1

decisis application of law in the I.C.J. The term is Latin and means, "to stand by that which is decided." The I.C.J.'s opinions apply only to the parties before it. Nevertheless, the I.C.J. may cite its former opinions as evidence that a legal principle exists. Other sources of international law may include *jus cogens* norms, equity, and soft law. The I.C.J. is permitted to apply equity to resolve disputes if the parties so agree, and this has happened frequently in cases to delimit the territorial boundaries between two or more states.

After sources, the book delineates information on international organizations as subjects of international law. International organizations, like the United Nations and its many entities, help maintain international peace and security. This book also examines non-governmental entities like the Red Cross, intergovernmental companies and producer associations.

Following international organizations, this book discusses the relationships between states and individuals. Individuals possess rights and duties under international law. Individuals have rights associated with citizenship and human rights. Among their duties, they are not to commit war crimes or crimes against humanity, like genocide.

Next, this book addresses issues related to international jurisdiction and conflict of laws. It sets out the different types and principles of jurisdiction, jurisdictional conflicts, theories of sovereign immunity, and diplomatic and consular immunity. Some non-state actors, namely individuals, have inflicted terror on states. Because of universal jurisdiction, any state may prosecute such individuals or extradite them to another state or the International Criminal Court for prosecution.

This book then presents information related to international dispute settlement, perhaps the most important obligation states face after the requirement to protect their population and territory.

Under international law, states must resolve disputes peacefully. Toward this end, they may utilize negotiation, inquiry, mediation, alternative dispute resolution, courts, satisfaction or apologies, and seek the good offices of the U.N. Secretary-General.

In the penultimate chapter, this book examines international rights and responsibilities of states. States incur international responsibility when they, by act or failure to act, breach an international obligation to another state or individual. This breach creates rights and duties between the affected states, individuals, or international organizations. This chapter discusses what acts may be attributed to the state, the breaches that require injury to be actionable, the circumstances that preclude a finding of wrongfulness, and the remedies available to states to repair the harm they have caused other nations.

In the final chapter, this book delineates issues concerning the use of force and the laws of war. This controversial topic addresses ultimate breakdowns in state relationships, leading them to engage their military instruments. A considerable body of treaties and customary principles has developed to define war and regulate its conduct. Wars may be internal or international. The United Nations and its predecessor, the League of Nations, have attempted to resolve these crises. Nuclear war poses the most dangerous challenge to the world community as it has the potential to destroy significant parts or all of planet earth as humankind has come to know it.

B. Why the World Needs International Law [§2]

Because states may resort to massive violence to resolve their disputes, the world needs international law. International law is vital to the maintenance of international peace and security. In a peaceful world, states can trade goods and exchange their people for the benefit of all. This encourages the building of trust. When states know that other states will abide by the rule of law, they can expect a level playing field.

CHAPTER II

II. Historic Foundations

A. The Guiding Principle [§3]

The Baron de Montesquieu, a French philosopher who lived from 1689 to 1755, perhaps best stated the guiding principle of international relations. He said, "different nations ought in time of peace to do one another all the good they can, and in time of war as little harm as [possible]." Baron de Montesquieu, *The Spirit of Laws* 7 (Legal Classics Library Ed. 1984).

His philosophy provides direction for an international legal system founded on peace and security. During peace, nations should endeavor to assist each other for the common good of humanity. During war, they should limit the damage and destruction to the other country or countries. Such a policy facilitates the rebuilding of lives and territories following the devastation of war.

This philosophy is in keeping with that of Sun Tzu, the Chinese military philosopher, who wrote *The Art of War*. Sun Tzu said, "Generally in war the best policy is to take a state intact; to ruin it is inferior to this." Sun Tzu, *The Art of War* 77 (Samuel B. Griffith trans., Oxford University Press, 1971). Thus in war, Sun Tzu urges participants to commit little damage, as this is in their best interest. Unfortunately, nations have not always followed this advice and have inflicted harm that takes decades, if not centuries, to repair. Even when they conquered a particular territory, all they achieved is the right to correct the damage.

B. The Development of International Law [§4]

International law developed out of wars and efforts to trade. It has advanced its principles to regulate wars and trade among nations, recognizing that trade is best carried out among nations at peace. The main wars that gave rise to international law include

5

both those among European states and those between European states and the indigenous peoples they encountered in the new worlds.

Early on, St. Augustine, who lived from 354-430, suggested that certain types of wars, those consistent with Christian values, might be considered just. *See* Mary Ellen O'Connell, *International Law and the Use of Force: Cases and Materials* 106 (Thomson West 2005). Two principal theorists and the Peace of Westphalia further advanced precepts of international law. Depending on the country, both Francisco de Vitoria and Hugo Grotius can lay claim to being called the father of international law. This book refers to Francisco de Vitoria, who lived from 1480 to 1546, as the Spanish father of international law and to Hugo Grotius, who lived from 1583 to 1635, as the Dutch father of international law. Both men made substantial contributions to development of international law jurisprudence. The Peace of Westphalia, which brought to conclusion the Thirty Years War among European States that began in 1618, also advanced principles of public international law.

1. Francisco De Vitoria [§5]

Vitoria was a theologian for whom law merged with religion. He wrote the book *On the Indians Lately Discovered* in 1557, several decades after the Spanish encounter with the Indians of the New World. Vitoria examined legal norms from a moral perspective. He believed that law was dictated by God, and therefore divined from a higher source than man.

For Vitoria, law merged with theology to create a system of mutual rights and duties based on the premise of human equality. Vitoria postulated that Indians had rights and duties. The rights of Indians included their designation as the true owners of their lands with "dominion in both public and private matters." *See* S. James Anaya, *The Rights of Indigenous People and International Law in Historical and Contemporary Perspective*, 1989 Harvard

Indian Law Symposium 191, 194 (1990) (citing F. Vitoria, *De Indis et de Ivre Belli Reflectiones* (Classics of International Law ed. 1917)). When the Spanish discovered them, Vitoria proclaimed that the Spanish did not receive automatic title upon Indian lands. Similarly, he said that if the Indians had discovered the Spanish, they would have not received title to Spanish lands. *Id.* at 195. This title concept reverberates throughout international law.

Nevertheless, Vitoria maintained that the Catholic Church obtained rights over Indians, which derive from natural law (*jus gentium*). As pagans not in the state of grace, Indians were duty bound to allow foreigners to travel to their lands, trade among them, and preach the gospel. If Indians refused, the Spaniards could declare a just war, which would be one sanctioned by God and the Catholic Church. *Id.*

From the Indians' perspective, however, such an obligation must have seemed confusing, as this was their first encounter with the Spaniards and their Catholic Church. The term "just war" continues to surface centuries later as leaders seek to rally their populations to engage in massive violence by proclaiming a noble cause.

2. Hugo Grotius [§6]

Grotius wrote of the natural law rights of all peoples, including strangers to true religion. Grotius said that natural law "is the dictate of right reason. It indicates whether an act is morally right or wrong, according as it complies or disagrees with rational nature itself. Such an act is consequently either prescribed or forbidden, as the case may be, by God, the author of nature." Hugo Grotius, *De Jure Belli Ac Pacis* 40 (W.S.M.Knight translation 1922). Most importantly, Grotius believed that even people who did not worship the Europeans' God, or "strangers to true religion," had legal rights. *See* S. James Anaya, *supra* §5, at 196.

7

Grotius argued that natural law and custom should be established by consent. States should agree on the law to govern their relations. He also believed that law was out there in the universe to be divined by those with special gifts to retrieve it. Ultimately, some international law scholars have argued that Grotius removed the religious grounds for a just war. *Id.* Rather, he focused on state consent and natural law to justify certain acts.

3. The Peace of Westphalia [§7]

The 1648 Peace of Westphalia was a series of treaties that ended the Thirty Years War between the Holy Roman Empire (which by then consisted primarily of Germany) and several European states, namely Spain, France, and Sweden. Because the war lasted so long, the Peace of Westphalia is sometimes referred to as the "Peace of Exhaustion."

The Peace of Westphalia ended the political hegemony asserted by the Catholic Church, as referenced in Vitoria's work. It also established a treaty-based system for peace and cooperation in Europe. The Peace of Westphalia furthered Grotius' view that law and custom should be based on consent.

Equally important, the Peace of Westphalia ushered in the era of the independent territorial state founded on three concepts: (1) territorial integrity; (2) exclusive jurisdiction; and (3) non-intervention in the domestic affairs of other states. These three principles became the foundation for the modern conception of states.

As states evolved, they created rules to regulate themselves through treaties and customary practices. They ultimately formed international organizations of states to oversee various relationships, including those involving trade. The League of Nations ceased to exist and transferred its assets to the United Nations in 1946. The U.N. oversaw decolonization, leading to the creation of more states and the development of more entities that regulate trade among states. During the same time, the rights of individuals evolved to recognize that individuals possess human rights that must be protected by their states and that could be enforced against their states. Simultaneously, the world recognized that individuals had the capacity to inflict enormous terror on states. In response, individuals are required not to engage in international crimes such as war crimes or crimes against humanity. If they do, any country may assert jurisdiction no matter where the crime took place.

International law continues to progress toward creating a more peaceful world.

CHAPTER II

CHAPTER III

III. States

A. Four Criteria of State Formation [§8]

An entity must meet four criteria to be considered a state. It must have (1) a permanent population; (2) a defined territory; (3) a government; which is (4) capable of interacting on the international plane. Upon obtaining the four criteria and achieving statehood, the nation becomes free to independently govern its own population, within its own territory, and set its own foreign policy. This ability equates with sovereignty, the power and control over territory and people. States possess international legal capacity, meaning they can enter into treaties, and can sue and be sued in world courts.

The Montevideo Convention on Rights and Duties of States of 1933 codified the four principles into treaty form. It was signed by the North and South American states of Argentina, Brazil, Chile, Colombia, Cuba, Dominican Republic, Ecuador, El Salvador, Guatemala, Haiti, Honduras, Mexico, Nicaragua, Panama, Paraguay, Peru, United States, Uruguay, and Venezuela. *See* Convention on Rights and Duties of States (Inter-American, Dec. 26, 1933), 49 Stat. 3097 T.S. 881, 165 L.N.T.S. 19, 3 Bevans 145.

1. Permanent Population [§9]

A group of people must permanently reside in the entity's territory. Nevertheless, there is no limitation on how small the population may be. As of 1 November 2007, the United States Census Bureau projected the world's population at 6,628,432,160 people. The world's smallest populations can be found in the Vatican with approximately 950 people, Tuvalu with over 12,000, and Nauru with nearly 14,000. The largest populations can be found in China with 1,322,000,000 people, India with 1,120,000,000, and the United States with 303,000,000.

2. Defined Territory [§10]

There is no size limitation, meaning that a state may be situated on a small or large landmass. The smallest land areas can be found in the Vatican with 0.15 square miles; Monaco with 0.75 square miles; and Nauru with 8 square miles. The Vatican and Monaco are so tiny that you can walk through them in less than 15 and 30 minutes respectively. Because its population resides on such a micro land area, Monaco is considered the most densely populated state in the world with a projected 42,861 people per square mile.

The three states with the largest land areas are Russia (6,562,112 square miles); China (3,600,946 square miles); and the United States (3,537,437 square miles). China is far more densely populated because it contains a billion more people on a landmass that is only 63,509 square miles larger than the United States.

Globalization has led to more links between populations and land areas than ever before, with Chinese citizens making clothes and furniture for U.S. citizens. Similarly, a U.S. citizen can telephone a U.S. credit card or computer company only to be serviced by someone in India. When Hurricanes Katrina and Rita hit the Gulf Coast states in 2005, U.S. citizens telephoned a 1-800 number that connected them to Indian operators who gave advice on where to seek aid within the United States. Companies may be based in one country and owned by citizens or corporations from another country. For example, Australian, German, and Japanese corporations own U.S. entertainment conglomerates. This makes territory seem a shifting concept.

3. Government [§11]

The country must contain a government that controls the territory and is habitually obeyed by the population. This is a stringent requirement at the beginning of obtaining statehood, but once statehood has been obtained, the lack of a government does not affect status. The country of Italy possesses a parliamentary government that may form and reform itself often within a year. Constant changes of governments do not affect Italy's status as a nation state. Similarly, during the several-week period in November and December of 2000, when a dispute arose in the United States as to who won the presidential election and became head of the government, the United States was still considered a state.

If a government loses control over the territory, but its population continues to accord it allegiance, then it may be considered a government-in-exile. The government of Kuwait became one in exile when the Iraqis ousted it from its territory in 1990. Government-in-exile status may be temporary until the government can regain control over the territory. If it cannot after a passage of a significant amount of time, then it may lose its status as a government.

4. Capacity to Operate on the International Plane [§12]

The government must be competent to conduct international relations with other states and international organizations. It must possess the ability to negotiate and enter into treaties with other states and enjoy privileges and immunities within other states. This includes the privileges to assert sovereign immunity for its governmental acts or to send diplomats to other countries.

A state may cede part of its capacity to conduct international relations to another state without affecting its status as a state. For example, because there are no diplomatic relations between the United States and Cuba, the United States government

13

requested that Switzerland conduct relations with Cuba on its behalf. The Swiss Embassy accredits U.S. diplomats and represents U.S. interests in Cuba. The United States does not lose its status as a state because it has given up its capacity for this one situation. If, however, a government were to cede its capacity to conduct all foreign relations to another state, then its status as a foreign nation would come into question.

B. Variety of States [§13]

States vary in their diversity. The following information delineates some of the different types of states.

1. Micro-States [§14]

Small states, like the Vatican, Nauru, and Monaco, contain tiny territories and small populations. Although micro in size, these governments function as full members of the international community.

2. Failed States and Rogue Nations [§15]

Failed states are those whose governments lose control over people and territory. A state that loses the ability to protect its people from massive violence on this scale has failed to exercise one of the principal components of sovereignty. Cycles of revenge and hatred make it difficult for any government to function effectively.

Between April and July 1994, one segment of the Rwandan population, the Hutus, committed genocide against another segment of the population, the Tutsis. The genocide took the lives of 800,000 people and left 95,000 children orphaned. Between 1972 and 1973 in neighboring Burundi, the Tutsis, which dominated the army, massacred more than 100,000 Hutus after an uprising against the Tutsi government. A more recent example developed in Darfur, Sudan, after various groups known as the Sudan Liberation Army (SLA), the Justice and Equality Movement (JEM), and the Janjawid began fighting against or on behalf of the Sudanese government. The conflict forced hundreds of thousands of refugees to flee attacks on their villages, homes, and personhood.

Rogue nation is a term frequently applied to states perceived as violating international law. This term is employed in the eye of the beholder.

Some states considered South Africa and Rhodesia to be rogue nations during the apartheid period when they refused to provide equal rights to all of their citizens. For other states, Iraq became a rogue nation when it invaded Kuwait in 1990 and ignored United Nations resolutions calling for it to withdraw. Even before it invaded Iraq in 2003 in search of weapons of mass destruction that were never found, the United States was branded a rogue nation in its own media after it was voted off the U.N. Human Rights Commission. As a Commission member, the United States had opposed resolutions reducing the cost of HIV/AIDS drugs and acknowledging a human right to adequate food.

Obviously, the country characterized as a rogue nation is likely to vociferously disagree with the application of the label to its conduct. No entity within the United Nations system takes an official vote to brand a country as a rogue nation.

3. Economic Unions [§16]

States may come together to form economic and strategic unions, such as the European Union or the East African Community. The European Union (EU), formerly known as the European Community (EC) or European Economic Community (EEC), was established on November 1, 1993. It is now a union of twenty-five independent states based on the continent of Europe, *see* <http://europa.eu.int/>. It was formed to enhance political, economic, and social co-operation among its members. Admission is conditioned on respect for the U.N. Charter, the rule of law, democracy, human rights, the inviolability of all frontiers, and nuclear non-proliferation. Further, a state seeking membership must demonstrate respect for ethnic groups and national minorities, and commitment to resolving its disputes with other states peacefully.

Whether a state meets these goals must be viewed through the eyes of the other members.   Turkey, for example, sought admission to the EU's predecessor grouping five decades ago. The EU agreed to consider Turkey if it would commit to democratize by eliminating its army's role in national politics and the death penalty, while augmenting freedom of speech and religion, according to an article by Christopher Caldwell, *Bordering on What?* N.Y. Times Mag. 46, 48 (Sept. 25, 2005). Caldwell reported that it was only after Muslim Turkey charged the EU with being a Christian club that the EU consented to opening membership talks, which began on October 3, 2005. In the meantime, the French Prime Minister suggested delaying talks until Turkey recognized the Greek part of Cyprus, and the German Christian Democratic leader urged Turkey to be content with a "privileged partnership," rather than member status. *Id.* at 48.

On January 2, 2002, twelve European states created the Eurozone comprising 300 million people. The twelve states eliminated their separate national currencies, such as the French Franc and Spanish Peseta, and adopted the Euro as their currency. During August 2005, the Euro traded at a ratio of 1 Euro to 1.25 U.S. dollars. By March 2008, the dollar had sunk to trade at 1 Euro to 1.58 U.S. dollars, making European goods more expensive in the United States and U.S. goods less expensive in European countries.

Since establishing currency is one aspect of sovereignty, several European states chose to give up this aspect of control over their economies. Three states chose to forego joining the

16

Eurozone. The United Kingdom continues to use the pound sterling as its currency, while Sweden and Denmark maintain their respective krona.

The East African Community (EAC) is the regional intergovernmental organization of the Republics of Kenya, Uganda, and the United Republic of Tanzania. The EAC headquarters are located in Arusha, Tanzania. These three East African countries cover an area of 1.8 million square kilometers and have a population of 82 million who share a common history, language, culture, and infrastructure. The EAC website, <http://www.eac.int>, proclaims it aims to widen and deepen co-operation among the partner states in the political, economic, and social fields for their mutual benefit.

4. Federated States [§17]

Federated states are composed of multiple components. The United States, which comprises fifty states and the District of Colombia, shares this feature in common with many nations. Germany, Switzerland, Australia, Brazil, India, Mexico and Canada are additional examples of federated states. Mexico's official name is the United Mexican States and it contains 31 states and a federal district.

Switzerland, for example, is composed of 26 cantons or states. It possesses the four official languages of German, French, Italian, and Romansh, all of which appear on the Swiss Franc, the country's currency. Romansh is primarily used for communicating with Romansh-speaking persons within a tiny part of the country, while German, French, and Italian enjoy equal status in Parliament, the federal administration, and the army. For more information about Switzerland, *see* <http://www.swissemb.org/country/sglance.pdf>.

Sometimes countries may refer to their federal components as cantons like Switzerland, or provinces like Canada. No matter the name, these federated entities contain a government that is separate from the national one and is responsible for local affairs.

5. States-In-Training [§18]

States-in-training refer to insurgent communities and movements of national liberation. They may have been once colonized and/or governed by the mandate system established at the end of World War I by the League of Nations. After World War II, the mandates became trust territories with the trustee state obliged to prepare the trust territory for full independence.

States-in-training often lack complete control over territory, which is one of the four criteria for statehood. After a period of decolonization and negotiation in the 1940s, 1950s, 1960s, and 1970s, many states-in-training succeeded the colonizing state on the continents of Africa and Asia, and in the Middle East. British Palestine became Israel, giving rise to the Palestinian Liberation Organization to seek statehood for the Palestinian people.

6. Associated Nations [§19]

Some territorial or non-territorial communities, such as Puerto Rico and the Cook Islands, choose to associate themselves with other states. As such, they possess a special hybrid, or in-between, status where they are not a federated component of the state, but neither are they a fully sovereign state. Through a referendum, Puerto Rico or the Virgin Islands, for example, may someday exercise their right to self-determination by becoming an independent sovereign state or a federated component of the United States.

The Cook Islands' constitution, *see* <http://www.ck/govt.htm#con>, sets out its special relationship with New Zealand as a free association that may in the future change to full independence or another status. The Cook Islanders are New Zealand citizens. The Queen or King of England is the head of state of the Cook Islands, as she or he is of New Zealand.

7. Subjugated Nations [§20]

Subjugated nations comprise states within states, like the Navajo Nation or Cherokee Indians, whose territory is surrounded by the United States. Native American peoples were initially completely sovereign until they ceded their power to act on the international plane. Only a complete sovereign can enter into treaties with other sovereigns as tribes initially did with the U.S. government. Currently, Native Americans possess limited self-governance within their territory, and are thus subjugated to, or dependent on, the United States government.

In *Cherokee Nation v. State of Georgia*, 30 U.S. 1 (1831), the Supreme Court considered whether the Cherokee Nation, an Indian tribe, constituted a foreign state as defined by the U.S. Constitution. If they were a foreign nation, the Cherokees could avail themselves of the original jurisdiction of the Supreme Court and sue the state of Georgia to restrain Georgia from executing certain laws, which they believed would annihilate them as a political society and seize lands protected by treaties with the United States government.

The Cherokees were initially completely sovereign over their territory, and were acknowledged as such in their treaties with the United States. However, their territory became part of the United States in the same treaties in which they have acknowledged themselves to be under the protection of the United States.

In *Cherokee Nation v. State of Georgia*, Chief Justice Marshall concluded that these treaties changed their status to domestic dependent nations. Marshall stated that they were in a state

19

of pupilage, resembling that of a ward to his guardian. They are thus under the control and dominion of the United States. Because the Cherokees were no longer a foreign nation, they could not sue the state of Georgia in the Supreme Court and obtain an injunction prohibiting Georgia from seizing their lands.

In essence, the Cherokees became a subjugated nation that ceded their right to operate on the international plane to the United States government. With these changed circumstances, the Cherokees lost rights associated with the completely sovereign state.

C. Acquisition of Territorial Sovereignty [§21]

Once formed, states may acquire sovereignty over additional territory. They may purchase territory from another state, as the U.S. did when it bought Louisiana from France. If they conquer territory during a war, the territory shifts to its new occupiers. The legitimacy of this change will be determined by the legality of the war. In earlier times, states could discover and occupy uninhabited territory.

A territory is considered *terra nullius* when no one occupies it. Any state may claim sovereignty over such areas through a combination of discovery and continuous occupation. As Vitoria, the Spanish father of international law, indicated in relation to the Indians the Spanish encountered in the New World, no state can claim occupied territory without some succession of rights from the true owners.

A title may be considered inchoate or incomplete if the state only proclaims that it discovered the territory, that is merely seeing the land, but without any act of taking possession. Possession must be completed within a reasonable time. Acquiring territorial sovereignty includes the duty to protect the territory and to

20

protect the rights of other states within the territory. In the 1928 *Island of Palmas (Miangas)* case between the United States and the Netherlands, the Permanent Court of Arbitration said that territorial sovereignty involves "the exclusive right to display the activities of a state." *See Island of Palmas Case (The Netherlands v. United States),* 2 Rep. Int'l Arb. Awards 829 (Perm. Ct. Arb. 1928).

Consider, for example, the case titled the *Legal Status of Eastern Greenland (Denmark v. Norway),* 1932 P.C.I.J., Ser. A/B., No. 53, where the Permanent Court of International Justice, the predecessor court to the International Court of Justice, had to analyze the sovereignty claims of Denmark and Norway over Eastern Greenland. Norway issued a proclamation on July 10, 1931, placing portions of Eastern Greenland under Norwegian control on the theory that Eastern Greenland was *terra nullius,* not occupied by anyone. The court said that Norway was required to base its claim on (1) discovery, and (2) continued display of authority. To satisfy the latter, Norway could demonstrate (a) intention and will to act as a sovereign, and (b) some actual exercise or display of authority.

Denmark asserted that its claim to title over Eastern Greenland was "founded on the peaceful and continuous display of state authority over the island." Denmark showed that it had established colonies on Greenland after its initial discovery as early as the 10th century, although these colonies subsequently vanished. It also put forth Danish treaties with other countries that mentioned Greenland, and recognized Denmark's rights over Greenland. Norway became a party to various bilateral and multilateral agreements in which Greenland was described as Danish or in which Denmark excluded Greenland from the operation of the agreement, an indication of sovereign control. Norway had also promised not to contest Danish sovereignty over the whole of Greenland.

21

The court ruled that Norway's proclamation of July 10, 1931 was invalid and stated that Denmark possessed a valid title to sovereignty over Greenland. Denmark had both discovered Greenland and displayed continuous authority over the island. Greenland, the largest island in the world at 856,160 square miles, became an integral part of Denmark under its Constitution of June 5, 1953. One of the ironies of description is that Greenland contains more ice than Iceland, which is mostly green.

Individuals, by contrast, may purchase an island for their private domain, but they may not proclaim this island a state. Individuals do not possess territorial rights on the international plane.

D. State Succession [§22]

States may evolve and change from one entity to another. State succession occurs when one state succeeds another. The Vienna Convention on Succession of States in Respect of Treaties, 1946 U.N.T.S. 3, U.N. Doc. A/CONF.80/81 (1978), defines succession of states as "the replacement of one State by another in the responsibility for the international relations of the territory." This Convention opened for signature on August 23, 1978, and entered into force on November 6, 1996. Hereinafter, this treaty will be referred to as the State Succession treaty or VCOSS.

Issues of state succession arise when: (a) a state absorbs all of a predecessor state; (b) a state takes over part of another state's territory; (c) a state becomes independent of another state; and (d) a state arises from a predecessor that has been dismembered. *See* Damrosch, *infra* §29, at 348. Within the last century, state succession has resulted from peace treaties, decolonization, unification, merger, and dissolution of states.

The decolonization of Africa and Asia resulted in the creation of dozens of new states in the 1950s and 1960s. The merger of Tanganyika and Zanzibar resulted in the United Republic of Tanzania in 1964. The dissolution of Yugoslavia gave birth to several new states in the 1990s. On 17 February 2008, Kosovo declared independence from Serbia, becoming the seventh state to be carved from former Yugoslavia. The unification of East Germany and West Germany in 1993 led to the reconstitution of one state of Germany. As a result of these and other statehood changes, the United Nations membership has nearly quadrupled since its formation in 1945 with 51 original members. Montenegro became the 192nd member when it was admitted to the United Nations on 8 June 2006.

Nevertheless, when states form unions, but retain considerable autonomy and keep their status as states, this does not give rise to state succession issues. In 2005, the European Union sought to adopt a new constitution, which had to be approved by all 25 member nations. Nine countries had accepted the constitution before France and the Netherlands voted against the proposed European Constitution in the summer of 2005. Their vote jeopardized the new constitution. But because France and the Netherlands maintain their status as independent states, their citizens had a right to reject further integration with other states.

When state succession does occur, the new state has options. It may enter the world community *tabula rasa*, a phrase meaning a clean slate. Or, the new state may succeed to some or all rights and obligations of its predecessor state. This depends on the nature of the obligations, which are discussed herein.

1. Public and Private Laws [§23]

One issue concerns whether the new state keeps its old laws. This depends on whether the laws are public or private. Public law is the political law for the effective administration of the country. It does not survive state succession. For example, a socialist state changing to a capitalist market economy state would need different public laws. Private law governs relations between individual citizens (such as private contracts for real estate purchases). Private law is unaffected by state succession if the laws are consistent with the new regime. However, if laws are inconsistent with the new regime, then private law does not succeed. Damrosch and her colleagues note, "succession is, in effect, a presumption, which can be rebutted by positive legislation of the new state." *See* Damrosch, *infra* §29, at 352 (citing 1 D.P. O'Connell, *State Succession in Municipal Law and International Law* 101-141 (1967).

2. National Debt [§24]

A state may owe national debt to individuals, corporations, charities, other states, or international organizations. The financial obligation may be issued as bonds or can arise through loans to fund public projects, such as constructing roads or funding wars.

For example, on January 1, 1791, at the beginning of its statehood, the United States national debt was $75 million. By January 15, 2004, it surpassed the $7 trillion mark. On October 18, 2005, the U.S. debt passed $8 trillion at $8,003,897,406,911.24 and $9 trillion on November 2, 2007, according to the U.S. treasury website <http://www.publicdebt.treas.gov/opd/opdpenny.htm>. Another website, <http://www.brillig.com/debt_clock/>, calculated each U.S. citizen's share at $29,930.39, based on an estimated 2007 population of 303,423,301.

When an indebted state is absorbed by another entity and the debtor entity retains fiscal independence, the debtor-creditor relationship is unaffected. The debtor entity, although part of a new international person, remains responsible for repayment of the debt. Thus, were the United States to merge with Canada or Mexico, and maintain fiscal independence, U.S. citizens would remain responsible for their $9 trillion in debt. A separating state, however, does not succeed to the national public debt of the predecessor state, but it remains responsible for the localized debt connected to its territory. Thus, for example, if Texas were to become the Republic of Texas, it would only be responsible for the U.S. debt associated with Texas.

3. Local Debt [§25]

Local debt is owed by a state in respect to specific territory. This debt is "incurred for funds expended or used in connection with a particular project in the territory directly affected by absorption or separation." Damrosch, *infra* §29, at 354. For example, a state may issue road or education bonds to build bridges or fund school expansion in a particular part of its territory. If no agreement is concluded to the contrary, the new state assumes the predecessor's debts associated with the territory. *Id.*

This became a particular issue when colonies gained independence. Some new states sought to have no responsibility for the debts of the predecessor colonial state, but usually in the state succession treaty they were held responsible for debt connected to the colonial territory.

The general rule is that change in sovereignty does not affect local debts if the unit is unaffected by change. *Id.* In other words, the debt follows the debtor with territorial shifts. For example, if Russia had borrowed money to build roads in Alaska before selling Alaska to the United States, these debts would follow Alaska to the United States, which would become responsible for repayment. If Alaska had remained a part of Russia and Russia sold a different part of its territory to another state, then Russia would still be responsible for Alaska's debts.

4. Public Property [§26]

The general rule is that public property follows the territory where it is located. *Id.* at 352 (citing Restatement (Third) §209(1)). However, the successor state may agree to permit the predecessor state to retain certain public property, like military

25

bases. It will then acquiesce to the removal by the predecessor state of public property from the successor state's territory. This issue arose with the break up of the Soviet Union, which then became Russia, Georgia, Ukraine, and several other independent republics in 1991. In order not to create more nuclear weapons states, the nuclear weapons that had been spread throughout the U.S.S.R. were moved to just Russia.

5. Legal Obligations [§27]

What happens to obligations arising from violations of international law? Some commentators have referred to obligations "contracted by the predecessor State with a view to attaining objectives contrary to the major interest of the successor State or of the transferred territory" as odious debts. *See* Damrosch, *infra* §29, at 356.

The general rule is that the successor state has no responsibility under international law for international delicts, such as those associated with prosecuting a predecessor's war. The predecessor state continues to be responsible for its international law violations. *Id.* For example, the United States spent approximately $1 trillion to fight wars in Afghanistan and Iraq between 2002 and 2007. If it were absorbed by another state, the new state would not be responsible for the U.S. debt associated with this war.

In another example, West Germany created a Hardship Fund, *see* <http://www.claimscon.org/index.asp?url=hardship/overview>, in 1980 to compensate Jewish victims of Nazism from Soviet bloc countries who suffered considerable damage to health during the Holocaust and emigrated to the West after 1965. After reunifying with East Germany on October 3, 1990, West Germany remained obliged to meet its own commitments.

6. State Succession to Treaties [§28]

Under VCOSS, *supra* §22, the treaty obligations of the predecessor state do not automatically pass to the successor state. The predecessor must devolve these rights. *Id.* at art. 8. Devolution agreements are known as passing of the torch agreements. One state agrees to convey its treaty obligations to another state. This is similar to parties passing contract rights from one to another through assignment. For example, in 1989, Russia agreed to succeed to the Soviet Union's treaties, including its United Nations membership and Security Council seat.

Some states, particularly newly independent ones, will issue Unilateral Declarations whereby they will pick and choose the treaties to keep or discard. *Id.* at art. 9. With newly independent states, the clean slate metaphor applies. They can continue treaties or disavow them. The new state simply declares that the predecessor state's treaties will remain in effect while it examines them to determine which ones will be adopted and which ones will be terminated.

Certain treaties, such as boundary agreements, are not affected by state succession. *Id.* at art. 11. However, legitimate boundary disputes may be submitted to the International Court of Justice for resolution. Rights of transit on international waterways or over another state may also not be affected by state succession. This is similar to an easement in domestic property law, which passes with the land to the next purchaser.

The Moving Treaty-Frontiers Rule affects the addition of a portion of territory to an existing state. The territory passes out of the treaty regime of its former sovereign into the treaty regime of its new sovereign. For example, when the United States purchased Louisiana from France, the U.S. acquired sovereignty over Louisiana, which became bound by U.S. treaties.

27

With the uniting of two or more states, all previous treaties continue in force, unless there is an agreement to the contrary or they are contradictory. *Id.* at art. 31. If the treaties are contradictory, then the state must decide which one is to remain in force. For example, when West Germany, a member of NATO, unified with East Germany, a member of the Warsaw Pact, this created a problem as NATO and the Warsaw Pact were competing military organizations. West Germany was the dominant economic partner in the unification and thus the new state of Germany became a member of only NATO. The Warsaw Pact was officially dissolved on July 1, 1991. With separating states, all treaties also continue in both territories unless a treaty is related to a particular part of the territory. *Id.* at art. 34. Then it moves with the new territory.

E. Recognition of States [§29]

Recognition occurs when one state acknowledges that another state possesses the essential elements of statehood. There are two views on recognition. With the constitutive view, the act of recognition by other states constitutes the new state and confers international legal personality on the entity. Under the declaratory view, states merely declare what already exists by their act of recognition. With the declaratory view, the existence of a state depends on facts and whether those facts meet the criteria of statehood. Once the entity meets the four criteria, it becomes a state and it may exist without being recognized.

Diplomatic exchange or entering into a treaty between two states implies recognition. An observer or court looks to acts of recognition, or the lack thereof, to decide whether an entity is a state. Some scholars perceive a duty to recognize because a state is not a state without recognition under the constitutive view of recognition. However, Professor Ian Brownlie says in his book, *Principles of Public International Law*, "Recognition, as a public act of state, is an optional political act and there is no legal duty in this regard." *See* Ian Brownlie, *Principles of Public International Law*

90 (5th Ed. 1998), as cited in Damrosch et al., *International Law: Cases and Materials* 293 (4th Ed. 2001) (hereinafter "Damrosch, *supra* §29").

In other words, a state can chose to recognize or not recognize a new state, as it deems appropriate. Political issues play an important role in states' decisions to confer recognition. The United States recognized the state of Israel on May 14, 1948, yet several Arab nations have never recognized Israel. Immediately after Kosovo declared independence from Serbia in 2008, several nations, including the United States, recognized the new entity, but Israel did not. Israel declared it did not recognize breakaway states.

F. Recognition of Governments [§30]

Recognition of governments differs from recognition of states. The latter looks at the nature of the entity. Specifically, recognition of states concerns whether an entity meets the four criteria to be considered a state. The former examines the political occupants of the entity, including what individuals or groups claim to speak for the state. Further, does that group have effective control over the territory and is it being habitually obeyed by the bulk of the population? As with state recognition, political concerns may play a role in a state's decision to recognize a government.

1. *De Jure* and *De Facto* Governments [§31]

A *de jure* government is considered the lawful government of a state. It assumes power according to the state's constitution or the traditional means of transfer within the state. If the state has a democratic election system, then *de jure* governments must be elected according to the appropriate process. If the state possesses a monarchy, then the head of state must become so according to the customary means.

The head of state and the head of government may be occupied by the same person, as in the United States where the president is both head of state and head of government. In the United Kingdom, by contrast, the reigning monarch is head of state and the prime minister is head of government. He or she is elected according to a parliamentary system where the party, which holds the majority of seats in the government, determines who among its members becomes the prime minister. Following this process legitimizes the government as *de jure*.

A *de facto* government assumes power by employing extra constitutional means, such as through a coup or a revolution. This government may oversee the country if it has effective control over the territory and is habitually obeyed by the population. A *de facto* government may become *de jure* through the passage of time and with recognition by other states and its people of its legitimacy.

2. Unrecognized Governments Can Bind a State [§32]

Unrecognized governments can also bind a state. The 1923 Tinoco Claims Arbitration involved a dispute between Great Britain and Costa Rica. *See The Tinoco Claims Arbitration (Great Britain v. Costa Rica)*, 1 Rep. Int'l Arbitral Awards 369 (Perm. Ct. Arb. 1923). The Tinoco regime came to power by coup and maintained control over Costa Rica for thirty months, during which it entered into certain contracts and oil concessions. The restored government nullified the Tinoco contracts, including an oil concession to a British company. Costa Rica argued that since Great Britain never recognized the Tinoco regime, it could not claim that the Tinoco regime could legally confer rights upon its citizens.

The sole arbitrator, William Howard Taft, disagreed. He said that non-recognition does not outweigh the evidence of the *de facto* character of the Tinoco government. A *de facto* government may come to power contrary to the country's constitution. If it maintains a peaceful administration, with the acquiescence of the people for a substantial period of time, it is the government of the country and can bind the country.

3. Governments-In-Exile [§33]

If a *de jure* government loses effective control over the state's territory and takes up residence in another state, then it becomes a government-in-exile. States may recognize governments-in-exile on the premise that another group, such as those who staged a coup or a purported revolution, illegally occupies the territory, and the legitimate government will be restored to power in the foreseeable future. When Iraq overran Kuwait in 1990 and proclaimed Kuwait as its 19th province, the Kuwaiti government became one in exile. Because it was recognized as the *de jure* government of Kuwait, it could claim the state's assets in other countries and request military assistance. The world community responded and forced Iraq back into its own territory where it has been contained.

Governments-in-exile differ from provisional governments. National Liberation Movements are considered provisional governments until they acquire control over territory and are habitually obeyed by their people. Governments-in-exile previously had control over the territory but lost it while maintaining the connection to the people.

4. Governments as Plaintiffs and Defendants in National Courts [§34]

Recognition of government issues may arise when governments become plaintiffs or defendants in the national courts of other states. First, when a foreign government tries to sue in a court of another state, national courts may look to their Foreign Ministry or State Department to determine whether the executive branch has recognized the entity. In some instances, only a recognized foreign government may be permitted to sue in courts of another country.

Second, a foreign government may become a defendant in a court and wish to assert sovereign immunity to dismiss the suit. Courts may look to whether its executive branch has recognized the government to determine whether the entity should be granted immunity from suit.

Third, an act of a foreign government may come into question, and courts have to determine whether the government has been recognized. In *Autocephalous v. Goldberg*, 917 F.2d 278 (7th Cir. 1990), the Turkish military government, which came into being after the Turkish invasion of Cyprus, issued decrees providing that all abandoned property now belonged to the Turkish government. After the Turkish invasion of Cyprus forced Greeks to flee and abandon their churches, the Church was vandalized and everything of value was removed. This included four Byzantine Mosaics that belonged to the Kanakaria Church.

The U.S. court refused to give legal effect to the nationalization decrees of an unrecognized government. Turkey was the only state that recognized the military government's legitimacy. Most other states considered its actions of invading and issuing the divestment decrees to be illegal. As a consequence, the purchaser of the four Byzantine Mosaics was forced to return the mosaics to the Kanakaria church. She lost her entire investment.

By contrast, in the 1933 *Salimoff v. Standard Oil of New York* case, 262 N.Y. 220 (1933), the court gave effect to the decrees of the Soviet Government, which succeeded the Russian government. Russian nationals sought the return of oil lands confiscated in Russia by the successor Soviet Government. The court declared that the Soviets were a government, and "its decrees have force within its borders and over its nationals." *Id.* at 226.

Rather than create the state, the court said, "Recognition … simply gives to a *de facto* state international status." *Id.* at 226–227. While a court could not recognize a state, it could say that the Soviets are "a government, maintaining internal peace and order, providing for national defense and the general welfare, carrying on relations with our own government and others." *Id.* at 227.

The court maintained that "To refuse to recognize that Soviet Russia is a government regulating the internal affairs of the country, is to give fictions an air of reality which they do not deserve." *Id.* The court was, in effect, taking the declaratory view of recognition; i.e., that recognition would merely declare what already exists.

In conclusion, the four criteria determine whether or not an entity is a state. A state can acquire or lose territory by a variety of lawful means. States may choose to join other states or break up into component parts. States opt to recognize other entities as states, but there is no duty in this regard. Government status is determined by the population; that is, whether they habitually obey the individuals comprising the government. The government must exercise control over the territory initially, but it can still be considered a government after losing control if the people continue to accord it allegiance.

CHAPTER III

CHAPTER IV

IV. Sources of International Law

A. In General [§35]

The two primary sources of international law include conventional or treaty law and customary law developed through state practice. All states and their tribunals recognize these two types of international law.

Some tribunals, such as the International Court of Justice, also recognize the following two categories as a subsidiary means for determining rules of law: general principles of law recognized by civilized nations, and the teachings of the most highly qualified publicists. Also, the I.C.J. may decide a case *ex aequo et bono*, meaning in equity and good, if the two parties so agree.

At least one arbitral tribunal viewed United Nations General Assembly resolutions as a potential source of international law to the extent that they represent viewpoints among a variety of states and economies. Some scholars have argued that these same resolutions might be viewed as evidence of state practice, which could create customary law if states vote a certain way out of a sense of legal obligation.

The Restatement of Foreign Relations Law declares that the United States recognizes customary and treaty law as primary sources of international law. Customary international law is defined as general and consistent practice of states that is followed from a sense of legal obligation. The Restatement permits general principles common to the major legal systems of the world to be invoked as supplementary rules of law. **See** Restatement (Third) of Foreign Relations Law §102(4)(1984).

B. Treaty Law [§36]

The Vienna Convention on the Law of Treaties, 1115 U.N.T.S.

331, U.N. Doc. A/CONF.39/27 (1969) (hereinafter "VCLT" or "Vienna Convention on the Law of Treaties"), codifies customary law with respect to treaties. Article 2 of the VCLT defines a treaty as "an international agreement concluded between States in written form and governed by international law, whether embodied in a single instrument or in two or more related instruments and whatever its particular designation." A nation may be a negotiating state, meaning that it "took part in the drawing up and adoption of the text of the treaty," or a contracting state, meaning that it "consented to be bound by the treaty, whether or not the treaty has entered into force." A "party" refers to a state that "has consented to be bound by the treaty and for which the treaty is in force." A "third State" is one that is not a party to the treaty." *Id.*

Treaties may be bilateral (between two states), trilateral (between three states), or multilateral (between four or more states). Extradition treaties between two states represent common examples of bilateral treaties. NAFTA, the North American Free Trade Agreement between the U.S., Mexico, and Canada, is a trilateral treaty.

Multilateral treaties may be limited to the initial signatories or they may be open to all states to sign and join. The latter type of treaty may codify existing customary law, make new law, or combine the two functions. Administrative or regime treaties represent multilateral treaties open to all states. The Law of the Sea treaty, for example, creates a regime for regulating a resource common to all mankind.

States may also enter into non-binding gentlemen's agreements. These are concluded in the personal names of their representatives and are not submitted for ratification through the customary process. They often contain vague language or mere declaration of purposes and there is no remedy for breach.

36

Whether created as treaties or as gentlemen's agreements, these contracts between states can be violated by one of the parties. In 1939, for example, the Soviet Union and Nazi German governments signed economic and non-aggression pacts, which they announced to the world. They also concluded a secret protocol to the non-aggression pact giving the Baltic States to the Soviets and dividing Poland between them. These pacts lasted almost two years before German leader Adolf Hitler desecrated the non-aggression pact and secret protocol by invading the Soviet Union. The secret protocol was rumored to exist for decades, but was not officially confirmed until 1989 when the Soviet Union became Russia again and the documents were released to the general public.

1. Consent to Be Bound By Treaties [§37]

To create legal rights, duties, and obligations, states must manifest intent to be bound by their agreements. According to Article 11 of the VCLT, a state can indicate its consent to enter into a treaty through "signature, exchange of instruments constituting a treaty, ratification, acceptance, approval, or accession, or by any other means if so agreed." *Id.*

Only the leader with authority to speak for a state can sign a treaty binding the state. Otherwise, the treaty is considered *ultra virus* and the state is not bound.

Ratification signifies the "international act so named whereby a State establishes on the international plane its consent to be bound by a treaty." *Id.* at art. 2. This usually means submitting the executive's treaty-making power to legislative control, meaning that while the executive may negotiate the treaty on behalf of the state, the legislature must give its final stamp of approval. The state's internal law may require that all treaties be subject to subsequent ratification by the legislature before it becomes binding on the state.

Under Article 12 of the VCLT, if negotiating states agree that signature will have the effect of binding a state, a state may accept a treaty by signature alone or by signature subject to ratification. The state's acceptance will depend on the state's constitutional provisions.

With accession, a state becomes a party to a treaty to which it was not an original signatory. The treaty must permit states to subsequently accede to a treaty, according to Article 15 of the VCLT. A state may accede to a treaty before or after it becomes binding, depending on the treaty's terms.

According to the U.S. Constitution, treaties require a two-thirds vote of the Senate to bind the U.S. However, a president can disavow a treaty without receiving the consent of the Senate. *See Goldwater v. Carter*, 444 U.S. 996 (1979) (dismissing the case filed by Senator Barry Goldwater who claimed President Jimmy Carter could not terminate a 1954 mutual defense treaty with Taiwan without the advise and consent of the Senate or the approval of both Houses of Congress).

U.S. presidents sometimes opt to submit a document as an international agreement, another euphemism for treaty. These require a majority vote from both Houses of Congress to become the law of the land. The U.S. president can also conclude executive agreements. These are signed in the name of the president and are not submitted for ratification or a vote. As with all gentlemen's agreements, these executive agreements do not bind the United States. The other state receives only the word and assurances of the current U.S. president, which subjects the agreement to being disavowed by a subsequent U.S. president or even by the president who originally signed it.

2. Treaty Observation [§38]
Under Article 26 of the VCLT, the Latin maxim, *pacta sunt*

servanda, governs treaty observation. Every treaty in force is binding upon the parties to it and must be performed by them in good faith. Article 27 provides that a party may not invoke internal law as justification for failure to perform a treaty.

For example, United States law contains a rule that a later statute supersedes an earlier treaty. A domestic court may apply the statute, but the U.S. remains responsible under international law for performing its treaty obligations to other states. Domestic issues are only relevant when they affect the capacity of the state to bind itself to a treaty.

3. Treaty Application and Interpretation [§39]

Treaties apply to all the territory of each party, unless it otherwise appears from their terms, according to Article 29 of the VCLT. For example, with state succession, two states with various treaties may merge and create a situation where dissimilar treaties apply to different segments of the combined country. This requires the merging states to negotiate which treaty will become the binding law of the land.

While treaties can make new rules between the parties, they cannot apply these regulations retroactively, according to Article 28 of the VCLT. Nevertheless, legal concepts can change over time, leading to different interpretations of the treaty's ordinary meaning.

Treaties must be interpreted in good faith, using the ordinary meaning in light of its purpose. Under Article 31(4) of the VCLT, special meanings may be established in treaties. This is similar to a requirement in domestic contract law, which interprets the terms using plain meaning, unless the parties have clearly established a unique meaning. These special understandings of certain terms must be set out clearly so that all parties understand the significance of the change.

Courts may take into account the practice of the parties and relevant rules of international law in interpreting their treaties. A unilateral interpretation of an international agreement, whether made by the executive, legislative, or judicial organs of one of the contracting states, is not binding upon the other contracting states.

4. Treaty Amendment and Modification [§40]

Articles 39-41 of the VCLT govern amendment and modification. A treaty may be amended by all parties or by a two-thirds vote when the treaty so specifies. Proposals must be given to all state parties to provide them an opportunity to take part in the negotiation to amend the treaty.

Under Article 41 of the VCLT, two or more parties to a multilateral treaty may modify a treaty if (1) the treaty permits such modification; or (2) the modification in question is not prohibited by the treaty. Further, if states choose the second option, the modification must not affect rights of other parties or the performance of their obligations, and the modification can not be incompatible with the purpose of the treaty. This permits a limited number of states to modify a treaty just between them if the modification best serves their particular interests.

5. Treaty Reservations [§41]

According to Article 2(d) of the VCLT, a reservation is "a unilateral statement, however phrased or named, made by a State, when signing, ratifying, accepting, approving or acceding to a treaty, whereby it purports to exclude or to modify the legal effect of certain provisions of the treaty in their application to that State." A state cannot reserve to the core essence of a treaty. For example, if a treaty bans a particular weapon, a state cannot reserve the right to use that weapon. With the international treaty to ban landmines, other states rejected the United States' efforts to exempt certain types of landmines.

The negotiating states elected to preserve the integrity of the treaty rather than compromise in order to attract the world's largest economy.

Moreover, a treaty reservation modifies the effect of a treaty provision for the reserving state in its relations with all other states. However, the reservation has no influence on the treaty provisions between the non-reserving states. The original treaty provisions continue to apply to their international relations.

What happens when other states object to a reservation? The General Assembly requested an I.C.J. advisory opinion on this issue when certain states sought to reserve to provisions of the Genocide Convention. In the *Reservations to the Convention on the Prevention and Punishment of the Crime of Genocide* case, 1951 I.C.J. 15, the General Assembly asked whether the reserving state could be regarded as being a party to the Convention while still maintaining its reservation if the reservation is objected to by one or more of the parties to the Convention but not by others. By seven votes to five, the I.C.J. held that the reserving state could be regarded as being a party to the Convention if the reservation is compatible with the object and purpose of the Convention.

The General Assembly also questioned the I.C.J. about the legal effect of a reservation between the reserving state and (a) the parties who object to the reservation and (b) the parties who accept the reservation. The court answered that an objecting party to the reservation could in fact consider the reserving state as not being a party to the Convention. An accepting party, however, could consider the reserving state to be a party to the Convention.

Finally, the General Assembly wanted the I.C.J. to determine the legal effect on the treaty when an objecting state is a signatory to the Convention, but has not yet ratified it or by a state entitled to sign or accede but which has not yet done so. There is no legal effect when an objecting state is entitled to sign or accede but has not yet done so. The I.C.J. indicated that the legal effect takes place only upon ratification. Until that moment, the objection merely serves as a notice to the other state of the eventual attitude of the signatory state.

The five dissenting judges declared that these questions were "purely abstract," as they did not mention any particular states or particular reservations. They surmised that the integrity of the terms of the Convention was more important than universal acceptance and that the interests of the international community would be better served by losing a party to the Convention if a state insisted on certain modifications.

The Convention on the Prevention and Punishment of the Crime of Genocide entered into force on January 12, 1951. *See* 78 U.N.T.S. 277. By the end of 1950, the U.N. Secretary-General had received notice of 18 reservations to the Convention on the Prevention and Punishment of the Crime of Genocide. Eight states had proposed reservations to articles IV, VI, VII, IX, and XII. Article IV provides that "[p]ersons committing genocide or any of the other acts enumerated in article III shall be punished, whether they are constitutionally responsible rulers, public officials or private individuals." Article VI permits both municipal tribunals and an international penal tribunal to assert jurisdiction. Article VII eliminates the option to consider genocide as a political crime for extradition purposes. Article IX sets forth the compulsory jurisdiction of the International Court of Justice. Article XII permits the state to extend the application of the Convention to any and all territories for which the contracting party is responsible.

Fifty years later, 132 nations had become a party to the Genocide Convention. Thirty of those nations had reserved against various provisions. Some states eventually withdrew their initial reservations, including eleven states that reserved against Article IX on submitting a dispute to the International Court of Justice. Some states objected to the reservations of others. The Australian Government, for example, refused to accept any of the reservations put forth by Bulgaria, the Philippines, the Byelorussian Soviet Socialist Republic, Czechoslovakia, the Ukrainian Soviet Socialist Republic, the Union of Soviet Socialist Republics, Poland and Romania. As of October 3, 2000, 28 states continued to actively reserve against at least one provision, according to the website <http://www.preventgenocide.org/law/convention/reservations/>.

6. Withdrawal from Treaties [§42]

A state may withdraw from a treaty according to its terms and not incur international responsibility. After the I.C.J. decided in 2004 that the United States must provide new hearings for 51 Mexicans on death row in United States, *see Mexico v. U.S.*, 2004 I.C.J. 1, *infra.* at §106, the United States withdrew from an optional protocol to the Vienna Convention on Consular Relations that gave the tribunal jurisdiction to hear such disputes. The withdrawal followed a February 28, 2005 memorandum from President George W. Bush to Attorney General Alberto R. Gonzales directing state courts to abide by the decision of the I.C.J. The I.C.J. decision required American courts to review and reconsider claims that inmates' cases had been hurt by failure of local authorities to allow them to contact their consular officials. The United States possessed an international legal right to withdraw from the optional protocol.

In a follow-up case, *Medellín v. Texas*, 128 S.Ct. 1346 (2008), the United States Supreme Court concluded that neither I.C.J. decision nor the President's Memorandum independently required states to provide consideration and review of Medellín's and the other Mexican nationals' claims. The Court also found that the Vienna Convention does not constitute

43

directly enforceable domestic federal law. It affirmed the Texas Court of Criminal Appeals dismissal of Medellín's request for a writ of review to challenge his state capital murder conviction and death sentence.

7. Treaty Denouncement or Suspension [§43]

What happens when a nation suspends or denounces compliance with a treaty? According to Article 57 of the VCLT, a treaty can only be suspended "in conformity with the provisions of the treaty" or "at any time by consent of all the parties after consultation with the other contracting States." Without this compliance, a state may still be held responsible under international law for performing its obligations to the other party or parties to the treaty.

This issue arose in the *Case Concerning the Gabcikovo-Nagymaros Project (Hungary v. Slovakia)*, 1997 I.C.J. 7. Hungary and Czechoslovakia entered into a treaty on 16 September 1977, to provide for diversion of the Danube River, which formed the countries' common boundary for approximately 85 miles, and to build structures. The Danube was to be diverted into a by-pass canal in Czechoslovakian territory. A structure downstream at Nagymaros was to generate additional power and moderate the flow of waters released. If not moderated, this flow could have adversely affected water management and navigation further down the Danube.

In May 1989, Hungary suspended its work on the project in response to public protests about the potential environmental impact. The public was concerned about the project's effects on the water quality, plants, and animals in the Danube basin, and on the availability of water in particular localities. In the 1980s, Czechoslovakia made provisional plans under the name "Variant C" in anticipation that Hungary would abandon the project. Variant C called for a dam at Cunovo, on Czech territory.

Hungary unilaterally denounced the 1977 treaty on May 19, 1992, proclaiming a state of necessity or grave and imminent peril. The I.C.J. considered whether Hungary's suspension and later abandonment of the project could be justified by the defense of necessity. The court responded negatively because environmental concerns did not amount to a necessity when Hungary could show no grave and imminent peril. Czechoslovakia's "Variant C," on the other hand, was also an intentionally wrongful act.

The law of treaties determines whether a convention is or is not in force, and whether it has or has not been properly suspended or denounced. The I.C.J. determined that the Vienna Convention on the Law of Treaties defines the conditions by which a treaty may be lawfully denounced or suspended. The law of state responsibility determines whether the suspension or denunciation of a convention, seen as incompatible with the law of treaties, involves the responsibility of the state. The latter set of laws determines whether the denunciation or suspension of a treaty was a wrongful act. In this case, the treaty remained in force and Hungary remained obligated to Czechoslovakia to fulfill the terms.

8. Treaty Termination [§44]

Treaties are of unlimited duration unless their provisions specify a sunset clause, stating either a definitive termination date, or circumstances that will cause them to terminate. A treaty may also give the parties the right to terminate either with or without justification. To terminate, denounce, or withdraw from a treaty, a party must do so according to appropriate provisions of the treaty. If nothing is specified in the treaty, states may terminate or suspend the agreement by consent of all parties.

A state may seek to terminate a treaty by claiming a supervening impossibility of performance. In this instance, the performance of the treaty must be truly impossible and not just impracticable or difficult. States have also sought to terminate treaties by claiming a fundamental change of circumstances prohibits the state from performing its obligations.

In the *Case Concerning the Gabcikovo-Nagymaros Project*, 1997 I.C.J. 7, Hungary claimed that both impossibility of performance and fundamental changes of circumstances justified its May 19, 1992 termination of its treaty with Czechoslovakia. The court found that the Vienna Convention on the Law of Treaties was not directly applicable, as both states ratified the Convention only after their 1977 treaty. However, because the Convention's Articles 60 to 62, which relate to termination and suspension, declare customary international law, they still apply to bind these states regardless of when they signed the Convention.

The 1977 treaty between Hungary and Czechoslovakia did not contain any provision on termination. The treaty established a longstanding and durable regime of joint investment and joint operation.

Hungary also asserted a right to terminate the treaty based on state necessity. However, the I.C.J. determined that was an insufficient ground for termination of a treaty. It can only be invoked to exonerate failure to implement a treaty. Even then, the duty to implement the treaty revives after the necessity vanishes. Parties must terminate a treaty by mutual agreement.

Hungary then argued that impossibility of performance under Article 61 of the Vienna Convention permitted it to terminate the treaty. Article 61 requires the "permanent disappearance or destruction of an object indispensable for the execution of the treaty" to rationalize the termination of a treaty on grounds of impossibility of performance. Here, the parties had rejected an amendment to allow impossibility of performance based on serious financial difficulties.

46

Hungary also defended its actions on grounds of *rebus sic stantibus*, the Latin phrase indicating that a fundamental change of circumstances has taken place. Hungary cited profound political changes, the project's diminishing economic value, the progress of environmental knowledge, and the development of new norms and prescriptions of international environmental law as examples of fundamental changes that warranted terminating the treaty.

The court did not find Hungary's changed circumstances argument to be compelling. It noted that the prevalent political conditions were not closely linked to the object and purpose of the treaty. While the environmental knowledge and growth of environmental law was unforeseen, the treaty's articles 15, 19 and 20 were designed to accommodate change so the parties could take into account such developments. For this to work, the existence of the circumstances at the time of the treaty's conclusion must have constituted an essential basis of the consent of the parties to be bound by the treaty.

Hungary then maintained that it could terminate the treaty because Czechoslovakia breached the agreement by planning, constructing, and operating Variant C. The I.C.J. replied that a breach must be material to give rise to counter measures by the injured state. Here, Czechoslovakia's Variant C does not constitute grounds for termination under the law of treaties. Hungary terminated the treaty on May 19, 1992, before Czechoslovakia violated the treaty by diverting the Danube waters in October 1992. Hungary's termination was thus premature, as Slovakia had not yet violated the treaty.

Hungary further argued that both parties repudiated the treaty through conduct. The I.C.J. responded that although both Hungary and Czechoslovakia failed to comply with their obligations, this reciprocal wrongful conduct did not bring the treaty to an end, nor did it justify its termination.

47

The court cited the Latin maxim *pacta sunt servanda*, meaning treaties must be observed in good faith. Czechoslovakia resisted efforts to terminate after Hungary sent notice. Czechoslovakia declared Hungary's notice to be without legal effect.

Moreover, Hungary failed to give sufficient notice of termination. It gave only six days' notice of termination with a May 19 declaration to take affect on May 25. The I.C.J. considered this to be insufficient notice when Hungary had yet to suffer injury.

The Court's final declaration said that Hungary's May 19th termination notice was without legal effect; that Slovakia as successor to Czechoslovakia became a party to the treaty; and that Hungary and Slovakia must negotiate in good faith to achieve the objectives of the treaty. Further, the Court mandated that Hungary compensate Slovakia for the damage it suffered after Hungary suspended and abandoned the works, and that Slovakia compensate Hungary for putting into effect its provisional solution.

9. Voiding and Void Treaties [§45]

A treaty may become voidable, meaning that a party may elect to void the treaty under certain circumstances. Other situations absolutely void a treaty.

With allegations of error, fraud, and corruption, a treaty becomes voidable, according to Articles 48-50 of the VCLT. The victim state has the option to sever certain provisions or invalidate the entire treaty.

With error, the mistake must relate to a fact (e.g., map errors) or a situation presumed to exist. Under Article 48(2) of the Vienna Convention on the Law of Treaties, if a state contributes to the error, it cannot invalidate the treaty. Word errors are not sufficient to terminate a treaty.

Fraud also makes a treaty voidable. Under Article 49 of the Vienna Convention on the Law of Treaties, a state may invoke "fraud as invalidating its consent to be bound by the treaty." When false statements, misrepresentations, or deceptions give rise to fraud, they not only make the treaty voidable, they also can destroy the basis of mutual confidence or trust between the parties. An analogy may be found in prenuptial agreements between parties about to marry. If one party deceives his or her partner about his or her assets by providing false statements or failing to reveal the true nature of their financial well being, the prenuptial agreement becomes voidable and trust is destroyed.

Corrupting a state's representatives into signing a treaty, which does not benefit the state, gives the state the option to void a treaty under Article 50 of the Vienna Convention on the Law of Treaties. States corrupt other states' officials by providing money or property bribes and sexual favors. The goal is to persuade the representative to commit to agreements that he or she would not otherwise, but for the vice.

Treaties are absolutely void if the state or its representatives have been subjected to coercion, if the consent to be bound was expressed in violation of internal law, or if the treaty conflicts with a *jus cogens* norm. Articles 51 and 52 of the VCLT provide that the expression of a state's consent to be bound by a treaty shall be without any legal effect if it is procured by threats against the state's representatives or by a threat or use of force against the state. Similar rules voiding contracts under domestic law can be found where one party threatened or used force to procure contract acceptance.

Note, however, that threats to use force against a state or to ruin a representative's career or harm his family are different from those to enact economic sanctions or recall diplomats. While the former will automatically void a treaty, the latter will not.

A treaty is similarly void where *ultra virus* representatives concluded the treaty because they lacked the competence to bind the state under internal law. An elected public official from Bavaria, for example, has no competence to sign a treaty on behalf of Germany.

Finally, the formation of a new *jus cogens*, or preemptory, norm will invalidate treaties that conflict with the new norm. *Jus cogens* norms are those that the entire international community agree are of such moral importance that no derogation can be permitted. Thus, a treaty between two states to trade their citizens to become slaves would have been invalidated by the formation in the 1800s of the *jus cogens* norm prohibiting slavery and the slave trade.

C. Customary Law [§46]

Under the Statute of the International Court of Justice, the Court may cite international custom as evidence of a general practice accepted as law. U.S. foreign relations law also considers customary law to be a source of international law. Scholars have written extensively about customary principles. Vattel opined in the late 18th century that certain maxims and customs consecrated by long use and observed by nations in their mutual intercourse with each other became a kind of law. *See* Mark W. Janis, *An Introduction to International Law* 42 (4th Ed. 2003). British professor J. Brierly defined customary law as "a usage felt by those who follow it to be an obligatory one." *Id.* (citing J. Brierly, *The Law of Nations* 60 (4th ed. 1949). Webster's Dictionary defines custom as "a practice so long established that it has the force of law." *Random House Webster's College Dictionary* 335 (1996). To paraphrase the U.S. Supreme Court, you can think of a customary principle as a universal law of international society. *See United States v. Smith*, 18 U.S. (5 Wheaton) 153, 161 (1820).

States create customary law through their voluntary practices accepted as law. The general practice must include both a physical

50

act (the practice) and a mental component (*opinio juris* or the belief that they are acting in conformity with an international legal principle).

Numerous questions arise when trying to assess whether states have created legal principles through their acts. *See* Damrosch, *supra* §29, at 59–62. Who speaks for the state? This depends on the state. Within the United States, the President and Secretary of State speak for the country. In the United Kingdom and Germany, the prime ministers and ministers of foreign affairs speak for their countries. Thus, by their actions and statements, leaders signal they are creating legal principles.

How much time is required? Some customary principles may come into existence after a short period if a group of states adopt the same practice at the same time. The president of one country may announce or proclaim a legal principle and act accordingly. If other states immediately adopt the practice, a new legal principle may come into existence seemingly overnight.

How many states are needed to create a new legal principle? This depends on the law at issue and if the practice is general or regional to a group of states. If it is a general principle, then a variety of states from different economic and political groupings may need to consent to create a new principle. If it is a regional principle, say North American customary law, then only three states would need to consent. Thus, if one state proclaims the right to kidnap the citizens of the other two states, and the other two states follow suit, then a regional custom could come into existence. This would subject all North American inhabitants to being kidnapped at will when they are suspected of committing a crime in one of the other two states.

How much consistency is required to form a new customary principle? There must be consistency to create and sustain the principle, but some derogation may be permitted. However, systematic derogation during the formation period would indicate that a principle has not been created. Once the principle has come into existence, derogation indicates that a state has violated the rule and becomes responsible under international law to the victim state.

Are dissenting and non-participating states bound by the practice? If a state dissents and does not participate during the formation of the customary law, then it is not bound by the law. It, in effect, becomes a persistent objector. In the example above addressing kidnapping, if one of the three states vigorously disagreed with creating a right to kidnap another state's citizens, that state would not be bound by the new rule. In this hypothetical, the objection of one state within a three-state region would destroy the concept of a regional custom. If the other two states consented, then they would just create a local custom between them.

What is the evidence of *opinio juris*, or the longer *opinio juris sive necessitatis?* I.C.J. cases reference this Latin phrase as the perception that a given behavior is required by law or is legally obliged. In *The North Sea Continental Shelf Cases (Federal Republic of Germany v. Denmark) (Federal Republic of Germany v. Netherlands)*, 1969 I.C.J. 3, the I.C.J. explained that acts must "be carried out in such a way, as to be evidence of a belief that this practice is rendered obligatory by the existence of a rule of law requiring it... . The States concerned must therefore feel that they are conforming to what amounts to a legal obligation." *See* Damrosch, *supra* §29, at 94 (citing 1969 I.C.J. 3).

International elites listen and read the statements of leaders to determine whether they are acting because they feel legally obliged to do so. States indicate a sense of *opinio juris* when they act as if they are duty bound to act. A practice may start from voluntary, unilateral acts expecting acquiescence or emulation. A practice may also start from a treaty to which other states have committed. Ultimately, there needs to be a chain reaction indicating international consensus.

1. General Custom [§47]

The *Paquette Habana*, 175 U.S. 677, 20 S.Ct. 290, 44 L.Ed. 320 (1900), discusses the creation of a general principle of customary international law that binds all states, despite some derogation during its formation. The conflict arose during the Spanish (Cuban) American war. The plaintiffs were two Spanish nationals of Cuban birth who lived in Havana and owned separate fishing vessels that flew the Spanish flag. The vessels' cargo consisted of fresh fish when they were seized and condemned as prizes of war. The crew had no knowledge of the war or the blockade. The ship carried no arms or ammunition on board and made no attempt to run the blockade or resist capture.

The Supreme Court considered whether the armed vessels of the U.S. could legally capture these fishing smacks during the war with Spain. The answer depended on whether a customary law exempting fishing boats from seizure had developed that would bind the United States.

The court declared that states by their practice had created the following customary rule, "[C]oast fishing vessels, pursuing their vocation of catching and bringing in fresh fish, have been recognized as exempt, with their cargoes and crews, from capture as prize of war." 175 U.S. at 686. The Supreme Court asserted that this ancient usage among civilized nations began centuries ago and gradually ripened into a rule of international law.

The Supreme Court examined several acts and evidence of *opinio juris* to indicate that the rule existed. In 1403 and 1406, Henry IV of England issued orders protecting fishing vessels from seizure. The Holy Roman Emperor Charles V and Francis I of

53

France concluded a treaty on October 2, 1521, that followed Henry IV's practice of permitting fishing vessels to come and go in peace. In 1536, Dutch edicts permitted herring fishing during war times.

Nevertheless, there was some derogation during the formation of the practice. While early French practice permitted admirals to authorize fishing during times of war, the French curtailed this practice in 1681 and 1692 due to the failure of their enemies to reciprocate the treatment. The French resumed the customary practice by June 5, 1779, when Louis XVI addressed a letter to his admiral informing him not to disturb fishermen.

The United States became a state in 1776, and by 1785 it was following the practice. In 1785, the U.S. and Prussia (the predecessor state of what is now modern day eastern Germany, northern Poland, and a small portion of Russia) agreed that if war arose between them, "all women and children, scholars of every faculty, cultivators of the earth, artisans, manufacturers, and fisherman, unarmed and inhabiting unfortified towns, villages or places, and in general all others whose occupations are for the common subsistence and benefit of mankind, shall be allowed to continue their respective employments, …but if anything is necessary to be taken from them for the use of such armed force, the same shall be paid for at a reasonable price." *Id.* at 690-691.

The United States continued the practice in 1846. In its war with Mexico, the United States recognized the exemption of coastal fishing boats from capture in letters from the Secretary of the Navy. The 1848 U.S.-Mexico peace treaty asserted the words from the 1785 U.S.-Prussia treaty.

States in the east adopted the practice as well. The Empire of Japan permitted fishing to continue during its war with

China. The Supreme Court cited Takahashi, International Law, 11, 178, for its note that Japan promulgated an ordinance in August 1894, which established prize courts and ordained that the enemy's vessels are exempt from detention, including boats engaged in coast fisheries, as well as ships engaged exclusively on a voyage of scientific discovery, philanthropy, or religious mission. *Id.* at 700.

The Supreme Court spent considerable time looking at the evidence of the rule, and it then strictly applied the rule to the facts. While it noted inconsistencies, the Court said these interruptions were not, in effect, claims to abandon the rule and start another rule. The Court declared that the capture of the two fishing vessels was unlawful and without probable cause. It ordered that the "decree of the District Court be reversed, and the proceeds of the sale of the vessel, together with the proceeds of any sale of her cargo, be restored to the claimant, with damages and costs." *Id.* at 714.

2. Regional Custom [§48]

Countries can create regional custom through consistent practice accepted as law throughout a group of states linked by geographic qualities. As with a general custom, some derogation may be permitted but when one country persistently objects, the custom does not apply to it.

The *Haya De La Torre* case, which is often referred to as the *Asylum Case (Colombia v. Peru)*, 1950 I.C.J. 266, addresses the issue of whether a regional customary principle had been established that would bind Peru although it had not signed particular conventions that contained the rule. On October 3, 1948, Victor Raul Haya de la Torre was the leader of the American People's Revolutionary Alliance when a military rebellion broke out in Peru. The Peruvian government suppressed the hostilities on the same day and opened an investigation.

On October 4, 1948, the President of Peru issued a decree, charging the American People's Revolutionary Alliance with having organized and directed the rebellion. The next day, the Minister of Interior denounced Haya de la Torre in a note addressed to the Minister for the Navy. By October 11, the Examining Magistrate opened judicial proceedings against Haya de la Torre and ordered his arrest on October 25. Two days later, on October 27, a military junta seized power. The junta immediately began court marshals and summary executions.

On November 16, Haya de la Torre was ordered to report to the Examining Magistrate. He was charged with the crime of military rebellion. He did not report. Instead, on January 3, 1949, he sought asylum in the Colombian embassy in Lima. On January 4, 1949, Colombia requested safe passage for him out of Lima, which Peru refused.

Colombia claimed the right as the state granting the asylum to Haya de la Torre to qualify his offence as political for asylum purposes. Colombia proclaimed this right as a principle of American international law, a regional custom local to American states. Colombia cited three treaties to support its claim: the Bolivian extradition treaty signed on July 18, 1911; the Havana Convention on Asylum signed on February 20, 1928; and the Montevideo Convention of 1933. Colombia alleged that these treaties codified regional custom, and therefore bound Peru, even if it did not sign them.

The I.C.J. required Colombia to prove that the custom was established in such a manner as to bind Peru by showing consistent and uniform usage and an acceptance of the practice as law. The I.C.J. found the cases Colombia cited to be contradictory, and full of uncertainty, inconsistency, fluctuations, discrepancies, and political expediency. The I.C.J. did not find a customary practice giving one state the right to unilaterally characterize an offence as political for asylum purposes. Further, the I.C.J. found that even if there were such an established custom, it could not be invoked against Peru, which had persistently objected to such a claim at every term and had not ratified the Montevideo Convention.

Colombia lost on the merits, meaning that Peru did not have to provide safe passage to Haya de la Torre so he could depart its territory. Nevertheless, Peru did not possess the right to enter Colombia's embassy and retrieve him as long as he was on Colombia's territory.

3. Special Custom [§49]

A special or local custom may be created between two states. For example, two states may agree to create a right of passage through the territory of one state in favor of another state. They must specify between them what is included within the right.

In the *Case Concerning Right of Passage Over Indian Territory* (*Portugal v. India*), 1960 I.C.J. 6, the I.C.J. adjudicated whether Portugal or India established a local custom between them. Portugal had two enclaves (Dadra and Nagar-Aveli) on the Indian peninsula surrounded by India. These were Portuguese colonies that grew out of the era of Vasco Da Gama, who was the first explorer to complete the all water trade route between Europe and India. A rebellion broke out in the enclaves (supposedly sponsored by India with the blessings of Prime Minister Nehru) to overthrow Portuguese rule. Portugal attempted to send military weapons to help the government maintain its sovereignty over the enclaves. India objected, claiming that Portugal did not have a right of passage through India to get to its colonies.

Portugal claimed that it had a right of passage through Indian territory to maintain sovereignty over its enclaves. In domestic law, a right of passage appears similar to an easement between two properties permitting one property owner the right to traverse through another property owner's land to get to his property. After reviewing the history between Portugal and India, the I.C.J. concluded that Portugal did not have a right of passage to bring armed forces, armed police, arms, and ammunition through India to its territories. In its prior relations with Britain, which had colonial authority over India when the Portuguese colonies were established, Portugal only received a right to transport private persons, civil officials, and goods through India to its enclaves.

Because Portugal failed to prove a special or local custom between it and India, it was left with territories that it could not defend. India ultimately obtained sovereignty over the enclaves.

4. Conflicts Between Treaties and Customary Rules [§50]

Sometimes treaty and customary rules may conflict. International law has developed four principles of interpretation in this situation. The first concerns the Latin maxim *lex specialis derogat generali*, which means the specific prevails over the general. Between a treaty rule and a customary rule, the more specific will govern the particular situation.

Courts will also take into account the parties' intent and ask whether they intended to replace a treaty rule with a customary rule. If they did manifest such intent through their language or actions, then the treaty rule will govern.

Another rule examines whether the customary rule or the treaty rule was later in time. The more recent of the two should be applied to govern the situation. This rule is subject to regular presumptions of interpretation, according to Articles 31-32 of the VCLT.

The general presumption, nevertheless, is that treaties should not derogate from general custom. Countries are bound by customary principles and should obey them. Treaties can supplement customary rules, but they should not conflict with them. Thus, in the hypothetical on kidnapping in §46, to the extent that international law forbids kidnapping, two states would not be able to establish a local custom or treaty between them to kidnap each other's citizens. *See generally* Sherri Burr, *From Noriega to Pinochet: Is There an International Moral and Legal Right to Kidnap Individuals Accused of Gross Human Rights Violations?*, 29 Denver. J. of Int'l Law & Policy 101-114 (Spring 2001).

D. General Principles of Law [§51]

The I.C.J. can consider general principles of law common to the major legal systems as supplementary rules of law. In his book *International Law in Theory and Practice* 50-55 (1991), Professor Oscar Schachter distinguished five categories of general principles of municipal or domestic law. He asserted that some general principles of law are principles of municipal law (1) "recognized by civilized nations;" (2) "derived from the specific nature of the international community;" (3) "intrinsic to the idea of law and basic to all legal systems;" (4) "valid through all kinds of societies in relationships of hierarchy and co-ordination;" and (5) founded on "the very nature of man as a rational and social being." *See* Damrosch, *supra* §29, at 118 (citing Oscar Schacter, *International Law in Theory and Practice* 50-55 (1991)).

Damrosch and her colleagues note that the I.C.J. rarely cites general principles in majority court opinions, unless they have risen to the status of customary law or have been referenced in treaties. Rather, individual or dissenting opinions sometimes reference general principles. The I.C.J. tends to use certain generally recognized rules as those that have acquired the status of customary law.

The following are examples of general principles of law common to all nations. Common general principles include those requiring (1) good faith; (2) the obligation to repair a wrong; and (3) estoppel. Estoppel prevents a person from asserting a claim or fact that is inconsistent with his prior position in another proceeding. Others of a general character forbid abuse of rights or retroactive applications of legal principles. Analytical general principles embrace *pacta sunt servanda*, requiring that treaties be obeyed in good faith, and *nemo plus iuris transfere potest quam ipse habet*, which forbids people from transferring more rights than they possess. *Id.* at 121.

Some general principles relate to the administration of justice and the rules for the determination of preliminary objection in trials. Consider, as an example, the principle of *res judicata*, a Latin phrase to indicate the issue before the court has already been decided by another court.

General principles that relate to legal logic include the Latin maxims *lex posterior derogat priori*, which means the later supersedes the earlier law, if both have the same source, and *nemo judex in sua causa*, which means that no one can be a judge in his own case. The latter does not always apply in the International Court of Justice. A rule of the court permits a party to a contentious case to appoint a judge if the other party has a judge on the court. This differs from the rule in municipal law that excuses judges with connections to one of the parties. *Id.* at 121-122.

E. *Jus Cogens* Norms [§52]

Jus cogens norms can preempt and void a treaty. There are four criteria for identifying peremptory norms under Article 53 of the Vienna Convention on the Law of Treaties. First, these are norms of general international law. Second, they have to be accepted and recognized by the international community of states as a whole. Third, they permit no derogation. Fourth, they can be modified only by new peremptory norms.

Strong examples of such norms are the prohibitions against slavery, torture, and genocide. The freedom of the high seas represents another example.

The effect of Article 53 of the Vienna Convention on the Law of Treaties is to limit the treaty-making power of states by invalidating treaties that conflict with peremptory norms. Article 64 of the Vienna Convention on the Law of Treaties voids and terminates existing treaties that conflict with any peremptory norm, including new emerging ones. The function of a *jus cogens* norm is to protect the society and its institutions from harmful consequences of individual agreements.

Jus cogens norms restrict the freedom of the parties, as the rules are absolutely binding. What are the consequences if a *jus cogens* norm voids a treaty? Treaties voided by Article 53 suffer two consequences. First, the *jus cogens* norm eliminates the consequences of any act performed in reliance on any provision that conflicted with the peremptory norm. Second, the *jus cogens* norm requires the parties to bring their mutual relations into conformity with the peremptory norm.

Treaties voided by Article 64 similarly undergo two consequences. First, Article 64 releases the parties from any obligations to further perform the treaty. Second, Article 64 has no effect on any rights, obligations, or situations of the parties that do not conflict with a *jus cogens* norm.

States in effect possess moral duties. They must maintain law and order within their boundaries. They must defend their territory against external attacks. They must provide care for the bodily and spiritual welfare of their citizens at home and protect their citizens living abroad. Treaties that prevent states from fulfilling one of these essential tasks may be considered immoral and consequently void. The bottom line is that international law has some rules that do not require state consent.

F. Teachings of Scholars [§53]

Scholars through their writings have systematized international law. Famous publicists in England include Ian Brownlie and Sir Hersch Lauterpacht. In the United States, Abe Chase, Richard Falk, Louis Henkin, Myers McDougal, Michael Reisman, and Oscar Schachter have been cited in numerous opinions for their contributions to international law. The writings of scholars published in The Hague Academy's *Recuil des Cours* are viewed with deference. United States courts often cite to law review articles and treatises by scholars, as the Second Circuit did in the *Filartiga* case, 630 F.2d 876 (2d Cir. 1980), which is discussed in the section 80 on torture.

There are also famous associations of scholars, such as the International Law Commission, whose 34 members propose draft treaties; the *Institut de Droit International*, which possesses 120 members and associate members and was awarded the 1904 Nobel Peace Prize; and the International Law Association, which has over 3,700 members divided into branches, including the American Branch. The American Society of International Law (ASIL) meets annually in the spring to consider pressing questions of international law. The Jessup International Law Moot Court competition is held in association with the ASIL annual meeting and offers law students from around the world an opportunity to brief and argue international legal issues. In 2005, for example, the University of Queensland (Australia), as applicant, defeated the International Islamic University (Malaysia), as respondent, before a Championship Round panel that included Dame Rosalyn Higgins, an I.C.J. judge from the United Kingdom. After a conference on transnational law in 2004, the Association of American Law Schools moved to establish an International

Association of Law Schools to facilitate communications and exchanges between various law schools around the world.

The writings of scholars may be considered problematic if the writing is nationalistic, rather than reflective of general international consensus. Some scholars have links to their government, which may affect their objectivity. Despite these problems, courts look to objective scholarly writing to indicate sufficient systematization of various international legal rules and principles.

For example, in *United States v. Smith*, 18 U.S. 153, 5 L.Ed. 57, 5 Wheat. 153 (1820), the Supreme Court wrote, "There is scarcely a writer on the law of nations, who does not allude to piracy as a crime of a settled and determinate nature; and whatever may be the diversity of definitions, in other respects, all writers concur, in holding, that robbery, or forcible depredations' upon the sea ... is piracy." 18 U.S. at 161. The Court used citations to scholars to buttress its conclusion that "the crime of piracy is defined by the law of nations with reasonable certainty." *Id.* at 160.

G. Equity [§54]

The I.C.J. can apply equity to resolve disputes, if the parties so agree. In the cases delimiting the continental shelf between two or more states, the I.C.J. has frequently applied equity and referenced the use of equitable principles. In his 1991 book *International Law in Theory and Practice,* Professor Oscar Schachter perceived five uses of equity. He noted that equity has been used as (1) a basis for individualized justice; (2) considerations of fairness, reasonableness, and good faith; (3) a basis for certain specific principles of legal reasoning associated with fairness and reasonableness (such as estoppel, unjust enrichment, and abuse of rights); (4) standards for the allocation and sharing of resources and benefits; and (5) as a broad synonym for distributive

63

justice. *See* Damrosch, *supra* §29, at 129 (citing Oscar Schacter, *International Law in Theory and Practice* 50-55 (1991)).

States frequently cite equity to justify their demands for economic and social arrangements and redistribution of wealth. As Professor Damrosch and her colleagues observe in their international law text, international lawyers (especially in Europe) often refer to decisions based on equity as *infra legem* (within the law), *praeter legem* (outside the law) and *contra legem* (against the law). *Id.* A court decision is considered *infra legem* when a rule leaves court margin of discretion within current law. The decision becomes *praeter legem* when the issue is not covered by a relevant legal rule and the court must go outside the law to resolve the conflict. A *contra legem* decision cited a relevant rule, but went against the rule in resolving the conflict. Courts may depart from the law to avoid unjust enrichment.

When it comes to applying equity, courts are mindful of the maxim that is found in various legal systems, "he who seeks equity must do equity." Equity relates ultimately to fairness, as the I.C.J. and other courts have observed in various cases.

1. The Diversion of Water from the Meuse (The Netherlands v. Belgium) [§55]

In *The Diversion of Water from the Meuse* (*The Netherlands v. Belgium*) case, 1937 P.C.I.J. Ser. A/B, No. 70, 76-78, the Permanent Court of International Justice considered a dispute between the Netherlands and Belgium over construction of locks and canals to alter the water level and rate of flow of the Meuse River. Judge Hudson said in his individual concurring opinion, "It would seem to be an important principle of equity that where two parties have assumed an identical or a reciprocal obligation, one party which is engaged in a continuing non-performance of that obligation should not be permitted to take advantage of a similar non-performance of that obligation by the other party." He also repeated maxims such as "Equality is equity," and "He who seeks equity must do equity," in concurring with the court's decision to reject the Netherlands' claim against Belgium when the Netherlands had been the first to put a lock on the Meuse River. *Id.* at 77.

2. The Corfu Channel Case [§56]

The United Kingdom sued Albania after it placed mines in the Corfu Channel that damaged British warships and took British lives. In *The Corfu Channel Case (United Kingdom v. Albania)*, 1949 I.C.J. 4, 22, the Court maintained that Albania had a duty to warn Britain of the imminent danger of the mine fields based on "elementary considerations of humanity, even more exacting in peace than in war."

3. The Cayuga Indians Case [§57]

The Cayuga Indians were a tribe split between the U.S. and Canadian borders. The Canadian Cayugas claimed they had not received their fair share of revenue payments for land ceded to the U.S. *See The Cayuga Indians Case, American and British Claims Arbitration*, Nielsen Reports 203, 307 (1926). The arbitration tribunal determined that the claim of the Cayugas was founded "in the elementary principle of justice that requires us to look at the substance and not stick in the bark of the legal form." *Id.* at 313.

The tribunal determined that special circumstances made the equitable claim of the Canadian Cayugas especially strong, particularly their lack of international status, their dependent legal position, and that the 1926 treaty between the U.S. and Canada required decisions be made on principles of law and equity. The tribunal held that the Canadian Cayugas were entitled to money damages because they had not received their fair share of the revenues.

H. Soft Law [§58]

Two categories constitute soft law, which are considered flexible forms of law: voluntary codes and guidelines, and General Assembly resolutions. Some scholars refer to these types of rules, along with general principles of law, as gap fillers to cover legal holes when no treaty or customary rule exists.

The United Nations and the World Bank have prescribed foreign investment codes and norms of conduct for transnational corporations. The World Health Organization and the Food and Agricultural Organization have codified food standards. Non-governmental organizations, such as the International Olympic Committee (I.O.C.), set out standards for their members and participants. The I.O.C. provides participating athletes with information on substance abuse and doping, and has been known to strip athletes of medals who violate these rules.

Of the 8,000 General Assembly resolutions and decisions issued between 1946 and 2000, Professor Damrosch and her co-authors contend that fewer than 100 "express general rules of conduct of states." Damrosch, *supra* §29, at 145. Nevertheless, at least one arbitrator found that General Assembly resolutions could be indicative of international law. Sole arbitrator Rene Jean Dupuy considered this issue in the case of *Texaco Overseas Petroleum v. Libya Arab Republic*, 17 I.L.M. 1 (1978), to determine what level of compensation Libya should pay after it issued decrees nationalizing the assets of two oil companies. Libya relied on General Assembly resolutions for its proposition that it alone may determine compensation.

The arbitrator did not dispute Libya's sovereign right to nationalize the assets of the two oil companies. Rather, he criticized its failure to appropriately compensate the oil companies. Dupuy considered the legal effect of several General Assembly resolutions to determine the legal standard of compensation. He concluded that General Assembly Resolution 1803, titled

"Permanent Sovereignty over Natural Resources," which passed by a vote of 87 for, 2 against, and 12 abstaining on December 14, 1962, could be considered as evidence of international law. He noted that the majority of 87 included the developed and developing worlds, all geographic areas and economic systems. He also asserted that Resolution 1803 represented a compromise because it recognized state sovereignty over natural resources and principles of international compensation.

With the other resolutions he considered, namely 3171 and 3281, the market economies had voted against them and several developing countries had abstained. Dupuy concluded that only Resolution 1803 reflected the state of customary international law existing in the field. His order required Libya to pay just compensation to the nationalized oil companies. In conclusion, both international and national courts may draw on several sources of international rules to decide conflicts involving states.

CHAPTER V

V. International Organizations

A. The United Nations and Its Specialized Organs [§59]

Public international organizations are entities created by treaties and comprised primarily or entirely of states. The primary global entity is the United Nations, which was established on October 24, 1945, by 51 countries. By 2006, its membership had grown to 192 states.

The United Nations Charter endows the organization with four primary purposes: (1) maintain international peace and security; (2) develop friendly relations among nations; (3) cooperate in solving international problems and in promoting respect for human rights; and (4) become a center for harmonizing the actions of nations. Charter of the United Nations, June 26, 1945, T.S. 993, 3 Bevans 1153 (hereinafter "U.N. Charter)."

The U.N. is not a world government. It is composed of six main organs:

- The General Assembly, which has 192 members;
- The Security Council, which has 15 members;
- The Secretariat, which is led by the Secretary-General;
- The Economic and Social Council;
- The Trusteeship Council; and
- The International Court of Justice.

Other U.N. offices include the UNHCR (the United Nations High Commission for Refugees); the UNDP (the United Nations Development Programme); and the UNICEF (the United Nations Children's Fund). They report to the General Assembly or the Economic and Social Council. We will discuss each of the six main organs in turn along with other global entities.

1. The General Assembly [§60]

Only states can become members of the United Nations. All members are represented in the General Assembly. Each member state may have from one to a maximum of five representatives, but only one vote. In its advisory opinion entitled *Conditions of Admission of a State to Membership in the United Nations*, the I.C.J. determined that Article 4 of the U.N. Charter required candidates for admission to be "(1) a State; (2) peace-loving; (3) must accept the obligations of the Charter; (4) must be able to carry out these obligations; (5) must be willing to do so." *See* I.C.J. Advisory Opinion of 28 May 1948.

The General Assembly meets annually from September to December. At the September opening of the General Assembly, presidents, prime ministers, kings, queens, and other leaders from all over the world descend on the New York headquarters to give speeches and interact with each other. Most General Assembly decisions are made by a simple majority vote. Certain decisions require a two-thirds majority, such as recommendations on (1) international peace and security; (2) admitting new members, suspending members' rights and privileges, or expelling members; (3) electing non-permanent members to the Security Council; (4) approving the United Nations budget; and (5) amending the United Nations Charter. *See* U.N. Charter, *supra* §59.

Often, decisions are reached through consensus rather than by voting. As discussed previously with reference to the Libya-Texaco case, General Assembly resolutions may be considered evidence of customary law, depending on the tribunal.

In 2000, the U.N. hosted a millennium summit on development, which put forth eight objectives covering poverty, sexual discrimination, hunger, primary education, child mobility, maternal health, the environment, and disease. By the year 2015, the member states pledged to reduce by half the proportion of people living on less than a dollar a day and reduce by half the proportion of people who suffer from hunger. They also committed to ensure that all boys and girls complete a full course of primary schooling; to eliminate gender disparity in primary and secondary education; and to reduce by two-thirds the mortality rate among children under five.

According to the publication *Basic Facts about the United Nations*, available at <www.un.org/aboutun/basicfacts/unorg.htm>, the United Nations budget for 2000-2001 was $2,535,000,000. Member dues are calculated as a percentage of the budget based on the state's share of the world economy, adjusted to take into account factors like per capita incomes. Countries are also assessed a share of peacekeeping costs, which amounted to another $2 billion in the year 2000. Other organs that are funded separately include international tribunals, and programs like the U.N. Development Program and UNICEF.

A member that fails to pay dues in a timely manner may lose its ability to vote in the General Assembly if the arrearage equals or exceeds the amount of the contributions due from it for the preceding two full years. Nevertheless, the General Assembly may permit the member to continue voting if it becomes satisfied that the arrearage was due to circumstances beyond the member's control. Although all U.N. members are required to pay assessments in full by January 31 of a given year, few do so. In 1997 and 1998, for example, only 27 out of the then 187 members (or 14.4%) paid assessments in full by the deadline for those years. This means that 85.6% of states did not pay their bills on time.

The United States, as the world's largest economy, is assessed approximately 25 percent of the annual general budget, and any specialized funding for peacekeeping or other specialty operations. As such, the U.S. is the biggest financial contributor to the United Nations. Beginning in the early 1980s, the Reagan

Administration withheld United States dues to protest certain United Nations activities and encourage reform.

When word leaked that the U.N. teetered on bankruptcy due to the missing component of its budget, U.S. citizens contributed to the budget. School children sent coins and dollars. Individuals sent checks. Television and entertainment mogul Ted Turner pledged a billion dollar trust fund for the U.N.

On January 16, 1998, Ambassador Bill Richardson, the U.S. Delegate to the United Nations, said in a speech to the Kennedy School, "Today, America is a debtor nation at the United Nations - to the tune of one billion dollars.... I believe that if America is to remain the world's 'indispensable nation' this unacceptable situation must be rectified." *See, e.g.* <http://www.globalpolicy.org/finance/chronol/fin1998_A.htm>. Although President Clinton called for payment in full, Congress refused to heed his demand for much of his presidency.

Instead, Congress conditioned U.S. payment of arrearages to specific benchmarks, encouraging the U.N. to downsize and eliminate overlapping programs and activities. Congress also sought to reduce the U.S. share of the U.N. budget from 25 to 22 percent. The April 27, 1999 Committee on Foreign Relations report from Senator Jesse Helms observed that had the reduction been in place during the previous five years, U.S. taxpayers would have saved "at least a half billion dollars in assessed contributions to the United Nations and its specialized agencies."

The advocacy for the U.N. continued into the next U.S. presidential administration. Jane Roberts, a 62-year-old retired French teacher and tennis coach, sought 34 million Americans to donate at least one dollar to the United Nations Population Fund (UNFPA) after President George W. Bush refused to release the $34 million Congress approved for UNFPA.

72

The U.S. never lost its vote in the General Assembly, although it was ousted from the United Nations Human Rights Commission and the International Narcotics Control Board in 2001. At the time, the U.S. owed the U.N. $582 million in back dues.

2. The Security Council [§61]

The Security Council contains 15 members, which include five permanent ones and ten rotating members elected for two-year terms. Each Security Council member has one representative with one vote. Decisions involving procedural matters require nine affirmative votes. Decisions on all other matters require nine affirmative votes, and must include the concurring votes of the permanent members. A negative vote by a permanent member acts as a veto, effectively killing the measure.

The five permanent members are China, France, Russia, the United Kingdom, and the United States. Together, these five nations successfully fought the Nazi German government and its allies during World War II. They have veto power over all Security Council decisions, with the exception of procedural matters.

The primary purpose of the Security Council is to maintain international peace and security. The Security Council may convene at anytime, whenever peace is threatened. Any United Nations member can be invited to participate in a Security Council meeting if it is a party to a dispute that the body is considering. The Security Council endeavors to resolve conflict peacefully, and may undertake to mediate various disputes, urge the parties to seek mediation or arbitration by third parties, or suggest submitting the dispute to the International Court of Justice.

The Security Council may deploy peacekeeping troops to help parties maintain a truce or to keep opposing forces apart.

The Security Council makes recommendations to the General Assembly on the appointment of a new Secretary-General and on the admission of new members to the United Nations.

For decades, the United Nations and international law scholars have put forth proposals to reform the Security Council to better reflect current global economic realities. One proposal would expand the Security Council to a body of 24, with 11 permanent members and 13 rotating members. This plan would add six new permanent members without veto power and three new two-year spots for rotating members. For the six permanent spots, four nations (Brazil, India, Germany, and Japan) launched an ambitious global lobbying campaign in 2005. Three African nations (Egypt, Nigeria, and South Africa) also lobbied to become permanent members.

The *New York Times* reported that the process became highly politicized when Argentina and Mexico opposed Brazil, China and the two Koreas opposed Japan, and the United States opposed giving any new members veto power out of concern that it would paralyze the Security Council. *See* Joel Brinkley, *As Nations Lobby to Join Security Council, the U.S. Resists Giving Them Veto Power*, New York Times, sec. 1, p. 14 (May 15, 2005). Since this issue has already been debated for decades, the discussions will likely continue for many more years without resolution.

3. U.N. Secretariat [§62]

The United Nations Secretariat carries out the substantive and administrative work of the United Nations. The Secretariat consists of departments and offices with a staff of 8,900 under its regular budget and another 7,500 under special funding. The staff is drawn from 170 countries. The Secretariat is headquartered in New York, with offices in Geneva, Vienna, Nairobi, and other locations. Agreements between the United Nations and the host nation set out the relationship.

For example, the agreement between the U.S. and the U.N. provides that the headquarters district shall be inviolable and prohibits U.S. federal, state, and local officials from entering the premises without the consent of the Secretary General. The headquarters treaty entered into force on November 21, 1947. *See* 11 U.N.T.S. 11, 61 Stat. 3416, T.I.A.S. No. 1676, 12 Bevans 956.

The Secretary-General is the chief administrative officer of the Secretariat. The General Assembly appoints the Secretary-General based on a recommendation from the Security Council. Secretary-Generals have been elected from Europe, Asia, South America, and Africa. Boutros Boutros-Ghali, the international lawyer and diplomat from Egypt, was the only Secretary-General to serve just one term of appointment from 1992-1996.

On January 1, 1997, Kofi Annan of Ghana became the seventh Secretary-General of the United Nations. He was reelected for a second five-year term that began on January 1, 2002 and ended when he was succeeded by Ban Ki-moon on January 1, 2007. Secretary-General Annan was the first to serve from sub-Saharan Africa and the first to be elected from the ranks of U.N. staff, having joined the U.N. in 1962 to work for the World Health Organization. He also served in the office of the U.N. High Commissioner for Refugees and as Under-Secretary-General for Peacekeeping at a time when nearly 70,000 military and civilian personnel were deployed in U.N. operations around the world. Secretary-General Annan shared the Nobel Peace Prize with the United Nations in 2001. The Nobel Peace Prize has been awarded to several other U.N. Agencies and associated individuals, including the refugee and labor agencies, and U.N. Secretary-General Dag Hjalmar Agne Carl Hammarskjöld of Sweden, the legendary diplomat who perished in a plane crash while serving his second term in office.

4. The Economic and Social Council [§63]

The Economic and Social Council currently has 54 members (twice the original number of 27). Its members are elected by the General Assembly for 3-year staggered terms. Each member has one vote and a majority vote decides questions.

The Economic and Social Council meets throughout the year. Its primary purpose is to coordinate the economic and social work of the U.N. and its family of organizations. It has a host of subsidiary bodies. For example, the Commission on Human Rights monitors the observance of human rights throughout the world. Other bodies focus on social development, the status of women, crime prevention, narcotic drugs, and environmental protection.

5. The Trusteeship Council [§64]

The Trusteeship Council was established to provide international supervision for 11 trust territories administered by seven member states, and to ensure that adequate steps were taken to prepare the territories for self-government or independence. Trust territories were initially set up by mandates from the League of Nations, the predecessor organization to the United Nations.

When South Africa sought to dissolve its mandate by incorporating South-West Africa (a German colony until 1920) into the Union of South Africa, the General Assembly asked the I.C.J. for an advisory opinion. The Court held unanimously that South Africa was not competent to modify the international status of South-West Africa without the consent of the U.N. *See International Status of South-West Africa*, Advisory Opinion of 11 July 1950. It also decided by 12 votes to 2 that South Africa continued to have the international obligation to submit reports and transmit petitions from the inhabitants of that territory, with supervisory functions to be exercised by the United Nations. The territorial boundaries and people of

South-West Africa eventually formed the independent Republic of Namibia, which joined the U.N. on April 23, 1990.

By 1994, all trust territories had attained independence, either as separate states or by joining neighboring countries. On December 15, 1994, Palau, the last trust territory in the Pacific Islands, became the U.N.'s 185th member state. The Trusteeship Council now consists of the five permanent members of the Security Council. It meets when an occasion arises. It is practically defunct. There have been calls from some scholars to revive the Trusteeship Council to assist failed states. *See, e.g.,* Gerald B. Helman and Steven R. Ratner, *Saving Failed States*, 89 Foreign Policy 3 (Winter 1992-1993). However, Professor Ruth Gordon criticizes this approach as top down. She proposes, instead, to rebuild failed states by "focusing on the peoples themselves, without preconceived ideas of the answers or the solutions." Ruth Gordon, *Saving Failed States: Sometimes a Neocolonialist Notion,*" 12 American Univ. J. of Int'l L. & Policy 903, 973 (1997).

6. International Court of Justice [§65]

The International Court of Justice is the main judicial organ of the United Nations. Article 93(1) of the U.N. Charter provides that "[A]ll members of the United Nations are *ipso facto* parties to the Statute of the International Court of Justice." Situated in the Peace Palace in The Hague, a city in The Netherlands, the Court functions in the official languages of French and English. Information about the entity and its decisions can be found on its website <http://www.icj-cij.org>.

The 15 judges are elected jointly by votes of the General Assembly and the Security Council. There are always judges from the five permanent Security Council members: China, France, Russia, the United Kingdom, and the U.S. A gentlemen's agreement partitions the other ten judges by geographic regions.

I.C.J. judges are elected to nine-year staggered terms. Five judges are chosen every three years. When a vacancy occurs for the U.S. judge, for example, the State Department Legal Advisor may form a committee to solicit nominations and recommendation letters. Some international law professors have been known to actively campaign for the position by calling their acquaintances all over the country, while others prefer to rest on their laurels. The committee provides a recommendation to the Legal Advisor, who ultimately forwards a recommendation to the President who communicates the nominee's name to the U.S. Representative to the United Nations. Thomas Buergenthal, a Holocaust survivor and former law professor from George Washington University, was elected the U.S. judge on March 2, 2000. He is eligible for reelection in 2009.

The I.C.J. primarily decides contentious cases, or disputes between countries. There is no *stare decisis*, requiring the court to follow its prior opinions or precedent, in international law. The I.C.J. cannot make international law; rather, it determines the law that states have created through their treaties, customary practice, and other sources indicating their consent. It then applies the relevant law to resolve disputes.

During the 60 years between 1947 and 2007, the I.C.J. issued orders and/or opinions in 110 contentious cases between states, some of which included two or more phases to first resolve objections to jurisdiction or other matters before reaching the merits. As a court of original jurisdiction and final appeal, the court issues an average of one to three opinions a year. Some disputes occupy several years of court time, from initial application to resolution.

The I.C.J. does not possess an independent enforcement mechanism. Article 94 of the U.N. Charter, *supra* §59, requires U.N. members to comply with I.C.J. judgments. If a party to a case fails to conform its actions to the ruling, then the other party can seek recourse in the Security Council, which has the authority under Article 94(2) of the U.N. Charter to "decide upon measures to be taken to give effect to the judgment."

The I.C.J. may also issue advisory opinions upon receiving requests from the General Assembly, the Security Council, and other U.N. specialized agencies. Between 1947 and 2007, the I.C.J. issued 24 advisory opinions, some containing two phases, at the request of various U.N. entities.

In the *Case Concerning Reparations for Injuries Suffered in the Service of the United Nations*, Advisory Opinion of 11 April 1949, the I.C.J. considered a request for an advisory opinion on several questions. The first issue concerned whether the U.N. possessed international legal capacity to bring claims against a *de facto* or *de jure* government for injuries to itself or its agents. The court answered affirmatively, as the U.N. is an international legal person. As a subject of international law, the U.N. possesses international rights and duties, including the capacity to maintain its rights by bringing claims. The I.C.J. concluded that members had clothed the United Nations with the international legal personality necessary to carry out its duties.

The second issue concerned whether the U.N. had the right to bring a claim against a state to obtain reparations for injuries suffered by a U.N. agent while on duty. The court again answered affirmatively, as its members have endowed it with the capacity to bring international claims when necessitated by the discharge of functions. Such a claim would result from a breach by a member of its international obligations. The measure of reparations should depend upon the amount of damage that the organization suffered.

A third question considered whether the United Nations could bring a claim for damage to the victim. The court found this to be an implied right under the principle of functional necessity. The traditional rule that diplomatic protection is exercised by the national state does not involve the giving of a negative answer to the question. The rule rests on two bases. First, the defendant has breached an obligation toward the national state in respect of its nationals. Second, only the party to whom an international obligation is due can bring a claim in respect of its breach. Here, the question presupposes that the injury from which the reparation is demanded arises from a breach of an obligation designed to help the agent in performance of his duties.

The Court also addressed whether the U.N. or the state had superior right of diplomatic protection. It concluded that both could bring an action. The U.N. could bring an action against the state even if the defendant state is also the state of nationality.

This case makes clear the United Nations can sue states for injuries to itself and its agents. Further, it does not matter whether or not the agent is a national of the injuring state.

7. The U.N. System [§66]
The following international organizations are linked to the U.N. through cooperative agreements:

- The International Monetary Fund;
- The World Bank;
- World Health Organization;
- The International Civil Aviation Organization;
- International Labour Organization; and
- The Universal Postal Union.

All of these organizations are autonomous bodies created by intergovernmental agreements, with wide-ranging international responsibilities in the economic, social, cultural, educational, health, and related fields. The International Labour Organization, for example, is headquartered in Geneva, Switzerland, and was created by forty-five countries in 1919 by Part XIII of the Versailles Peace Treaty ending World War I. The ILO seeks social justice and higher living standards for the world's workers. In 1946, the ILO became the first specialized agency associated with the United Nations. The ILO was awarded the 1969 Nobel Peace Prize for its activities on behalf of laborers.

B. Nongovernmental International Organizations [§67]

Under Article 71 of the U.N. Charter, *supra* §59, non-governmental organizations (NGOs) have consultative arrangements with the Economic and Social Council. NGOs cover the entire array of human activity. They may be involved in humanitarian, health, human rights and environmental matters, as well as professional and scientific associations. NGOs do not have full status as international legal persons. For examples, they cannot sue and be sued in the I.C.J.

In the development field, some NGOs collaborate with the World Bank. According to the Duke University website <http://docs.lib.duke/edu/igo/guides/ngo/>, the World Bank classifies NGOs into three main operational groupings. First, hundreds of thousands of *community-based* organizations function in a narrow geographic region. Second, 6,000 to 30,000 *national* organizations operate in one country. Third, hundreds of *international* organizations function in two or more developing countries. International NGOs channel billions of dollars every year into developing countries. CARE and Oxfam, two humanitarian organizations that fight global poverty, exemplify well-known international NGOs.

The International Committee of the Red Cross, based in Switzerland, is an NGO with important functions under the

81

Geneva Conventions on the Laws of War. The Red Cross delivers humanitarian supplies to areas ravaged by hostility, famine, natural disasters and sometimes genocide. The film *Hotel Rwanda* illustrates the Red Cross' role. The International Committee of the Red Cross has won the Nobel Peace Price three times, in 1917, 1944, and 1963. The international community clearly values its services as an instrument for assisting the peace process.

C. Intergovernmental Companies and Producer Associations [§68]

States also create international entities to conduct financial or commercial activities. The Bank of International Settlements, for example, was established by a 1930 multinational convention. This public multinational financial institution operates under a Swiss charter and is governed by Swiss law.

Scandinavian Airline Services (SAS) and Air Afrique are aviation consortia, a group of countries offering airline services. SAS was established by Denmark, Norway, and Sweden. Air Afrique was founded in 1961 as a joint venture between France and its former colonies (Benin, Burkina Faso, Central African Republic, Chad, Congo, Côte d'Ivoire, Mali, Mauritania, Niger, Senegal, and Togo).

The Organization of Petroleum Exporting Countries (OPEC) is a producer association that regulates the production of petroleum. They make voluntary agreements, setting ranges for prices and output. There are no sanctions for noncompliance, nor are there rewards for compliance among its members.

In conclusion, these various types of international organizations represent the efforts of states to regulate various activities between and among them.

CHAPTER VI

VI. Individuals

A. Rights of Individuals [§69]

Unlike states and the United Nations, individuals do not possess international legal personality. Individuals cannot acquire territory. A successful entertainer or entrepreneur, for example, may purchase an island, but she or he cannot turn it into a state. Individuals do not make treaties. Individuals also do not possess belligerent rights to seek military assistance from other states. Only states can do all of the above.

Moreover, individuals cannot sue directly in the International Court of Justice nor could they in its predecessor court, the Permanent Court of International Justice. Instead, individuals must be protected by their state of nationality in one of these international tribunals. When a state takes up the claim of its national, as the Greek government did in *The Mavrommatis Palestine Concessions* case, 1924 P.C.I.J., Ser. A, No. 2, an injury to a national becomes an injury to the state. The state is protecting its own rights. According to the P.C.I.J., the dispute enters the domain of international law as "a dispute between two States." *Id.* at 12. The P.C.I.J. also said in the *Mavrommatis* case, "It is an elementary principle of international law that a State is entitled to protect its subjects, when injured by acts contrary to international law by another State, from whom they have been unable to obtain satisfaction through the ordinary channels." *Id.*

Individuals can do the following. First, they possess nationality rights. Second, individuals can own property, which international law protects from unlawful takings by states. Third, individuals can commit war crimes, crimes against humanity, and crimes of aggression. As a consequence, they may be tried in national or international forums. Fourth, individuals possess human rights, which they can enforce in domestic courts or human rights

83

courts. In these courts, individuals may sue their national state or another state for human rights violations.

B. Nationality [§70]

Nationality connects individuals to states. Individuals may be a national of one or more states. The following subsections discuss the forms of nationality, whether individuals possess a right to nationality, the limitations on nationality, the necessity of a genuine link, and nationality transfers through annexation.

1. Forms of Nationality [§71]

There are two common forms of nationality. *Jus sanguinis* (also known as *jure sanguinis*) grants nationality status based on birth to nationals. It represents a holdover from Roman Civil Law as an outgrowth of nationality based on membership in a tribe or ethnic group. *Jus soli* (also known as *jure soli*) grants nationality based on birth within the territory. This is an outgrowth of feudal and common-law systems and continues today in the United Kingdom and the United States.

Some states, like Brazil and Mexico are more generous with granting nationality, while other states, like Japan, are parsimonious. There are Koreans who have lived in Japan for over three generations who do not possess Japanese nationality because Japan recognizes only *jus sanguinis* and the Koreans were not born to Japanese citizens. The United States recognizes both forms of nationality. Foreign parents have been known to go to a great deal of effort to give birth on U.S. soil. It seems as if the rich fly in and the poor walk.

2. The Right to a Nationality [§72]

Article 15 of the Universal Declaration of Human Rights asserts, "Every one has the right to a nationality," and "No one shall be arbitrarily deprived of his nationality nor denied the right to change his nationality." *See* G.A. Res. 217, U.N. GAOR, (III 1948).

Article 20 of the American Convention on Human Rights provides that every person has the right to a nationality, and particularly "the right to the nationality of the state in whose territory he was born if he does not have the right to any other nationality." *See* O.A.S. Official Records OEA/Ser. K/XVI/1.1, Doc 65, Rev. 1, Corr.1, Jan. 7 1990; 9 I.L.M. 101 (1970).

Nationality is important because international law abhors statelessness or people without a country. Article 1 of the United Nations Convention on the Reduction of Statelessness requires states to grant nationality to persons born in their territory who would otherwise be stateless. This Convention is available at <http://www.un.org/law/ilc/texts/statless.htm>. Article 2 applies these rights to foundlings, or abandoned babies, discovered within their boundaries. *Id.*

In a 1974 article in the *Yale Law Journal*, Professor Myres McDougal and two of his colleagues defined statelessness as "the loss of a community willing and able to guarantee any rights whatsoever." *See* Myres S. McDougal, Harold D. Lasswell & Lungchu Chen, *Nationality and Human Rights*, 83 Yale L.J. 900, 961 (1974) (citing H. Arendt, *The Origins of Totalitarianism* 297 (1958)). Further, they noted that "[t]he powerlessness of the stateless person is most apparent in the limitation upon his freedom of movement, both of egress and of return.... Unable to enter the territory of a state lawfully, he is often compelled to do so clandestinely. His illegal entry continues to haunt him." *Id.*

Over 30 years later, their statements have become even more prophetic as states have moved in the wake of terrorism to vigorously enforce passport and visa requirements to enter and leave a country. In 2005, the United States began requiring even those entering on cruise ships for a day to bring passport in hand. Previously, cruise ship tourists were able to show a driver's license to enter the United States.

Nevertheless, the world's nations "are in virtual unanimity that statelessness is not to be imposed as punishment for crime." *See Trop v. Dulles*, 356 U.S. 86, 102, 78 S.Ct. 590, 2 L.Ed 2d 630 (1958). In *Trop v. Dulles*, the U.S. Supreme Court determined that a military deserter could not be deprived of his U.S. citizenship. The Court noted a United Nations' survey of the nationality laws of 84 nations of the world revealed "that only two countries, the Philippines and Turkey, impose denationalization as a penalty for desertion." *Id.* at 103 (citing Laws Concerning Nationality, U.N.Doc. No. ST/LEG/ SER.B/4 (1954). In the U.S., denationalization as a penalty for desertion would constitute cruel and unusual punishment and is thus prohibited by the Eighth Amendment.

3. Limitations on Nationality [§73]

There are limitations on conferring nationality. The Convention on Certain Questions relating to the Conflict of Nationality Laws, 179 L.N.T.S. 89 (April 12, 1930), provides, under Article 1, that each state determines who is a national, so long as the nationality laws are compatible with international law. Under Article 3, a person having two or more nationalities may be regarded as a national of all, depending on each state's law. Some states do not recognize dual nationality, whereas others do.

With dual nationality, the principle of dominant or effective nationality governs. Whichever nationality is the most dominant determines which state may exercise diplomatic protection over the national.

This sometimes becomes a problem for those who marry foreign spouses. In *United States ex rel. Mergé v. Italian Republic*, 22 I.L.R. 443, 14 U.N.R.I.A.A. 236 (Italian-U.S. Conciliation Commission 1955), the Commission ruled that the United States was not entitled to present a claim on behalf of its national who was born in New York. At the age of 24, she married an Italian national in Rome, thereby acquiring Italian nationality, and lived with her husband in Rome. The Commission found that U.S. nationality was not her dominant nationality because the Mergé family did not have a habitual residence in the United States and the permanent professional life of the head of the family was not established there.

States sometimes disagree on whether an individual has to give consent (express or implied) to assume another state's nationality. Some states assert that someone must give consent, while others maintain that consent is not necessary. Individuals who become naturalized citizens give consent by completing the naturalization process and pledging allegiance to their new country. California Governor Arnold Schwarzenegger, for example, became a naturalized citizen of the United States in 1984, while retaining the Austrian nationality he has held since birth, making him a dual national.

States cannot confer nationality upon all the inhabitants of another state, or on all the people entering its territory. By traveling to Benin, for example, you cannot automatically become a Benin citizen, with all the rights and duties of citizenship. The duties of citizenship may include paying taxes and serving in the military to protect the country.

Swearing allegiance to another country can lead to the presumption that an individual has renounced her original citizenship. Margaret Randall, an author and photographer, acquired United States citizenship upon her birth in 1936. She subsequently moved to Mexico as an adult, and declared her allegiance on July 13, 1967. *See* <http://www.usdoj.gov/osg/briefs/1988/sg880072.txt>. She returned to the U.S. and married a U.S. citizen in 1984. She applied for permanent residency, but the U.S. Immigration and Naturalization Service (I.N.S.) denied her request and attempted to deport her under the McCarran-Walter Act. *See Randall v. Meese*, 854 F.2d 472,

473 (D.C. Cir. 1988). After a five year legal battle, the I.N.S. decided in 1989 that she had never lost her citizenship and should not have been subjected to deportation hearings.

4. Necessity of a Genuine Link [§74]

Many states assert no obligation to recognize citizenship without a genuine link between the purported national and the state claiming to exercise diplomatic protection.

The *Nottebohm* case between Liechtenstein and Guatemala involved whether Liechtenstein could bring a suit to protect the assets of one of its nationals. In Phase 1 of the case, Guatemala preliminarily objected to I.C.J. jurisdiction. Guatemala claimed its acceptance of the court's compulsory jurisdiction expired on January 26, 1952, a few weeks before Liechtenstein submitted its application. However, Liechtenstein submitted the case on December 17, 1951, before Guatemala's acceptance of jurisdiction expired. The court determined that once it had already acquired a case, it could not be deprived of jurisdiction.

In Phase 2 of *Nottebohm* (*Liechtenstein v. Guatemala*) 1955 I.C.J. 4, the I.C.J. deliberated the merits of the dispute. Liechtenstein claimed that Guatemala violated international law by arresting, detaining, expelling and refusing to readmit Frederich Nottebohm, and in seizing and retaining his property. Liechtenstein requested that Guatemala pay compensation for the harm it caused him.

Guatemala asserted that Liechtenstein could not defend Nottebohm, as it was not the proper state of nationality and there was no genuine link between the two. Nottebohm acquired German citizenship based on his birth in Hamburg in 1881. He moved to Guatemala in 1905, establishing his primary residence and place of business there. After Germany annexed Poland in 1939, Nottebohm applied for Liechtenstein nationality. After payment of 68,500 Swiss Francs (worth approximately U.S. $67,930 in April 2008, not including inflation) representing fees, taxes and security deposit to various Liechtenstein authorities, Liechtenstein waived its three-year residency requirement and Nottebohm took the oath of allegiance two weeks after his initial application.

Liechtenstein responded that Guatemala was precluded from attacking Mr. Nottebohm's nationality because it had acknowledged it on several occasions. On December 1, 1939, the Guatemalan Consul General in Zurich, Switzerland granted Nottebohm a visa based on his Liechtenstein passport.

The I.C.J. rejected Liechtenstein's claim and agreed that Guatemala did not have to recognize Liechtenstein's right to exercise protection over Nottebohm. It had merely acknowledged his passport.

The court examined whether the granting of nationality by Liechtenstein directly entailed an obligation on the part of Guatemala to recognize its effect. Under international law, nationality is a legal bond having as its basis a social fact of attachment, a genuine connection of existence, interests and sentiments, together with the existence of reciprocal rights and duties. States can only exercise juridical protection over a claimed national if the naturalization was based on juridical facts. Here, at the time of his naturalization, Nottebohm had been settled in Guatemala for 34 years. It was the main seat of his interest. He returned there after naturalization in Liechtenstein. He applied to go there after the United States released him in 1946. He would have gone there had Guatemala not refused to let him back in.

The I.C.J. also explored the necessity of genuine links between Nottebohm and Liechtenstein. Nottebohm and Liechtenstein had tenuous connections. Nottebohm had no settled abode there. He had no continuous residence. The only reason he went to Liechtenstein in 1946 was because Guatemala refused to readmit him. His only real link to Liechtenstein was his brother who had lived there since 1931. The bottom line is that unless naturalization is based on a real or genuine connection, other states do not have to recognize it.

5. Nationality Transfers Through Annexation [§75]

States have been known to conquer other states and immediately confer their citizenship on the occupants of the conquered state. After the German Reich annexed Austria, it conferred German citizenship on all Austrian citizens by a decree dated July 3, 1938. By a subsequent German executive order on November 25, 1938, the Reich deprived Jews residing abroad of German citizenship and subjected their property to confiscation. *See United States ex rel. Schwarzkopf v. Uhl*, 137 F.2d 898 (2d Cir. 1943).

Paul Schwartzkopf, for example, went through several nationality shifts and was affected by these laws. He was born a Jew in Prague, Bohemia and subsequently became a Czechoslovakia citizen in 1919 when Prague became a part of that country. Then he moved to Berlin and became a citizen of Germany in 1925. Two years later, he became a naturalized Austrian citizen. He was living in the United States when Germany annexed Austria. Three years later, he applied for United States citizenship, but was taken into custody as an enemy alien on December 9, 1941, after the U.S. declared war on Germany. The question became was he still an Austrian citizen or had he become a German citizen. *Id.*

The United States government considered the German takeover of Austria to be illegal. In considering the case of *United States ex rel. Schwarzkopf v. Uhl*, 137 F.2d 898, 902 (2d Cir. 1943), the Second Circuit noted that "under generally accepted principles of international law Germany could impose citizenship by annexation (collective naturalization) only on those who were inhabitants of Austria in 1938." However, the new nationality could only be conferred on or made eligible for election to those inhabitants who remained in the territory. The court concluded that the new allegiance was not transferred to inhabitants who voluntarily departed before the annexation and never elected to accept the sovereignty of the new government. *Id.*

Even though Austria had ceased to exist and there was no purported government-in-exile, the court observed that former nationals of an invaded country had the right to flee and establish a residence abroad. They could elect a new nationality and remain stateless until they had acquired it. While Schwarzkopf may no longer be Austrian, since the country did not exist, he was not German either. Thus he could not be retained as an enemy alien in the United States.

C. International Legal Responsibility of Individuals [§76]

International law recognizes individual responsibility for certain crimes against the law of nations, such as piracy, hijacking, genocide, torture, and violations of the laws of war.

1. Piracy [§77]

Webster's Dictionary defines a pirate as "a person who robs or commits illegal violence at sea or on the shores of the sea." *See* Random House Webster's College Dictionary 1029 (1996). While Hollywood has romanticized pirates in films ranging from the 2003 *Pirates of the Caribbean: The Curse of the Black Pearl* to the 1923 *The Love Pirate*, governments and private companies who have been victimized by such figures do not view them through rose-colored lenses. Piracy remains a problem for the international community, as Somali pirates tried to hijack a luxury cruise ship as recently as November 8, 2005. *See* <http://news.bbc.co.uk/2/hi/africa/4418748.stm>. The crew of the Seabourn Spirit vessel evaded the attackers by changing course and heading out into open water.

In April 2008, Somali pirates hijacked Dubai-flagged and French-flagged vessels. During the same month, pirates fired on a Japanese oil tanker in the Gulf of Aden and used rocket-propelled grenades to hijack a Spanish tuna boat.

Because these type of crimes take place on the high seas, capturing and punishing pirates can prove an elusive endeavor. All states agree that such individuals, when captured, should be brought to justice for their crimes. The United States Constitution grants Congress the power to "define and punish Piracies and Felonies committed on the high Seas, and Offences against the Law of Nations." *See* U.S. Const. Art. 1, §8, cl. 10. Congress deemed piracy as "robbery and murder committed on the high seas." *U.S. v. Smith*, 18 U.S. 153, 158 (1820) (referencing "8th section of the act of Congress of 1790, ch. 9"). The Court noted the general practice of all states was to punish "all persons, whether natives or foreigners, who have committed this offence against any persons whatsoever... ." *Id.* at 162. Thomas Smith was convicted of committing piracy on the high seas against a Spanish vessel.

Nevertheless, at least one scholar has argued that piracy is "solely a municipal law crime, the only question of international law being the extent of a state's jurisdiction to apply its criminal law to an accused foreigner acting outside the territorial jurisdiction of the prescribing state." *See* Janis and Noyes, *International Law: Cases and Commentary* 137 (2nd ed. 2001) (citing Alfred P. Rubin, *The Law of Piracy* 360 (2nd ed. 1998).

Over time the definition of piracy has expanded to cover acts committed on aircraft as well as ships. Article 101 of the United Nations Convention on the Law of the Sea, 1833 U.N.T.S. 3, U.N. Doc. A/Conf. 62/122 (1982), defines piracy as "illegal acts of violence or detention, or any act of depredation, committed for private ends by the crew or the passengers of a private ship or a private aircraft, and directed: (i) on the high seas, against another ship or aircraft, or against persons or property on board such ship or aircraft; [and] (ii) against a ship, aircraft, persons or property in a place outside the jurisdiction of any State."

2. Hijacking [§78]

Black's Law Dictionary defines the word hijack as "To commandeer (a vehicle or airplane), esp. at gunpoint." *See Black's Law Dictionary* (8th ed. 2004) (hijack). Hijacking is universally condemned as an international crime.

If a state possesses a person who has hijacked a vessel within its jurisdiction, it has many options. It may extradite the offender to another state, send him to the International Criminal Court, or bring him to justice within its national courts. It may assert universal jurisdiction, even if the hijacker is not one of its nationals and the crime did not take place on its territory.

3. Genocide [§79]

Black's Law Dictionary defines genocide as an "international crime involving acts causing serious physical and mental harm with the intent to destroy, partially or entirely, a national, ethnic, racial, or religious group." *See Black's Law Dictionary* (8th ed. 2004) (genocide). Article II of the 1948 Convention on the Prevention and Punishment of the Crime of Genocide lists five categories of acts that constitute genocide: (1) Killing members of the group; (2) Causing serious bodily or mental harm to members of the group; (3) Deliberately inflicting on the group conditions of life calculated to bring about its physical destruction in whole or in part; (4) Imposing measures intended to prevent births within the group; and (5) Forcibly transferring children of one group to another group. *See* 78 U.N.T.S. 277 (hereinafter "Genocide Convention").

Article 4 of the Genocide Convention further provides that persons who commit, conspire, direct, attempt or comply in

93

genocide shall be punished, even if they are "constitutionally responsible rulers, public officials or private individuals." The courts of their nationality state, the courts in the territory where the crime took place, or international penal tribunals may punish persons who commit genocide. Several cases alleging that individuals committed genocide are now pending before the International Criminal Court.

4. Torture [§80]

The Convention Against Torture and Other Cruel, Inhuman or Degrading Treatment or Punishment, 1465 U.N.T.S. 85, G.A.Res. 46 (XXXIX 1984) (Annex), defines torture as "any act by which severe pain or suffering, whether physical or mental, is intentionally inflicted on a person for such purposes as obtaining from him or a third person information or a confession, punishing him for an act he or a third person has committed or is suspected of having committed, or intimidating or coercing him or a third person...." The United States is also one of many parties to this Convention, but it is not a party to the Rome Statute of the International Criminal Court, U.N.Doc 32/A/CONF. 183/9, 37 I.L.M. 99. Article 7(2)(e) of that treaty defines torture as "the intentional infliction of severe pain or suffering, whether physical or mental, upon a person in the custody or under the control of the accused...." However, the same Article excludes "pain or suffering arising only from, inherent in or incidental to, lawful sanctions" from the definition of torture.

The torturer may be punished by his or her national state or by another country. Because torture has been condemned as a universal crime, torture cases can be brought in any jurisdiction. In 1980, the Second Circuit said in *Filartiga v. Pena-Irala*, 630 F.2d 876, 890 (2d Cir. 1980), "for purposes of *civil liability, the torturer has become like the pirate and slave trader before him hostis humani generis*, an enemy of all mankind." The court held that it possessed jurisdiction over Americo Norberto Pena-Irala, who was accused of kidnapping and torturing to death Joelito Filartiga. Dr. Joel Filartiga, Joelito's father, brought the action in New York, after his daughter discovered Pena living in Brooklyn. The U.S. Immigration and Naturalization Service arrested Pena and the Filartigas served him with a summons. All parties were citizens of Paraguay and the action took place in Paraguay. The U.S. Alien Tort Statute provides original jurisdiction over an alien for a tort committed in violation of the law of nations or a treaty of the United States.

During the U.S. prosecution of the war on terror, U.S. Secretary of Defense Donald Rumsfeld approved the following harsh stress techniques to be applied to detainees under U.S. control in Afghanistan, Iraq, and Guantanamo:

- Stripping detainees naked;
- Using cameras to take pictures of naked detainees;
- Hooding detainees for interrogation and hooding them for long periods of time;
- Requiring detainees to assume "stress" positions for long periods;
- Prolonging sleep deprivation;
- Using dogs to intimidate prisoners during interrogation;
- Exposing detainees to heat, cold, or cold water;
- Using sensory assault, including exposure to loud music and bright lights;
- Isolating detainees for periods exceeding 30 days;
- Threatening prisoners with abuse.

In implementing the policy, their commanding officers told U.S. soldiers that the Afghan prisoners, for example, "were nobodies, just enemy combatants." Pictures subsequently leaked in 2004 showing U.S. soldiers abusing Iraqi prisoners in Abu Ghraib, Guantanamo, and other U.S.-controlled prisons. U.S. soldiers placed Iraqis in positions designed to humiliate them and administered electrical shocks associated with torture.

See Seymour M. Hersh, *Torture at Abu Ghraib: American soldiers brutalized Iraqis. How far up does the responsibility go*, New Yorker Mag. (May 10, 2004). In Guantanamo, the U.S. authorities held individuals from Afghanistan and allegedly abused them, including using females to smear seemingly menstrual blood on practicing Muslims and then prohibiting them from washing themselves. Some individuals died in U.S. custody. *See* Carol D. Leonnig and Dana Priest, *Detainees Accuse Female Interrogators*, The Washington Post, Feb. 10, 2005.

The United States eventually prosecuted nine soldiers. Six reached plea agreements and three were convicted. Private Lynndie R. England, who became the face of the scandal when she was photographed smiling next to naked detainees mounted in humiliating poses, was sentenced to three years in prison.

Much of this behavior, as well as certain types of assault and maiming, was sanctioned as acceptable interrogation methods by a formerly confidential memorandum for William J. Haynes II, General Counsel for the Department of Defense. The "Military Interrogation of Alien Unlawful Combatants Held Outside the United States" memo, which was released to the public on 2 April 2008 had been prepared by John C. Yoo in 2003 when he was a deputy in the Justice Department's Office of Legal Counsel. The memo declared that as Commander in Chief, the President of the United States has authority to suspend or terminate any part of any treaty during wartime, including the U.N. Convention Against Torture and Other Cruel, Inhuman, or Degrading Treatment or Punishment. Additionally, because the Convention is not self-executing, the memo found that it places no domestic legal obligations on the Executive Branch of the U.S. government and does not create any cause of action in U.S. federal courts. Similarly, the memorandum found that customary international law lacks domestic legal effect, and therefore can be overridden by the President at his discretion. The memorandum was eventually repudiated. Dan Eggen & Josh White, *Memo: Laws Didn't Apply to Interrogators*, Washington Post (Apr. 2, 2008).

U.S. Defense Secretary Rumsfeld was subsequently sued by a Guantanamo inmate challenging his detention as an enemy combatant in *Hamdi v. Rumsfeld*, 542 U.S. 507, 124 S.Ct. 2633 (2004). The Supreme Court held that due process required that a United States citizen being held as an enemy combatant be given meaningful opportunity to contest the factual basis for his detention before an impartial decision-maker.

While a government may sanction acts, such as those approved by Rumsfeld, they may still be illegal under either or both domestic and international law. Further, because of universal jurisdiction, even if a person is not brought to justice in his own territory, he may be brought to justice in another country. Rumsfeld was indicted for war crimes in Germany in 2007.

5. Violations of the Laws of War [§81]
The offending country, an enemy state, or international authorities may also punish violations of the laws of war.

After World War II, the occupying powers of the United States, the United Kingdom, the Union of Soviet Socialist Republics, and France established the Nuremberg Tribunal to try war criminals whose offenses had no particular geographic location. Because of the nature of the acts, the Nuremberg Tribunal possessed jurisdiction regardless of where the offending act was committed. The leaders, organizers, instigators and accomplices of the war were all considered liable for all criminal acts committed in the execution of a common plan.

The men put forth two common defenses. First, they proclaimed their acts were actions of sovereign states, and thus only the state was responsible. Second, international law cannot punish human beings; only states can.

The Nuremberg Tribunal rejected these defenses. International law imposes duties and liabilities upon individuals as well as on states. The Tribunal set forth two general categories of crimes for which international law could indeed punish individuals: war crimes and crimes against humanity. War crimes are violations of the laws or customs of war. The examples include murder, ill treatment of prisoners of war or deportation to slave labor camps, and wanton destruction of cities. Crimes against humanity include murder, extermination, enslavement, deportation and other inhumane actions committed against civilian populations, before or during the war, or persecutions on political, racial, or religious grounds.

The Nuremberg Tribunal considered that men, not abstract entities, commit crimes against international law and only by punishing individuals can the provisions of international law be enforced. Principles of international law that protect the representatives of states, such as sovereign immunity, cannot be applied to acts that are condoned as criminal to permit sheltering the acts from criminal responsibility.

Individuals have international duties that transcend the national obligations of obedience imposed by individual states. Soldiers taking orders to kill or maim cannot escape responsibility, but their punishment may be mitigated. Soldiers are trained in the laws of war. They can disobey an order that violates the laws of war.

During the Vietnam War, First Lieutenant Calley, a U.S. national, claimed that his troops were ordered by Captain Medina "to kill every living thing-men, women, children, and animals-and under no circumstances were they to leave any Vietnamese behind them as they passed through the villages enroute to their final objective." U.S. Court of Military Appeals, No. 26,875 (Dec. 21, 1973). While there was contradictory testimony as to whether Captain Medina issued such an order, the court found that an order to kill unarmed civilians would be illegal. The court stated, "For 100 years, it has been a settled rule of American law that even in war the summary killing of an enemy, who has submitted to, and is under, effective physical control, is murder." *Id.* Calley and another soldier opened fire on unarmed old men, women, and children in My Lai. When a few children remained standing, Calley personally shot them. He then came upon a group of 75 to 100 Vietnamese civilians and killed them as well. The court affirmed his conviction of the premeditated murder of not less than 22 Vietnamese civilians and of assault with intent to murder a Vietnamese child.

Wartime soldiers may sometimes find themselves in a double bind. If they follow the orders to commit war crimes or crimes against humanity, they may be liable in any jurisdiction for their behavior. If they follow the law, they may incur personal cost as they may be ostracized, demoted or suffer personal harm by their government, fellow troops, or even by those they tried to assist. In some instances, they have been executed by their comrades only to have the crime described as "friendly fire."

To illustrate these points, consider an incident depicted in the 1998 film *Saving Private Ryan*. A squadron, whose captain is played by actor Tom Hanks, debates what to do with a German prisoner of war during World War II. They captured the POW, but cannot take him with them on their mission to find Private Ryan. Several of the privates argue that they should kill the POW because if they let him go, he will end up behind enemy lines again. As the POW begs for his life, one man cites the Geneva Conventions and argues that it is illegal to kill him.

Finally, the captain ties a ribbon around the POW's eyes and tells him to march in a certain direction where he will be picked up by other U.S. troops. Towards the end of the film, the German POW returns to battle and kills the captain. This scene represents an excellent teaching analogy as the group took the correct action under international law, but it was costly on a personal level. More common, perhaps, is when an individual makes an expedient personal decision that later subjects him or her to prosecution under international law.

D. International Criminal Court [§82]

The Nuremberg Tribunal became the precursor to the International Criminal Court (ICC), which was created to provide a permanent forum for punishing individuals for international law violations. Its goals include the following: (1) justice and punishment; (2) deterrence; (3) record-keeping; and (4) the progressive development of international law.

One hundred twenty states participated in the "United Nations Diplomatic Conference of Plenipotentiaries on the Establishment of an International Criminal Court." They adopted The Rome Statute of the International Criminal Court and established the ICC on July 17, 1998. *See* U.N. Doc. 32/A/CONF. 183/9. The Statute entered into force on July 1, 2002. The ICC, composed of 18 judges elected to nine-year staggered terms (initially one-third were elected for three years, one-third for six years, and one-third for nine years), sits in The Hague. It operates in both English and French.

The court has jurisdiction over the crime of genocide, crimes against humanity, war crimes, and the crime of aggression. Article 6 of the Rome Statute defines genocide similarly to the Convention on Genocide discussed earlier in this chapter. Article 7 of the Rome Statute defines "crimes against humanity" to include acts such as murder, extermination, enslavement, deportation, torture, rape, enforced disappearance, and apartheid that are "committed as part of a widespread or systematic attack directed against any civilian population." War crimes are defined under Article 8 as "Grave breaches of the Geneva Conventions of 12 August 1949," such as willful killing and torture or inhuman treatment. War crimes also include "[i]ntentionally directing attacks against the civilian population," and "[a]ttacking or bombarding ... towns, villages, dwellings, or buildings which are undefended and which are not military objectives."

According to the ICC website <www.icc-cpi.int>, anyone who commits any of the crimes enumerated under the Statute after July 1, 2002, can be liable for prosecution by the Court. The ICC's chief prosecutor has brought cases against individuals based on the situations in the Sudan, Uganda, and the Congo.

Before the creation of the ICC, the U.N. Security Council established the International Criminal Tribunal for the former Yugoslavia (ICTY) in 1993 and the International Criminal Tribunal for Rwanda (ICTR) in 1994. Both tribunals are responsible for prosecuting individuals accused of committing genocide and other serious violations of international humanitarian law. The ICTY sits in The Hague and the ICTR maintains its offices in Arusha, Tanzania.

E. Extradition [§83]

States seek to cooperate in fighting crime by extraditing offenders from one country to another for trial and punishment. In a formal process, the requesting state presents an arrest warrant, statement of facts, relevant legal provisions, and evidence to justify apprehension and commitment for trial. Once a state receives a request, it must evaluate the situation, and decide to extradite or try the person. If the state rejects the request, then it must indicate reasons.

101

Most extradition treaties will not permit a state to surrender an individual charged with an offense that the state deems political or political in character, or for purely military offenses.

States who do not permit the death penalty may include provisions in their extradition treaties that prohibit extradition for certain offenses, unless the requesting party assures that it will not impose the death penalty for the alleged crime. Neither party is bound to deliver its own nationals, but may do so.

When Spain sought to extradite Chilean General Augusto Pinochet from the United Kingdom, it initially charged Pinochet with genocide, torture, kidnapping and murder related to the disappearance of 3,197 people after he seized power in a 1973 coup. The U.K. courts declared the initial warrant defective because (1) no offense was committed in Spain; (2) Pinochet was not a Spanish citizen; and (3) the U.K. had no jurisdiction over Pinochet. *See* Burr, supra §50, at 103.

Spain then amended its complaint to allege that Pinochet murdered Spanish citizens in Chile and committed the universal crimes of torture and hostage taking. These were triable offenses in the U.K. and Spain. The British government declared that Pinochet lacked immunity as a former head of state, and planned to arrest him until Baroness Margaret Thatcher intervened and reminded people of the aid Pinochet gave Britain during the Falkland/Malvinas Islands war against Argentina. Then, the British government permitted Pinochet to return to Chile on humanitarian grounds, stating he was too ill to stand trial. Rolled onto a plane in London, England, Pinochet walked off the plane in Santiago, Chile to a 21-gun salute and left for his beach house. He was subsequently indicted in Chile. Pinochet died in 2007.

The U.S. possesses extradition treaties, mostly bilateral, with over 100 nations. The U.S. and Mexico have developed an extradition process to keep criminals, particularly U.S. citizens, from seeking

102

refuge in Mexico. In the film *Thelma and Louise*, two women head towards Mexico after killing a man in Arkansas. Another film, *Going South*, opens with Jack Nicholson sneaking away, getting on a horse, and riding as fast as he can to cross the Rio Grande. On the other side of the river, he gets off his horse and starts screaming, "I'm in Mexico. I'm in Mexico. You can't touch me." In the scene, the sheriff and posse keep coming. By the time Nicholson realizes his pursuers are not going to stop at the border, his horse drops dead on him. He runs, but is apprehended.

These film scenes depict the feeling among U.S. criminals that Mexico will be their salvation. Mexico and the United States entered into five extradition treaties in 1899, 1902, 1925, 1939, and 1978. In 1990, the 1978 treaty became a source of conflict between the U.S. and Mexico and led to the case of *United States v. Alvarez-Machain*, 504 U.S. 655 (1992).

U.S. Drug Enforcement Administration (D.E.A.) agents arranged the kidnapping of Dr. Humberto Alvarez-Machain from his office in Guadalajara, Mexico. The D.E.A. agents hired Mexican nationals to transport him to El Paso, Texas, where he was transferred to Los Angeles to stand trial for participating in the alleged torture and killing of D.E.A. agent Enrique Camarena-Salazar. Dr. Alvarez-Machain challenged the jurisdiction of U.S. courts, claiming that he was brought to the United States in violation of the U.S.-Mexico extradition treaty.

The U.S. Supreme Court declared that the U.S.-Mexico extradition treaty did not deprive U.S. courts of jurisdiction because the treaty was silent on the issue of kidnapping. Since it did not forbid kidnapping, it was permissible. The court acknowledged that while the kidnapping of Dr. Alvarez-Machain may violate international law, it did not deprive U.S. courts of jurisdiction to try him.

Does legal silence mean an act is permissible? The answer was affirmative in the *Alvarez-Machain* case and in another international dispute between Turkey and France where the Permanent Court of International Justice wrote that international law permits all that it does not forbid. States have to give consent in order to give up freedom of action. *See* S.S. "Lotus" (*France v. Turkey*), 1927 P.C.I.J. Ser. A, No 10.

Justice Rehnquist said that Mexico knew the U.S. believed kidnapping was an acceptable means of procuring an offender for trial. In 1886, the Supreme Court held in *Ker v. Illinois*, 119 U.S. 436 (1886), that the court was not deprived of jurisdiction over Mr. Ker after he was forcibly abducted from Peru. There was no government involvement with Mr. Ker, who was kidnapped by a private messenger or bounty hunter. Nevertheless, Mexico was made aware, as early as 1886 of the *Ker* doctrine. The 1978 treaty did not establish a rule to curtail the effect of *Ker*.

In 1997, the U.S. and Mexico added a protocol to their extradition treaty. On November 13 of that year, President Clinton signed the Protocol to the Extradition Treaty between U.S. and Mexico. He transmitted the letter to the Senate for ratification on May 21, 1998. It entered into force on May 21, 2001. This protocol provides for "Delayed and Temporary Surrender," which permits the requested party to temporarily relinquish a person who has been convicted and sentenced in the requested party's jurisdiction so that the person may be prosecuted in the requesting party state before or during service of his or her sentence. The person shall be returned after conclusion of the proceedings. If the person is found not guilty, he receives credit for stay in the requesting country's prison. Nothing in this protocol, however, prohibits kidnapping.

Once the original *Alvarez-Machain* case proceeded to trial, the district judge granted Dr. Alvarez-Machain's motion for a judgment of acquittal on the ground that the government failed to present sufficient evidence to support a guilty verdict. The judge found that the U.S. government could not prove that Enrique Camarena-Salazar had been tortured, let alone by Dr. Alvarez-Machain.

Dr. Alvarez-Machain returned to Mexico and began a civil action against the U.S. Government that led to another U.S. Supreme Court decision during the summer of 2004. The doctor sued José Francisco Sosa, Antonio Garate-Bustamante, five unnamed Mexican citizens, the United States government, and four D.E.A. agents. Dr. Alvarez-Machain sought damages against the United States for false arrest under the Federal Tort Claims Act (F.T.C.A). He sued Sosa and other individuals for participating in his kidnapping under the Alien Tort Statute (A.T.S.).

The F.T.C.A. permits individuals to sue the U.S. government for personal injury caused by the negligent or wrongful act or omission of any government employee while acting within the scope of his office or employment. Pursuant to the A.T.S., U.S. district courts are given original jurisdiction over any civil action by an alien for a tort committed in violation of the law of nations or a treaty of the United States. The district court dismissed Alvarez-Machain's F.T.C.A. claim, but awarded summary judgment and $25,000 in damages on the A.T.S. claim. *See Alvarez-Machain v. United States*, No. CV 93-4072, 1999 U.S. Dist. LEXIS 23304, at *78 (C.D. Cal.).

A three-judge panel of the Ninth Circuit affirmed the district court's A.T.S. judgment, but reversed its dismissal of the F.T.C.A. claim in *Alvarez-Machain v. United States*, 266 F.3d 1045, 1064 (9th Cir. 2001). Sitting *en banc*, the full Ninth Circuit affirmed the three-judge panel's decision in *Alvarez-Machain v. United States*, 331 F.3d 604, 645 (9th Cir. 2003). The *en banc* panel cited a "clear and universally recognized norm prohibiting arbitrary arrest and detention" to support its conclusion that Dr. Alvarez-Machain's arrest amounted to a tort in violation of international law. *Id.* at 620.

105

In reversing the Ninth Circuit's *en banc* decision in 2004, the U.S. Supreme Court ruled that Dr. Alvarez-Machain was not entitled to a remedy under either the F.T.C.A. or the A.T.S. The Supreme Court, in *Sosa v. Alvarez-Machain*, 542 U.S. 692 (2004), determined that the U.S. had not waived immunity from suit, and that the A.T.S. did not apply to this type of violation. The U.S. Supreme Court was consistent in its actions towards the doctor. The U.S. Government not only had the right to kidnap Dr. Alvarez-Machain outside of the customary extradition process, but also could refuse to pay him any remedies. *See* Sherri Burr, *The U.S. Supreme Court and the Alvarez-Machain Cases: Recasting International Law*, 13 U.S.-Mexico L.J. 105, 107 (Spring 2005).

Mexico did not take this issue to the International Court of Justice, which may have reached a different outcome. Although the kidnapping was considered legal within the United States, Rehnquist acknowledged in his opinion that the same act may violate international law.

The U.S.-Mexico situation notwithstanding, most states comply with the formal extradition process. On 22 September 2007, Chile extradited former Peruvian President Alberto Fujimoro back to Lima to face charges of corruption and human rights violations for sanctioning death-squad killings. Fujimoro had been promptly arrested when he landed in Chile in November 2005. The Chilean Supreme Court ordered his extradition on 21 September 2007. Unfortunately for him, Fujimoro had left his previous refuge in Japan where he was immune from extradition because he is a Japanese national by birth to Japanese citizens. For more information, *see* Monte Hayes, *Ex-President of Peru Extradited from Chile to Face Charges*, Associated Press (Sept. 23, 2007).

F. Terrorists [§84]

The extradition process has been employed to counter terrorism while international law struggles to define it. The problem in defining terrorism is that one state's terrorist is another state's freedom fighter or political offender. Most treaties focus on whether the acts were targeted at political or governmental functions, as opposed to aircraft sabotage, hijacking, attacks on diplomats, and hostage taking.

The extradition treaties provide exceptions for political offenses and therein lies the problems. Who determines what is political? Must the target be governmental?

For example, under Article 2 of the International Convention for the Suppression of Terrorist Bombings, U.N. Doc. A/RES/52/164, "Any person commits an offence...if that person unlawfully and intentionally delivers, places, discharges or detonates an explosive or other lethal device in, into, or against a place of public use, a State or government facility, a public transportation system or an infrastructure facility: (a) [w]ith the intent to cause death or serious bodily injury; or (b) [w]ith the intent to cause extensive destruction of such a place, facility or system, where such destruction results in or is likely to result in major economic loss." This Convention was completed on December 15, 1997, and entered into force on May 23, 2001.

The treaty also punishes attempts to commit an offence as well as acting as an accomplice. Notice that the targets are public or governmental.

Under Article 2 of the International Convention for the Suppression of the Financing of Terrorism, *see* <http://www.un.org/law/cod/finterr.htm>, "Any person commits an offence within the meaning of this Convention if that person by any means, directly or indirectly, unlawfully and willfully, provides or collects funds with the intention that they should be used or in the knowledge that they are to be used, in full or in part, in order to carry out: (a) An act which constitutes an offence within the scope of and as defined in one of the treaties listed in the annex; or (b) Any other act intended to cause death or serious bodily injury to a civilian, or to any other person not taking an active part in the hostilities in a situation of armed conflict, when the purpose of such act, by its nature or context, is to intimidate a population, or to compel a government or international organization to do or to abstain from doing any act." The U.N. General Assembly in resolution 54/109 of December 9, 1999 adopted this Convention. With Article 2(b), the focus is on injuries to civilians, or to intimidate populations or force governments to act or refrain from acting.

For example, how should international law characterize the 2001 September 11th attacks on U.S. soil or the 2005 London bombings in the United Kingdom? The attack on the Pentagon was clearly aimed at a governmental target. The attacks of 9-11 on the World Trade Center, however, might be considered as aimed towards a private target, although its symbolism as an economic center was evident. Nevertheless, it instilled the most fear because nearly 3,000 people died and most of them were private citizens. Similarly, the 2005 London bombings struck a bus and three underground tube (subway) stations. Its purpose could only be to instill fear in the hearts of the general public, which took the direct hit.

In an extradition treaty that has a political offence exception, individuals could be extradited for the attacks on the World Trade Center and the London bus and tube stations, since their principal aim was to instill public fear. However, some countries could possibly decide not to extradite them for the attack on the Pentagon, which might be considered political in nature because the target was governmental.

Recent treaties, as indicated above, and the U.S. PATRIOT Act remove the distinction between private and governmental targets. The U.S. PATRIOT Act defines domestic terrorism in 18 U.S.C. 2331 (5) as "activities that—(A) involve acts dangerous to human life that are a violation of the criminal laws of the United States or of any State; (B) appear to be intended—(i) to intimidate or coerce a civilian population; (ii) to influence the policy of a government by intimidation or coercion; or (iii) to affect the conduct of a government by mass destruction, assassination, or kidnapping; and (C) occur primarily within the territorial jurisdiction of the United States."

Part B accords with international treaties that have looked at the nature and intent of the acts. However, it criminalizes an act regardless of whether the target is civilian or governmental.

G. Human Rights [§85]

Human Rights law is an exception to the rule that states are completely sovereign within their own territory. International law expresses concern with how states treat their own citizens and aliens. Under Article 55 of the U.N. Charter, equal rights and self-determination include higher standards of living, full employment, economic and social progress, and universal respect for human rights and fundamental freedoms.

The United Nations General Assembly adopted the Universal Declaration of Human Rights on December 10, 1948, with 48 states voting in favor; none against; and eight abstaining (including Saudi Arabia, South Africa, U.S.S.R, and Yugoslavia). *See* G.A. Res. 217, U.N. GAOR, (III 1948). Among its multitude of provisions are that everyone has the right to:

- Life, liberty and security of person;
- Be presumed innocent until proved guilty;
- Own property;
- Take part in government;
- Work and freedom of employment;
- Cultural participation;
- Rest and leisure;

- Education;
- Be equal before the law without discrimination;
- Freedom of peaceful assembly;
- Freedom of opinion and expression;
- Not be held in slavery or subjected to torture;
- Not be subjected to arbitrary arrest, detention, or exile; and
- Not be subjected to retroactive penal laws.

Further, the international community has adopted other conventions to clarify human rights. In 1965, the United Nations General Assembly adopted the Convention on the Elimination of All Forms of Racial Discrimination, 660 U.N.T.S. 195, to which the United States is a party. It condemns racial discrimination. It entered into force on January 4, 1969.

In 1966, the General Assembly adopted the International Covenant on Economic, Social and Cultural Rights, 993 U.N.T.S. 3. It entered into force on January 3, 1976. It provides that workers have a right to fair wages, safe and healthy working conditions, rest and leisure, and reasonable limitation of working hours. The United States is not a party to this covenant.

In 1966, the General Assembly adopted the International Covenant on Civil and Political Rights, 999 U.N.T.S. 171. It provides that all peoples have a right of self-determination; a right to life; and no one shall be held in slavery or subjected to torture. It entered into force on March 23, 1976.

There are several human rights conventions that protect families, women, and children. On December 18, 1979, the General Assembly adopted the Convention on the Elimination of All Forms of Discrimination Against Women, 1249 U.N.T.S. 13. The United States is not a party to this treaty, which entered into force on September 3, 1981. The Convention condemns discrimination against women in all forms and requires the parties to take steps to eliminate any discrimination. The United States is also not a party to The Convention on the Rights of the Child, 1577 U.N.T.S. 3, which applies to every human being below the age of 18. This treaty compels state parties to not discriminate against children and to ensure their protection and well-being.

These treaties and covenants may be enforced in national courts, if the state is a party, or in specially delineated human rights courts. More information about the European Court of Human Rights is available at its website, <http://www.echr.coe.int/echr>. The Inter-American Court of Human Rights website is available at <http://www.corteidh.or.cr/index_ing.html>.

CHAPTER VII

VII. International Jurisdiction, Conflicts, and Immunities

A. I.C.J. Jurisdiction [§86]

The International Court of Justice is the judicial arm of the United Nations and the successor court to the Permanent Court of International Justice, which was established under the auspices of the League of Nations. Its decisions are issued in English and French. It is both a court of original jurisdiction, meaning it finds all the facts, and of final appeal.

The I.C.J is composed of 15 judges, no two of whom may be nationals of the same state. The United Nations Security Council and General Assembly elect the judges by a majority vote of both bodies. The I.C.J. may have jurisdiction over legal disputes concerning (1) the interpretation of a treaty; (2) any question of international law; (3) the existence of any fact, which would constitute a breach of an international obligation; and (4) the nature and extent of the reparation to be made for a breach of an international obligation.

The I.C.J. reviews two types of cases: contentious cases between two or more states, and requests by United Nations entities for advisory opinions. The United Nations General Assembly, the Security Council or any of the Specialized Agencies may request an advisory opinion on international legal issues.

Only states may be parties to contentious cases. A state may choose a judge *ad hoc* to sit in the case if it does not already have one on the court and the other party does. This explains why sometimes decisions are made by a 16-judge panel rather than by 15 judges. The state must be a party to the court's statute and give either express or implied consent to jurisdiction. This consent may be derived from (1) an *ad hoc* agreement; (2) prior agreement in a bilateral or multilateral treaty; or (3) acceptance of the compulsory jurisdiction of the court.

This expression of consent may contain reservations that limit the jurisdiction to certain cases or restricts the court from taking others. The United States initially put forth four reservations when it accepted the court's compulsory jurisdiction.

When Nicaragua sued the United States in 1984 to challenge the mining of its harbors and other alleged acts of war, the United States disputed the jurisdiction of the I.C.J. to hear the conflict. The U.S. modified its acceptance of the compulsory jurisdiction of the I.C.J. three days before Nicaragua filed the suit. The I.C.J. ruled that the modification was not immediately effective because the U.S. needed to give six months' notice according to the terms of its own reservation.

In 1985, the U.S. withdrew from the compulsory jurisdiction after the I.C.J. pronounced that it possessed jurisdiction over the case of *Nicaragua v. United States*, 1984 I.C.J. 392. The U.S. chose not to participate in the merits of the case. The I.C.J. did agree with the United States' objection that centered on its multilateral treaty reservation that required all parties to a multilateral treaty must be before the court to permit it to hear a dispute concerning the treaty. The I.C.J. decided this meant that it could not apply the U.N. Charter or other multilateral treaties. It did find that it could apply customary international law.

The court noted the difficulty of international fact gathering when one party does not appear in the merits phase after there was marked disagreement between the parties as to the facts in the jurisdictional phase. The view of the facts of the party that chose not to appear in the merits phase, in this instance the United States, was not available. There was also secrecy surrounding certain conduct, thus making it difficult to obtain further information. The conflict was ongoing, requiring the Court to continue to gather facts throughout the case. In settled conflicts where the facts are clear, the I.C.J. focuses on applying law to the facts.

There have been other cases where the states have failed to appear. In the *Case Concerning U.S. Diplomatic and Consular Staff in Tehran (U.S. v. Iran)*, 1980 I.C.J. 3, Iran sent a letter expressing respect for the court while requesting the court not take jurisdiction over the matter. It did take jurisdiction and ultimately ruled against Iran.

In the *Nuclear Tests Cases (Australia v. France)*, 1974 I.C.J. 253, and *(New Zealand v. France)*, 1974 I.C.J. 457, France failed to appear to discuss its atmospheric testing near Australia and New Zealand. France subsequently issued a statement that it was terminating all tests. Since the I.C.J. concluded that the objective of Australia and New Zealand was to terminate all tests, it found no reason to continue the cases as the objective had been accomplished.

Australia and New Zealand sought to legally compel the termination of the test. When France issued its statement, it deliberately stated its conviction that its nuclear experiments had not violated international law, nor was it bound by any rule of international law to terminate the tests.

B. State Jurisdiction [§87]

States exercise three primary types of jurisdiction based on six principles. States possess jurisdiction to prescribe laws, execute them, and adjudicate disputes. This jurisdiction may be based on the following six principles: nationality, territorial, effects, protective, passive personality, and universal.

1. Types of Jurisdiction [§88]

Prescriptive or legislative jurisdiction refers to the authority of states to legislate and prescribe laws with respect to persons and things present within their territories. The conduct must take

115

place in all or in a substantial part of the territory. Nevertheless, conduct outside the state's territory that has a substantial effect within its territory may also be subject to the state's jurisdiction to prescribe laws.

Executive or administrative jurisdiction refers to the power of states to enforce laws. The executive or administrative branch of government is responsible for implementing legal rules.

Judicial or adjudicative jurisdiction refers to the competence of national courts to bring parties before them and to render authoritative judgments. With these types of jurisdiction, states may assert claims based on six principles.

2. Nationality Principle [§89]

The nationality principle refers to jurisdiction over persons or things possessing the state's nationality. The nationality must be effective, or provided through genuine links between the person and the state, to permit the state to exercise jurisdiction over the person. In the *Blackmer v. U.S* case, 284 U.S. 421, 52 S.Ct. 252, 76 L.Ed. 375 (1932), Chief Justice Hughes determined that the U.S. had jurisdiction over its citizen while he lived in France. Although residing in a foreign country, the Court found that Mr. Blackmer remained "personally bound to take notice of the laws that are applicable to him and to obey them." *Id.* at 438. This included a subpoena requiring him to appear as a witness on behalf of the United States in a criminal trial.

3. Territorial Principle [§90]

With the territorial principle, states may assert jurisdiction over their land and what happens therein. The subjective territorial principle permits jurisdiction over crime commenced within the state but completed abroad. The objective territorial principle grants states jurisdiction over crime commenced outside of the state but completed within the state.

In *American Banana Co. v. United Fruit Co.*, 213 U.S. 347, 356, 29 S.Ct. 511, 53 L.Ed. 826 (1909), Justice Holmes stated, "[T]he general and almost universal rule is that the character of an act as lawful or unlawful must be determined wholly by the law of the country where the act is done." In this case, the acts took place in Panama and Costa Rica, and Justice Holmes concluded that the U.S. lacked jurisdiction to criminalize acts within those countries.

4. Effects Principle [§91]

The effects principle is sometimes considered an element of the territorial principle. It grants the state jurisdiction over extra-territorial conduct that has an effect within the state. In *U.S. v. Aluminum Co. of America*, 148 F.2d 416 (2d Cir. 1945), the court considered whether two agreements between foreign companies violated U.S. laws. The 1931 agreement created an alliance between a French corporation, two German corporations, a Swiss corporation, a British corporation, and Aluminum Ltd., a Canadian corporation. The agreement called for the formation of a Swiss corporation to issue shares and fix quota on production. In 1936, the parties agreed to include imports into the United States.

The Second Circuit held that the 1936 agreement violated Sec. 1 of the Sherman Act, which prohibits contracts in restraint of trade. Congress can attach liability to the conduct of aliens because a state may impose liabilities for conduct outside its borders that has consequences within its borders. This liability is only for conduct that produces consequences within the state, regardless of intent.

5. Protective Principle [§92]

This principle permits domestic courts to exercise jurisdiction over acts, such as currency fraud, that threaten the existence of states. Thus, an Austrian citizen could manufacture fake Swiss francs while living in China, and Switzerland would have jurisdiction over his activities. He is subjected to being extradited to Switzerland to stand trial as his actions affect Switzerland's ability to control its economy.

6. Passive Personality (Nationality) Principle [§93]

This refers to the state's jurisdiction over persons who are legally responsible to their nationals. Under the passive personality principle, domestic courts may take jurisdiction over a citizen of another country who commits a tort or a crime against a state's nationals. In the *Case of the S.S. "Lotus" (France v. Turkey)*, 1927 P.C.I.J. Ser. A., No. 10, Turkey asserted jurisdiction over Lt. Demons, a French citizen, because his actions caused death to Turkish citizens and harm to a Turkish flag vessel.

7. Universal Principle [§94]

All states have jurisdiction over activities that are universally condemned as international crimes, war crimes, or crimes against humanity. Piracy, genocide, war crimes, and torture are examples of individual actions over which any state can exercise jurisdiction. This means that a person charged with such a crime can be extradited to any country in the world to stand trial.

C. Jurisdiction Over Vessels and Objects [§95]

States have jurisdiction over vessels that fly their flags. Aircraft vessels are the nationals of the state whose flag they fly. They have no right of innocent passage, although they may have a right of entry in distress. The downside is that they are subject to being shot down.

State aircraft are not permitted to fly over the territory of another state without authorization by a treaty or special agreement. Moreover, such privileges may be delineated by international agreements. The Soviets shot down Korean Airlines 007, a Korean flag vessel, in a tragic example when the airplane flew off course through Soviet airspace.

Maritime vessels are also nationals of the states whose flag under which they sail. In order for a state to offer diplomatic protection over a ship, there must be a genuine link between the state and the vessel. This is similar to the requirement for states to protect individuals.

They must show a substantial connection between the vessel and the state. It is not sufficient to register the ship in the state if it never docks there or does any business from the state's ports. A ship must sail under the flag of one state only. There is no dual nationality for ships.

In the *Case Concerning the S.S. Lotus (France v. Turkey)*, 1927 P.C.I.J. Ser. A., No. 10, a collision took place on the high seas between a French steamer, the S.S. Lotus, and a Turkish steamer, the Boz-Kourt. The Turkish boat sunk, taking with it eight Turkish citizens. When the French ship reached Constantinople, the Turkish authorities instituted criminal proceedings against Lt. Demons.

The court questioned whether Turkey could assert jurisdiction over Lt. Demons. Three jurisdictional principles were at issue. Lt. Demons, a French citizen, was the officer of the watch specifically responsible for making sure that a French flag vessel did not run into another ship. France could exercise nationality jurisdiction since both the accused and the vessel possessed its nationality. The accident took place on the high seas, which permits both states to exercise territorial jurisdiction. The victims were Turkish, giving Turkey passive nationality jurisdiction.

France argued that Turkey must point to a rule of international law giving it jurisdiction. Turkey argued that it possessed jurisdiction unless that jurisdiction conflicted with a principle of international law. The Court agreed with Turkey, noting that the "rules of law binding upon states … emanate from their own free will as expressed in conventions or usages generally accepted as expressing principles of law and established in order to regulate the relations between these co-existing independent communities... ." The Court made clear that restrictions upon the independence of states therefore could not be presumed. Turkey does not have to rely on a permissive rule; rather, it has the right to assert jurisdiction unless there is a prohibiting rule.

France also argued that international law recognizes the exclusive jurisdiction of the state whose flag is flown as regarding everything which occurs on board a ship on the high seas. The Court rejected this argument as well. On the high seas, the state that received effects from an offense can regard the offense as having been committed within its territory and it can prosecute the delinquent individual. Here, there were two ships, flying different flags, and consequently two different states had concurrent jurisdiction.

D. Conflicts of Law [§96]

When two states can exercise jurisdiction over the same set of facts, as in the *S.S. Lotus* case, that often creates conflict. International comity and *forum non conveniens* are two principles that courts use to resolve such disputes and decide on which of two forums would be the most appropriate.

1. International Comity [§97]

Under the comity principle, one nation accords respect to the legislative, executive, or judicial acts of another nation. Courts balance international duty and convenience with the rights of its own citizens. Courts have discretion to hear or dismiss a case on comity grounds.

To enforce foreign judgments and awards in another country's territory requires comity between nations and the willingness of respective courts to recognize and give effect to other courts' actions. This recognition promotes co-operation and serves justice and fair play by ensuring that disputes are tried only once.

2. *Forum Non Conveniens* [§98]

U.S. courts employ this doctrine to settle cases of concurrent jurisdiction and to avoid offending the interest of foreign states and defendants. A U.S. judge will refuse to adjudicate a case because the courts of another country would be the "fairer" place to hear the case. The judge considers the following factors:

1. The relative merits of adjudicating the dispute in another court;
2. The rights of the parties; and
3. The availability of a more appropriate forum for the plaintiff.

The use of *forum non conveniens* has expanded with the evolution of U.S. extraterritorial jurisdiction, which brought more cases within the purview of U.S. courts. *In re Union Carbide Corp. Gas Plant Disaster*, 809 F.2d 195 (2d Cir. 1987), was the biggest case to employ *forum non conveniens* after a gas plant disaster caused the deaths of over 2,000 Indian citizens and injuries to over 200,000 after exposure to a lethal gas known as methyl isocyanate. The government of India sought to keep the case in the U.S. where the law was more favorable to its position and would yield higher damages. However, the Second Circuit concluded that the district court's finding that Indian courts provided an adequate alternative forum could not be labeled as clearly erroneous or an abuse of discretion. *Id.* The district court had determined India to be the proper forum because, among other things, the relevant evidence was there; the Indian judiciary was developed, independent, and progressive; and the Indian tort law was suitable to resolve legal issues involving complex technology.

In *London Film Productions Ltd. v. Intercontinental Communications, Inc.*, 580 F.Supp. 47 (S.D.N.Y. 1984), a British corporation sued a New York corporation in the United States for

121

infringement of British copyrights that occurred in Chile and other South American countries. London Films alleged that Intercontinental was showing its motion pictures on television in South America. Intercontinental sought to dismiss the suit, claiming the court lacked jurisdiction. The wrongdoings did not violate U.S. law. The court determined that it possessed jurisdiction over whether an American corporation has acted in violation of a foreign copyright. The court noted that it was the only forum in which the defendant is the subject of personal jurisdiction. The court concluded that where "the balance does not tip strongly in favor of an alternative forum it is well-established that the plaintiff's choice of forum should not be disturbed." *Id.* at 50.

E. Foreign Sovereign Immunity [§99]

Foreign sovereign immunity exempts the personhood and possessions of the sovereign from arrest, detention, or other disturbance while visiting a foreign territory. All nations permit some form of this exemption.

1. Absolute Theory of Sovereign Immunity [§100]

The absolute theory of sovereign immunity affirms that the jurisdiction of a nation within its own territory is necessarily exclusive and absolute. Sovereigns are shielded from the jurisdictional reach of municipal courts on the theory that to implead the foreign sovereign could upset the friendly relations of the states involved. Under this theory, a U.S. court lacks personal, subject matter, *in rem,* and *quasi in rem* jurisdiction over a sovereign and its property.

The *Schooner Exchange v. McFaddon* case, 11 U.S. (7 Cranch) 116, 3 L.Ed. 287 (1812), depicts how the absolute theory of sovereign immunity may be applied to exempt a foreign sovereign's property from the jurisdiction of another sovereign's courts. The Schooner Exchange ship sailed on October 27, 1809, to Spain. On December 30, 1810, while peacefully on its voyage,

122

the ship was seized by Napoleon, Emperor of France and Italy. The Schooner Exchange became distressed during bad weather on the high seas, and entered U.S. ports seeking refreshment and repairs.

The original owners filed a libel, which is an admiralty lawsuit, in district court. They sought the return of their ship, claiming that the ship was their private vessel and not the public vessel of Napoleon. The district court dismissed the libel with cost, finding the ship immune and not subject to U.S. jurisdiction. The circuit court reversed.

The U.S. Supreme Court reversed the circuit court and affirmed the district court's finding that a public armed ship, in the service of a friendly foreign sovereign, was exempt from U.S. jurisdiction. The Court proclaimed that national ships of friendly nations enjoy the same immunity from arrest and detention as does the sovereign and foreign ministers. The Court never reached the merits of the underlying question as to whether the ship was illegally seized.

Once a domestic court refuses to take jurisdiction over a matter on sovereign immunity grounds, the plaintiff retains the option to sue the sovereign in its own courts. The plaintiff must determine whether the sovereign has waived immunity from jurisdiction over his or her claim.

There is some debate as to whether the sovereign, whose status changes, remains immune for life for actions while a sovereign. Clearly, international law provides immunity for the head of state. When the person loses that status, should he or she continue to be immune for acts committed while a sovereign? What if the sovereign is accused of committing international crimes against peace, war crimes, and crimes against humanity? Any state, including the national state, can assert jurisdiction over such crimes.

In Chile, for example, over 125 lawsuits were filed against Augusto Pinochet, the former president of Chile, for crimes allegedly committed while he was in office from 1973 to 1990. In Chile, Pinochet lost the sovereign immunity associated with being president once he left office. However, he acquired parliamentary immunity when he became a Senator-for-life, following his retirement as Commander-in-Chief of the Army. The Chilean constitution, passed during his military government, accorded him such status as a former president. On June 5, 2000, the Santiago Appeals Court voted to lift Pinochet's parliamentary immunity to allow him to be investigated in the lawsuits. The Chilean Supreme Court affirmed the lifting of immunity on August 26, 2004. For more information on this saga, Amnesty International, *see* <http://www.amnesty.org/>, and BBC News, *see* <http://news.bbc.co.uk/>, both tracked the factual development of the Pinochet cases, on their respective websites.

As the trial of former Serbian President Slobodan Milosevic entered its final stages before the International Criminal Court and the trial of former Iraqi President Saddam Hussein prepared to open in the fall of 2005 in Iraqi courts, a book argued that there should be no sovereign immunity defense for leaders accused of genocide. *See* Michael J. Kelly, *Nowhere to Hide: Defeat of the Sovereign Immunity Defense for Crimes of Genocide and the Trials of Slobodan Milosevic and Saddam Hussein* (Peter Lang Pub. 2005). Professor Kelly's book maintains that while current heads of state would retain immunity, those who had lost their status should lose immunity, and particularly when accused of crimes of genocide. Hussein was executed in 2006 and Milosevic was found dead in his cell in 2006.

2. Restrictive Theory of Sovereign Immunity [§101]
Under the restrictive theory of sovereign immunity, the sovereign is only immune when doing official sovereign acts, or *jure imperii*. The foreign sovereign can be sued when it engages

in commercial acts, or *jure gestionis,* and conducts itself similar to that of a merchant in the regular course of commercial conduct or a particular commercial transaction.

The Foreign Sovereign Immunities Act of 1976 codifies this separation of acts into U.S. law at Pub. L. No. 94-583, 90 Stat. 2891, as amended, Pub. L. No. 100-669 (1988), 102 Stat. 3969, 28 U.S.C. 1601 *et seq.* Several other states, including Australia, Canada, Pakistan, Singapore, South Africa, and the United Kingdom have codified similar statutes into their national law. *See, e.g.,* State Immunity Act, R.S.C. 1985, c. s-18 (Canada); Foreign States Immunities Act, 1985, 196/1985 (Australia); State Immunity Act, Act 19 of 1979 (Singapore); State Immunity Act, 1978, c.33 (United Kingdom); and Foreign States Immunities Act, 1981 S.A. Legal Admn. 87 (South Africa).

The *Texas Trading & Mill Corp. v. Federal Republic of Nigeria* case, 647 F.2d 300 (2d Cir. 1981), illustrates the restrictive theory of sovereign immunity. Nigeria entered into 109 contracts with 68 suppliers to purchase 16 million metric tons of Portland cement, worth approximately a billion dollars. Nigeria planned to use the cement for infrastructure construction. Based on its prior experiences, Nigeria anticipated that only twenty percent of the suppliers would perform. As a consequence, it overbought. When most of the suppliers fulfilled orders and began shipping the cement, Nigeria's docks and harbors became clogged with ships waiting to unload. Imports of other goods ground to a halt. More vessels carrying cement arrived daily as others steamed toward the Lagos/Apapa port.

To slow the tide, Nigeria unilaterally changed the terms of its letter of credit contracts requiring ships to convey to its Port Authority information concerning time of arrival two months ahead of time. It subsequently repudiated numerous contracts, and asked suppliers to settle. Many did; however, four American suppliers chose to sue Nigeria in U.S. federal district court. In

125

three of the cases, the U.S. district judge found jurisdiction and in one case the district court found jurisdiction lacking. The four cases were consolidated on appeal to determine whether Nigeria could invoke sovereign immunity to escape liability for breaching its contracts.

The Second Circuit found that Nigeria engaged in commercial activity when it entered into contracts and acquired letters of credit to purchase the cement. The Foreign Sovereign Immunities Act defines commercial activity as "a regular course of commercial conduct or a particular commercial transaction or act. The commercial character of an activity shall be determined by reference to the nature of the course of conduct or particular transaction or act, rather than by references to its purpose." *See* 28 U.S.C. Sec. 1603(d). Under this section, Nigeria could not use its intent to construct public infrastructure to escape liability. The restrictive theory of sovereign immunity permitted U.S. courts to exercise jurisdiction over Nigeria and the cases could proceed.

3. Waiver of Sovereign Immunity [§102]

States may also waive sovereign immunity. The effect of a waiver is to permit national courts to exercise jurisdiction over certain disputes. The sovereign's waiver of immunity may be either expressed or implied. Express waivers are often found in Friendship, Commerce, and Navigation treaties between two or more states. They may also be contained in contracts between a state and a private entity or person. Implied waivers may arise from agreements to arbitrate disputes.

Many states throughout the world, including Australia, Canada, Singapore, and South Africa, to name just a few, have passed some type of an immunity act. *See supra* §101. In the U.S., the Foreign Sovereign Immunities Act permits a U.S. court to take a case where the foreign sovereign has waived immunity, either explicitly or implicitly. *See* 28 U.S.C. §1605, (a)

126

(1). There are three kinds of waivers: (1) waiver of immunity from jurisdiction; (2) waiver of immunity from attachment in execution of a judgment or from execution of judgment (unless waived, foreign sovereign property is immune from attachment); and (3) waiver of immunity from attachment prior to entry of judgment.

Certain property of a foreign sovereign is always immune from attachment, such as funds of foreign central banks or monetary authorities held for their own account and property connected to military activities with either a military character or under control of military authorities.

4. Act of State Doctrine [§103]

The Act of State Doctrine refers to the special deference shown by national courts towards the public acts of foreign states done within their own country. This Doctrine functions similarly to foreign sovereign immunity because both defer to foreign sovereigns, and both compel domestic claimants to appeal to foreign courts. However, foreign sovereign immunity looks to the limits of the jurisdiction of national courts, whereas the Act of State Doctrine is concerned with the prescriptive jurisdiction of the foreign state, or their right to legislate laws. Further, the Act of State Doctrine can be asserted by both private and public entities seeking to escape liability for acts compelled by a sovereign nation. The following three cases demonstrate three examples of how the Act of State Doctrine has been applied by U.S. courts.

In *Underhill v. Hernandez*, 168 U.S. 250, 252 (1897), the Supreme Court stated, "Every sovereign state is bound to respect the independence of every other sovereign state, and the courts of one country will not sit in judgment on the acts of the government of another done within its own territory." The Court concluded that it could not adjudicate the acts of the defendant, which were imputable to the government of

127

Venezuela, even if those acts harmed the American citizen who brought the lawsuit.

Nearly seven decades later, the Court sustained the Act of State Doctrine in *Banco Nacional De Cuba v. Sabbatino*, 376 U.S. 398 (1964). In that case, an American Commodity broker complained about Cuban Law No. 851, which gave the Cuban President and Prime Minister discretionary power to nationalize, by forced expropriation, property or enterprises in which American nationals had an interest. The Cuban President and Prime Minister proceeded to nationalize the rights and interests of American companies, including those of the plaintiffs. Even if the U.S. State Department proclaimed the action a violation of international law, the Court said, "However offensive to the public policy of this country and its constituent States an expropriation of this kind may be, we conclude that both the national interest and progress toward the goal of establishing the rule of law among nations are best served by maintaining intact the act of state doctrine in this realm of its application." *Id.* at 436-437.

In 1990, U.S. Supreme Court Justice Antonin Scalia wrote in *W.S. Kirkpatrick & Co., Inc. v. Environmental Tectonics Corp. International*, 493 U.S. 400, 410 (1990), that the Act of State Doctrine has no application where "the validity of no foreign sovereign act is at issue."

In the *Kirkpatrick* case, foreign officials possessed an unlawful motivation in the performance of their official acts, the contracting for the construction and equipment of an aeromedical center at Kaduna Air Force Base in Nigeria. The officials sought to obtain bribes or commissions equal to 20% of the contract price. Scalia noted, "All parties agree that Nigerian law prohibits both the payment and the receipt of bribes in connection with the award of a government contract." *Id.* at 402. The U.S. courts could exercise jurisdiction over the dispute.

F. Diplomatic and Consular Immunities [§104]

The diplomat has several functions. The diplomat represents the sending state in the receiving state. The diplomat protects the interests of the sending state. The diplomat negotiates with the government of the receiving state on behalf of his government. The diplomat ascertains, by lawful means, conditions and developments in the receiving state and reports back to his government. The diplomat promotes friendly relations, and develops economic, cultural, and scientific relations. The diplomat can perform consular functions.

Consuls are concerned with international economic relations rather than political relations between the sending and receiving states. Traditionally, they have not been accorded the same immunities as diplomats. They have two primary immunities: (1) inviolability of consular archives; and (2) immunity of consuls for official acts. A state can tow a consul's car parked in a handicapped zone without a handicapped sticker, but cannot tow a diplomat's similarly parked car. Some diplomats have been known to take advantage of their immunity in crowded urban cities and park in front of water hydrants and other forbidden areas. When consuls act outside their official roles, they can be held liable for such violations of local law because they are not immune from either civil or criminal jurisdictions of domestic courts.

1. Diplomatic Immunity [§105]

With diplomatic exchanges, the sending state dispatches its diplomat to the receiving state, which accepts the diplomat and opens relations between the states. The Vienna Convention on Diplomatic Relations, 500 U.N.T.S. 95, codified the customary law on diplomatic relations into treaty form when states signed it in Vienna on April 18, 1961. It entered into force on April

129

24, 1964. The Optional Protocol on the Diplomatic Relations Convention is available at 500 U.N.T.S. 241.

Diplomatic immunity is accorded to the person, to his or her family, to the embassy premises, and to all correspondence of the mission, which is often referred to as the diplomatic pouch. "Inviolability" is the term used to indicate that the embassy premises and the personhood of diplomats and their families cannot be touched by the other state.

Diplomats possess absolute immunity from criminal jurisdiction. If they commit a crime, the sending state's option is to declare them *persona non grata*, a Latin phase meaning an unwelcome person. This gives the individual a certain amount of time to leave the territory before they will be stripped of their immunity. Under Article 9 of the Vienna Convention on Diplomatic Relations, a receiving state has the option to declare an individual *persona non grata* at anytime, even before they enter the territory. The receiving state does not have to give an explanation.

Diplomats are also immune from civil and administrative jurisdiction with few exceptions, such as issues involving real property, estates, and professional and commercial activity exercised outside of their official functions.

The embassy is viewed as the territory of the sending state, similar to an enclave. The archives and documents of the mission are also inviolable.

United Nations officials are accorded the same privileges and immunities as ambassadors, and its headquarters are granted the same status of embassies. The Agreement Between the United Nations and the United States of America Regarding the Headquarters of the United Nations, U.N.-U.S., June 26, 1947, 11 U.N.T.S. 11, requires that the headquarters district be inviolable and prevents United States police officers from entering the headquarters district without securing the consent of the Secretary-General. While the headquarters is located in New York City, it is under the control and authority of the United Nations. When a senior United Nations official was accused of using his position to solicit bribes in the Food for Aid program, Secretary-General Kofi Annan waived his immunity just hours before U.S. police arrested the official in 2005. For a news report of the story, *see Acting on new Oil-for-Food report, Annan lifts official's immunity, pledges further steps*, <http://www.un.org/apps/news/story.asp?NewsID=15336&Cr=iraq& Cr1=oil> (Aug. 8, 2005).

The receiving state can reject a diplomat and keep that person from becoming head of mission within its territory. When a diplomatic impasse occurs, the sending state either opts to send another person if it wishes to maintain diplomatic relations or elects to forego relations with a particular state. In some instances, the sending state declines to send another person.

The Reagan Administration refused to accept the credentials of Nora Astorga-Gadia de Jenkins after Nicaragua designated her as its next ambassador to the United States in 1986. Astorga, a lawyer who became a leading commander in the Nicaraguan civil war, served as Nicaragua's Deputy Minister of Foreign Affairs from 1984 to 1986. Soon after the U.S. rejection of Astorga, Nicaragua nominated her to become its ambassador to the United Nations. She served in both capacities jointly until her death from cancer in 1988. The U.S. government never officially recognized her in Washington.

As mentioned earlier, the customary law of diplomatic immunity was codified in the 1961 Vienna Convention on Diplomatic Relations. This Convention has been ratified by most states, and it constitutes one of the most widely accepted conventions. Article 29 states, "The person of the diplomatic agent shall be inviolable. He shall not be liable to any form of arrest or detention. The receiving State shall treat him with due respect and shall take all appropriate steps to prevent any attack on his person, freedom or dignity."

The *United States v. Iran* case, 1980 I.C.J. 3, arose most immediately out of the 1979 Iranian Hostage crisis, although the dispute between the two countries was long standing. Iran claimed 25 years of U.S. interference in its internal affairs, dating back to 1953. That year, the United States Central Intelligence Agency allegedly conspired to overthrow Dr. Mohammed Mossedegh, the elected Iranian prime minister and reinstate the Shah of Iran. The Shah was overthrown in 1979 after a harsh, brutal rule, involving secret police that imprisoned political activists. The U.S. admitted the Shah into U.S. territory to have surgery. Iranian students took over the U.S. embassy on November 4, 1979. For over three hours, embassy personnel called Iranian authorities seeking help. Iran did not send security forces to protect the embassy, nor did it rescue the hostages or persuade the students to terminate their actions. Twenty-eight hostages were diplomats, and four were members of the Consular Section of the Embassy.

After the U.S. sued Iran in the I.C.J., Iran contested jurisdiction. The Court found that the optional protocols to the Vienna Conventions on Diplomatic Relations and Consular Relations provided jurisdiction. Both countries were signatories of the treaties and their optional protocols concerning dispute resolution.

Once jurisdictional issues were resolved, Iran elected not to appear in the merits phase. While the Court noted the difficulty of discerning facts when there is a missing party, it observed that much about the dispute between the two parties was public information. The Court then used information in the news to determine Iran's concerns.

The Court considered whether Iran violated the two Vienna Conventions. The initiation of the embassy attacks could not be imputed to Iran. These were private acts by students. However, Iran was responsible for its own conduct. As the receiving state, it had a responsibility to ensure the protection of the U.S. Embassy and Consulates, their staffs, the archives, their means of communication, and the staff's freedom of movement. As the receiving state, Iran failed to protect the inviolability of the diplomats, archives, and documents.

2. Consular Immunity [§106]

In *U.S. v. Iran*, Iran was also held to have violated the Vienna Convention on Consular Relations and ordered to restore the Consulates at Tabriz and Shiraz to the U.S. government. The 1963 Vienna Convention on Consular Relations, 596 U.N.T.S. 261, was adopted two years after the Vienna Convention on Diplomatic Relations. It entered into force on March 19, 1967.

The *Case Concerning Avena and Other Mexican Nationals (Mexico v. U.S)*, 2004 I.C.J. 1, tested the role of consuls in assisting their citizens. On January 9, 2003, Mexico sued the United States for violating the Vienna Convention on Consular Relations. It based jurisdiction on the same optional protocol the U.S. used to sue Iran. Mexico charged that the U.S. had arrested, detained, tried, convicted and sentenced 54 Mexican nationals to death in violation of its international obligations to Mexico. Specifically, Mexico charged that the U.S. had violated Articles 5 and 36 of the Convention. Article 5 indicates the sending state shall have the right to protect its nationals, both individuals and corporate bodies. Article 36 addresses communication and contact with nationals of the sending state. This article gives the sending state the right to be informed when its nationals are arrested, committed to prison, or detained in any manner. The U.S. denied that it owed such obligations to dual nationals.

133

The I.C.J. ruled that the U.S. had to prove which individuals were also dual nationals with the United States to support its claim. Mexico presented birth certificates and declarations from 42 individuals stating that they never acquired U.S. nationality to prove the individuals were solely Mexican.

The I.C.J. found three separate rights under Article 36. First, the Mexican nationals should have been informed, without delay, of their right under Article 36 to contact their Consulate. This duty arose once the U.S. authorities knew the person was a foreign national or had reason to think so. The Court recommended that the U.S. routinely inquire about nationality at the time of arrest, as when reading suspects their "Miranda" rights. Second, the Mexican consular post should have been notified, without delay, of the Mexican citizens' detention if they requested such notification. Third, as the receiving state, the U.S. was obliged to forward, without delay, any communication addressed to the consular post by the detained person.

In March 2004, the I.C.J. concluded that the U.S. was in breach of its obligations to Mexico. Immediately following the decision, President Bush ordered the stay of execution for all Mexican nationals on death row to give U.S. courts time to review their sentences to determine if their rights had been violated by the failure to notify the Mexican consulate of their arrest, prosecution, and sentencing. Approximately a year later in March 2005, President Bush withdrew the U.S. from the Optional Protocol to the Vienna Convention on Consular Relations, which it had ratified in 1969 and used to take Iran to the I.C.J. in 1980. This withdrawal both prohibits the U.S. from suing to enforce rights under the Convention and from being sued before the I.C.J. on a consular matter.

In May 2005, the Supreme Court set aside an appeal by Jose Medellín, a Mexican citizen on death row in Texas, who was seeking to have his death sentence overturned based on the I.C.J.

decision. The court held any decision by it would be premature because President Bush had ordered state courts to revisit the issue, making Supreme Court intervention unnecessary in May 2005. The Supreme Court surmised that Texas courts would provide Medellin the review he sought.

In conclusion, this discussion of jurisdiction, conflicts, and immunities illustrates disputes between states. As jurisdictional principles have expanded, more states can assert control over the same set of facts. As a consequence, states have developed principles of comity and *forum non conveniens* to determine when it would be best to yield the case to another sovereign to resolve. States have restricted the implementation of sovereign immunity to recognize the increasing commercial roles of sovereigns. Diplomatic immunity remains as originally envisioned because states recognize that the advantages of according protection to their respective representatives outweighs any disadvantages.

CHAPTER VIII

VIII. International Dispute Settlement

A. Peace as a Goal [§107]

Peace and war are part of a continuum of state relationships. At any time, states engage in harmonious dealings, conflict, or war with each other. This chapter and the next two address these various stages of relationships. Chapter IX addresses issues concerning breaches of law that give rise to international rights and responsibilities. Chapter X lays out the legal obligations that arise when states engage in war, including their obligations to declare war and conduct it in a humane manner to minimize the harm to their respective populations and territories.

International law recognizes that the world community, nation-states, and their populations benefit from harmony. When interactions are pleasant, friendly states create positive peace, pursuing common goals with each other. They cooperate on diplomatic, political, social, cultural, and economic issues. They exchange diplomats and people. Students and teachers swap themselves to experience different living environments. Cultural entities host joint meetings and workshops. Rich nations may send volunteers to help educate and feed the populations of poorer states. Countries form economic unions or trade partnerships to benefit financially. Their respective populations most profit in these times.

Given these enormous advantages, international law, not surprisingly, requires states to settle their disputes peacefully. This requirement and the mechanisms to do so are the subject of this chapter.

When individuals are involved, conflict arises from time to time. Leaders create negative peace where they disagree and fail to resolve their differences. One nation accidentally or deliberately sinks the boat or downs the plane of another. The actor may immediately apologize and make restitution, thereby restoring the relationship to balance. Other leaders finding themselves in the same set of circumstances may justify their actions. The response to the rationalization determines whether the matter can be resolved peacefully through negotiation, arbitration, conciliation, enquiry, judicial decision, or other options discussed in this chapter. Successful resolutions return nations to positive peace. Ongoing quarrels, however, cause nations to descend into negative peace or worse, when they use their military instruments to resolve their disputes.

The Cooperative Monitoring Center (CMC), www.cmc.sandia.gov, is an arm of the U.S. government's Sandia National Laboratory. It was established to assist the arms control process. It has outlined a range of results based on whether there exists a state of minimum or maximum confidence between the parties. In a situation of minimum confidence, states distrust each other, they do not communicate well, and the public resists interaction. This usually results in minimal arms control, according to the CMC. Suspicious states, like paranoid neighbors, are more likely to purchase weapons to prepare for conflict.

When parties build conditions of maximum confidence between them, they operate with mutual trust, open communication, and public confidence, according to the CMC. This can lead to extensive arms control, as there is less need to stockpile weapons.

To encourage countries to grow from minimum to maximum confidence, the CMC encourages confidence-building activities, such as regional forums, cultural and technical exchanges, open travel and communication, economic trade and cooperation, participation in international organizations, joint projects, and regional arms control initiatives.

The next section of this chapter discusses state obligations to resolve disputes tranquilly so that they build maximum confidence between them. The last section provides an overview of the role of international entities, such as the United Nations, in assisting states to resolve their conflicts in a manner that does not threaten international peace and security.

B. State Obligations [§108]

By becoming members of the United Nations, 192 states have committed to resolve their disputes peacefully. Four provisions enshrine this commitment into the United Nations Charter. *See* U.N. Charter, *supra* §59.

Article 2(3) of the United Nations Charter provides, "All members shall settle their international disputes by peaceful means in such a manner that international peace and security, and justice, are not endangered." *Id.* at Art. 2(3). Under Article 2(4), "All members shall refrain in their international relations from the threat or use of force against the territorial integrity or political independence of any state, or in any manner inconsistent with the Purposes of the United Nations." *Id.* at Art. 2(4).

Moreover, under Article 33(1), "The parties to any dispute, the continuance of which is likely to endanger the maintenance of international peace and security, shall, first of all, seek a solution by negotiation, enquiry, mediation, conciliation, arbitration, judicial settlement, resort to regional agencies or arrangements, or other peaceful means of their own choice." *Id.* at Art. 33(1). Article 36(3) further provides that legal disputes, as a general rule, should be referred by the parties to the I.C.J. in accordance with the provisions of the Statute of the court. *Id.* at Art. 36(3).

The goal of the various options discussed in this chapter to resolve disputes peacefully is to encourage goodwill among nations. In harmonious situations, nations interact with maximum confidence. States may use any or all of the options discussed herewith to comply with such obligations.

1. Negotiation, Enquiry and Mediation [§109]

With negotiation, two or more parties to a dispute seek to resolve it directly between them. Just as individuals routinely negotiate to solve their conflicts, so do states. Indeed, negotiation is the primary method that states use to resolve disagreements. It happens so often that citizens are rarely aware of this behind-the-scenes activity. The news media tends to focus on the photo opportunities when the leader goes abroad to discuss a matter with her counterpart. The normal discussions do not take place in public view.

Diplomats, foreign ministers, or other representatives meet to set out their respective concerns with the goal of reaching a mutually satisfying outcome. The advantage to negotiation is that it seeks an ongoing relationship between the parties, by recognizing that they gain by resolving their immediate conflicts.

I.C.J. opinions sometimes refer to the parties' obligations to negotiate. In the *North Sea Continental Shelf Case*, 1969 I.C.J. 3, the I.C.J. said, "The Parties were under an obligation to enter into negotiations with a view to arriving at an agreement and not merely to go through a formal process of negotiation as a sort of prior condition for the automatic application of a certain method of delimitation in the absence of agreement; they were so to conduct themselves that the negotiations were meaningful, which would not be the case when one of them insisted upon its own position without contemplating any modification of it." Thus, states must negotiate in good faith, in open communication, with a goal to resolving their conflict without grandstanding.

With enquiry, the Secretary-General may be asked to investigate a dispute to determine an independent set of facts. For example, one party may claim that it accidentally harmed another nation. The victim state may believe the harm was intentional. Asking the Secretary-General to use his good offices to inquire into the situation and to determine the facts can help the parties considerably. During the time it takes to investigate the circumstances that led to the dispute, emotions may cool off, permitting the parties to eventually negotiate to reach a mutually satisfying resolution.

When emotions are too frayed to negotiate directly or the parties have taken intractable positions, they may bring in a third party to conduct mediation. The mediator may also be the Secretary-General or it may be another party. Before taking on the dispute, the Secretary-General may insist that the mediation be binding, requiring the parties in advance to obey his ruling.

For example, when France and New Zealand asked Secretary-General Javier de Perez de Cuellar from Peru to mediate their dispute, they agreed in advance to obey his ruling, which is available at 26 I.L.M. 1346 (1987). The conflict arose when two French agents sank the Rainbow Warrior, a vessel belonging to Greenpeace International, while in the Auckland, New Zealand harbor on 10 July 1985. The explosion caused the death of crewmember Fernando Pereira, a Netherlands citizen. New Zealand interviewed, arrested, and charged Major Alain Mafart and Captain Dominique Prieur with manslaughter and willful damage to a ship. After they plead guilty to manslaughter, the New Zealand Chief Justice sentenced them to 10 years in prison.

France and New Zealand attempted to negotiate their differences, but failed to reach a solution. They both formally approached the Secretary-General in June 1986 for a ruling. In his ruling, the Secretary-General set forth the facts, the violation of international law by France, and the international legal responsibility of the French government. He then ordered France to apologize to New Zealand for violating its sovereignty and its rights under international law, and to pay no less than U.S. $7 million to New Zealand for the harm caused. Further, he ordered New Zealand to release the two French agents to France to be immediately transferred to a French military facility in the isolated island of Hao in French Polynesia to serve three years. The Secretary-General's ruling further required France to give New Zealand reports on their situation every three months. Should any other differences arise, the Secretary-General ruled that either government could request binding arbitration.

2. Conciliation [§110]

An individual, a committee, or an institutional body can conciliate disputes. Conciliation commissions have been established to resolve both international conflicts and domestic clashes encompassing extreme strife between internal groups. Conciliation methods seek amicable, or friendly resolution of the dispute between the parties. Conciliation commissions may resolve either a single conflict or a series of disputes.

After the dissolution of apartheid, for example, South Africa set up the Truth and Reconciliation Commission to uncover the facts of what happened during the apartheid period when individuals disappeared and their bodies were never recovered. The Commission granted amnesty to those individuals willing to confess their crimes and reveal the full array of facts. The Commission became a force for healing the spiritual and psychological harm caused by apartheid as the perpetrators apologized and the victims became grateful to receive information on what happened to their loved ones.

The Truth and Reconciliation Commission "deliberately avoided a 'victors' justice' approach to the crimes of apartheid and chose instead one based on confession and absolution, informed by the principles of reconciliation, reconstruction, reparation and goodwill." *See Sosa v. Alvarez-Machain*, 542 U.S. 692, 124 S.Ct. 2739 (2004) [Declaration of Penuell Mpapa Maduna, Minister of Justice and Constitutional Development, Republic of South Africa, reprinted in App. to Brief for Government of Commonwealth of Australia *et al.* as Amici Curiae 7a, ¶3.2.1 (emphasis deleted)]. The South African Truth and Reconciliation Commission has been cited as a model to address internal strife in countries as diverse as the former Yugoslavia in Europe and Rwanda in Africa.

A host of treaties, like the Vienna Convention on the Law of Treaties and U.N. Convention on the Law of Sea, provide for conciliation. While any party to a dispute concerning these treaties may request conciliation, the recommendations are not binding.

3. Arbitration [§111]

Arbitration can take place with a sole arbitrator, as evidenced in the *Libya-Texaco* case, *supra* §58, or with a panel of arbitrators. With the latter, each party typically chooses one arbitrator, and the two arbitrators select the third. Both states together may also select a third arbitrator. With arbitration tribunals, parties typically share the cost. In creating the arbitral tribunal, the parties may specify the subject matter of the dispute; the rule of law and principles to be applied; the majority required for an award (51%, 2/3, 3/4) when there is more than one arbitrator; the time limit to reach an award; and the languages to be employed. The arbitral body may be set up *ad hoc* to hear one case or as a continuing body to handle a category of disputes.

The Iran-U.S. Claims Tribunal, with offices in The Hague, was established to hear claims of private Iranian citizens against

143

the government of the U.S., private U.S. citizens against the government of Iran, and government-to-government claims. The Tribunal consists of nine members, with three appointed by each government and three (third-country) members appointed by the six government-appointed members. The two governments share the cost. As of July 26, 2005, the Tribunal had resolved 3,936 cases by award, decision, or order. Approximately three-quarters of these cases (2,884) were for claims of less than U.S. $250,000. More information is available from the Tribunal's website at <http://www.iusct.org/index-english.html>.

It was an intermediary, the Government of Algeria, which negotiated the end to the U.S.-Iran hostage crisis and recommended the establishment of the Tribunal to resolve private and government-to-government disputes. Sometimes arbitration is compelled by treaty or may be invoked based on an optional clause in a prior treaty, contract, or Secretary-General ruling.

New Zealand invoked an arbitration clause in the Secretary-General's ruling on the *Rainbow Warrior* matter, *see* 26 I.L.M. 1346 (1987), after France removed the agents in late 1987 and early 1988 from Hao Island. France did so without informing New Zealand. Pursuant to the Secretary-General's ruling, three arbitrators were appointed, one by each party and one by both states.

During the arbitration proceeding, France justified its transfer of the agents by claiming *force majeure*, or absolute and material impossibility, and distress, or extreme urgency. It cited the illness of Major Alain Mafart and the pregnancy and dying father of Captain Dominique Prieur. The arbitration panel decided that France did not breach the Secretary-General's ruling by removing Major Mafart, but it did breach when it failed to

144

return him after his illness abated. Regarding Captain Prieur, the panel decided that France breached its obligations for failing to obtain consent from New Zealand before removing her, by removing her, and by failing to return her.

The arbitrators observed that compensation was available as reparation for material and non-material damage. They recommended the creation of a fund to promote close and friendly relations between the citizens of the countries, and required France to contribute U.S. $2 million to that fund.

4. Judicial Settlement [§112]

The International Court of Justice presents another option for resolving disputes between states. Under Article 36(2) of the Statute of the International Court of Justice, the I.C.J. possesses competence to consider "all legal disputes concerning: (a) the interpretation of a treaty; (b) any question of international law; (c) the existence of any fact which, if established, would constitute a breach of an international obligation; [and] (d) the nature or extent of the reparation to be made for the breach of an international obligation."

As mentioned before, the I.C.J. can render opinions in both contentious cases between two or more states and advisory opinions at the request of the Security Council, the General Assembly, or other organs associated with the United Nations when authorized by the General Assembly. Between 1947 and 2007, the I.C.J. issued orders and/or decisions in 110 contentious cases and responded to 24 requests for advisory opinions. Sometimes parties failed to appear, as Iran did when sued by the U.S. and France did after being sued by both Australia and New Zealand in 1971 for atmospheric nuclear testing in the South Pacific. Nevertheless, the I.C.J. proceeds under less than optimum circumstances to find the facts, determine the law, and render opinions.

After being asked by an organ of the U.N. to render an advisory opinion, the I.C.J. may invite other interested parties to state their views. The *Western Sahara* case came to the International Court of Justice as a request for an advisory opinion by the General Assembly. *See* The Western Sahara, Advisory Opinion of 16 October 1975, 1976 I.C.J. 12. The General Assembly was seeking to decolonize the Western Sahara from Spain when questions arose as to its legal status. Both Morocco and Mauritania claimed legal ties to the Western Sahara. Spain, Morocco, and Mauritania were invited to present their views on the issues before the I.C.J.

To resolve this dispute, the General Assembly requested answers to two questions. First, was the Western Sahara (Río de Oro and Sakiet El Hamra) at the time of colonization by Spain a territory belonging to no one (or *terra nullius*)? And, second, if the answer to the first question was in the negative, what were the legal ties between the territory and the Kingdom of Morocco and the Mauritanian entity?

After reviewing the history of the Western Sahara, the I.C.J. concluded that it was not *terra nullius* when colonized by Spain. In 1884, a country through "occupation" could legally acquire sovereignty over territory if the territory belonged to no one. However, if tribes and peoples having a social and political organization inhabited the territory, then it was considered occupied. Nomadic peoples organized into tribes occupied the Western Sahara. The territory, which forms part of the Saharan desert, is characterized by low and spasmodic rainfall. The nomads grazed their animals or grew crops where they found favorable conditions. They traversed the desert on more or less regular routes dictated by the seasons, and the wells and water holes available to them. These nomadic routes passed through some of southern Morocco, present day Mauritania, Algeria, and other states.

As to the second question on the legal ties between this territory and the Kingdom of Morocco and the Mauritanian entity, the I.C.J. concluded that there were legal ties between the Western Sahara and both the Kingdom of Morocco and the Mauritanian entity. The court stressed the need for a referendum to let the peoples of the Western Sahara decide their fate.

The General Assembly had submitted the case in 1975, seeking to avoid war. After the Spanish departed the Western Sahara in 1976, Morocco and Mauritania divided the territory between them. The indigenous Saharawis began fighting for independence. In 1976, the insurgents called the Polsario Front declared themselves to be a government-in-exile named the Saharawi Arab Democratic Republic. On 29 April 1991, the Security Council, in its Resolution 690 (1991), established the United Nations Mission for the Referendum in Western Sahara (MINURSO). It tracks developments on the Western Sahara, and more information may be obtained from its website, which is available at <http://www.un.org/Depts/dpko/missions/minurso/background.html>.

A U.N. peacekeeping force entered the Western Sahara in 1991 after a cease-fire was declared. Between 1991 and 2004, the United Nations spent more than $600 million on peacekeeping efforts in the Western Sahara and trying to arrange for a referendum.

The *Western Sahara* case illustrates that judicial decisions may have some role in resolving disputes by establishing the legal relations. However, if parties wish to wage war, there is nothing the I.C.J. can do to stop them. Further, a country may continue to ignore the I.C.J.'s decision, as Iran did, and the two parties may need to bring in a mediator to resolve the dispute. It was the Government of Algeria that brought an end to the U.S.-Iran hostage crisis by serving as an intermediary to reach a resolution that both sides could agree to and abide by.

Moreover, the I.C.J. has declined to give decisions where the claim lacks a dispute. For example, in two separate cases, Australia and New Zealand sued France seeking a declaration that atmospheric testing of nuclear weapons in the South Pacific oceans was inconsistent with the rules of international law. France did not make an appearance in either case. After the cases were filed, the French Minister said, "We have now reached a stage in our nuclear technology that makes it possible for us to continue our program by underground testing, and we have taken steps to do so as early as next year." *See Nuclear Tests Case (Austrailia v. France)* 1974 I.C.J. 253.

While the Australian Attorney-General believed this statement fell short of a commitment to no longer conduct atmospheric testing, the I.C.J. disagreed. The Court stated in *Nuclear Tests Case (Australia v. France), Id.* at 267, that "It is well recognized that declarations made by way of unilateral acts, concerning legal or factual situations, may have the effect of creating legal obligations." In this instance, the I.C.J. found that France had created a legal obligation of a binding character that it had a good faith obligation to observe. Thus, the I.C.J. found that the dispute had disappeared as France had already given Australia what it sought. The I.C.J. reached the same conclusion in *Nuclear Tests Case (New Zealand v. France)*, 1974 I.C.J. 457.

5. Regional Agencies or Arrangements [§113]

Regional groupings establish means to resolve disputes among their members. Among the more prominent regional agencies are the African Union, formerly known as the Organization of African Unity (OAU), *see* <http://www.africa-union.org>; the Organization of American States (OAS), *see* <http://www. oas.org>; the Arab League, *see* <www.arableagueonline.org>; the Organization for Security and Cooperation in Europe (OSCE), *see* <http://www.osce.org>; and the Organization of South-East Asian States (ASEAN), *see* <http://www.aseansec. org>. The OSCE describes itself as the world's largest regional security organization with 55 participating states that span the geographical area from Vancouver to Vladivostok.

The OAU has sought to resolve conflicts in Liberia and Sierra Leone. The OAS intervened to try to settle the El Salvador civil war crisis and to restore democracy in Haiti.

6. Satisfaction or Apologies [§114]

"I demand satisfaction," was a common refrain heard from the individuals who felt they had suffered a spirit or physical injury in the 1700s and 1800s. The demand was sometimes accompanied by a threat to duel if satisfaction was not forthcoming. From the context, it is clear that satisfaction corresponds to an apology.

Satisfaction has played a significant role in resolving disputes that border on violence within and among nation-states. Article 34 of the International Law Commission's Draft Articles on State Responsibility mentions satisfaction, along with restitution and compensation, as means for repairing injuries caused by internationally wrongful acts.

To return the situation to balance and restore confidence, nations must offer an effective apology that (a) acknowledges the harm they have caused the injured state; (b) offers to repair the harm; and (c) reassures that the damage will not be repeated. *See e.g.* Aaron Lazare, *On Apology* (Oxford Press 2004). Sometimes the Secretary-General, a mediator, arbitration tribunals, and judicial organs require satisfaction as part of their decisions. This obligates the state to apologize for its actions against another state.

After arbitrating the *Rainbow Warrior* dispute, French Prime Minister Michel Rocard apologized in May 1991 to New Zealand. When he returned to his country, however, France awarded Major Alain Mafart a medal for distinguished service. New

Zealanders greeted this action with horror, as it contradicted the apology. France also resumed nuclear testing in the South Pacific, although it claimed it was non-atmospheric testing.

This was not an example of an effective apology that healed a relationship. While the French leader acknowledged the damage and paid compensation to New Zealand, he undermined his apology by honoring Mafart, who was considered a murderer in New Zealand, and by resuming nuclear testing, which New Zealand felt threatened the health of its entire territory and people. The French leader's actions also put New Zealand on edge as France might bomb another ship if it came too close to monitoring its nuclear testing.

In his book, *On Apology*, Dr. Aaron Lazare writes, "Apologies have the power to heal humiliations and grudges, remove the desire for vengeance, and generate forgiveness on the part of the offended parties. For the offender, they can diminish the fear of retaliation and relieve the guilt and shame that can grip the mind with a persistence and tenacity that are hard to ignore. The result of the apology process, ideally, is the reconciliation and restoration of broken relationships." *See* Aaron Lazare, *On Apology* 1 (Oxford Press 2004).

The South African Truth and Reconciliation Commission provided examples of the power of apologies. After police officers recounted their crimes, they often broke down and cried, offering apologies even though the Commission did not require them. The victims of police violence often forgave the police officers. The Commission demonstrated how apologies could restore balance to painful situations when given with genuine heartfelt sentiment, indicating that the offender is truly sorry and the hurtful activity will not be repeated. The South African Commission demonstrated the role of apologies in healing internal conflict.

Apologies have also proved valuable in resolving external conflict between nations. Leaders have often apologized for the crimes of their nations against other states. A Japanese leader apologized to Korea for keeping females as comfort women during World War II, a situation that harmed the women both physically and emotionally, and caused psychic harm to their families and to the nation. In 2005, Japanese Prime Minister Junichiro Koizumi expressed "deep remorse and heartfelt apology" for his country's aggression toward many countries, particularly Asian nations, during its colonial rule. He noted the "tremendous damage and suffering" that Japan had caused these countries. *See* <http://www.kantei.go.jp/foreign/koizumispeech/2002/09/17sengen_e.html>.

In 1998, U.S. President Bill Clinton apologized to the Ghanaian people for the slave trade that robbed them of so many of their able-bodied souls, and to Rwandans for America failing to intervene to stop the genocide against 800,000 Tutsis and moderate Hutus. *See* Johanna McGeary, *Into Africa: Will Clinton's trip change the way Americans view Africa, and rewrite the terms of U.S. policy?*, Time, (April 6, 1998), *available at* http://www.cnn.com/ALLPOLITICS/1998/03/31/time/clinton.africa.html. The apologies were well received in both countries because the leader of the world's most important country acknowledged the hurt it caused by its actions and inactions.

In 2005, the United States the Department of Justice apologized to Hungarian Holocaust survivors whose possessions were stolen by U.S. Soldiers at the end of World War II. The apology was issued after the U.S. reached a $25.5 million settlement with elderly Jews to compensate them for their property losses. *See* Michael Christie, *US apologizes to Hungarian Jews over 'Gold Train,'* Reuters (Oct. 11, 2005), *available at* <http://www.alertnet.org/thenews/newsdesk/N11475027.htm>.

151

In 2008, Australian Prime Minister Kevin Rudd apologized in parliament to all Aborigines for laws and policies that "inflicted profound grief, suffering and loss." Some Aborigines criticized the apology because it was not accompanied with compensation for their suffering. All these incidents reveal the value of a heartfelt and well-meaning apology.

C. United Nations Obligations [§115]

Dealing with conflict requires balancing state interests with political realities. The world community has struggled to strike this balance beginning with the League of Nations, the brainchild of U.S. President Woodrow Wilson. President Wilson was accorded the Nobel Peace Prize in 1919 for his efforts, even though he failed to secure the U.S. Senate's ratification of the Covenant of the League of Nations and the Treaty of Versailles, which formally ended World War I. In 1921, the U.S. officially declared the war with Germany to be over.

The League was created to promote international co-operation and to achieve international peace and security. The Covenant of the League of Nations obliged its high contracting parties "not to resort to war," but instead to prescribe to "open, just and honorable relations between nations by the firm establishment of the understandings of international law as the actual rule of conduct among Governments... ." *See* <http://www.yale.edu/lawweb/avalon/leagcor.htm>. Despite its praiseworthy goals, the League died because it failed to provide for sufficient collective action to combat aggression. It depended on independent states to enforce its actions. The League stood by impotent in the 1930s as Germany and its fascist allies imposed their will on other states, without other nations responding until they themselves were under attack, which led to World War II.

The United Nations was created after World War II to maintain international peace and security through an organized procedure authorizing the use of force against an aggressor.

152

Both the Security Council and the General Assembly have been endowed with roles in maintaining international peace and encouraging nations to resolve their disputes peacefully. Article 24 of the U.N. Charter gives the Security Council primary responsibility for the maintenance of international peace and security. Only the Security Council can require enforcement by collective action against an aggressor.

Article 14 authorizes the General Assembly to "recommend measures for the peaceful adjustment of any situation." Under Article 12, the General Assembly cannot recommend measures while the Security Council is considering the same matter unless requested to do so by the Security Council.

U.N. peacekeeping measures have been authorized and deployed in several states around the world. U.N. peacekeeping operations seek to either avert imminent outbreak of hostilities or to secure a ceasefire and separate belligerents where violence has already occurred. U.N. forces have been sent to Egypt; the Congo (when newly independent from Belgium); Cyprus; Somalia; Kosovo; and during the Gulf War. The U.N. abandoned some areas, such as Rwanda in 1992, after its initial efforts failed.

The crisis in the former Yugoslavia became international as it dissolved into component states, such as Serbia and Kosovo, threatening international peace and security with violence. One group committed acts of systemic rape against another group, leading to mass exodus of refugees to neighboring territories. The U.N. intervened in 1999. The Security Council established the United Nations Interim Administration Mission in Kosovo, *see* <http://www.unmikonline.org/>, and authorized the bombing mission that ended the Serbian persecution of Kosovar Albanians. On 17 February 2008, Kosovo declared independence from Serbia, becoming the seventh state to be carved from the former Yugoslavia.

The U.N. has been most effective when the parties are ready to end the violence and have at least agreed to a ceasefire. In addition to deploying peacekeeping troops, the United Nations has sanctioned rogue members such as Rhodesia, South Africa, and Iraq after the invasion of Kuwait. The U.S. and U.S.S.R., two of the five permanent members of the Security Council, routinely vetoed sanctions against their activities in their respective spheres of influence during the Cold War.

In conclusion, peace on earth and good will toward all humankind may seem a utopia, considering the number of wars the international community has experienced since the enactment of the United Nations in 1945. However, if nations used the various means described under Article 33(1) of the U.N. Charter and discussed herewith to resolve their disputes peacefully, harmony in the world community would become a reality.

IX. International Rights and Responsibilities

This chapter discusses the rights and responsibilities of states that arise out of conflict. States incur international responsibility when they, by act or failure to act, breach an international obligation. The injuring state is responsible to the injured state to remedy the breach. The injured state may seek redress by asserting claims through diplomatic channels, or by employing dispute settlement options discussed in the preceding chapter. Under some circumstances, the injured state may resort to self-help or counter measures.

In determining whether acts, or failures to act, give rise to international responsibility, states, international entities, courts, and other tribunals, look at a number of issues. Can the act be attributed to the state? Did the state breach an international obligation? Did the state have responsibility for the act? Was the state injured? Were there circumstances that precluded a finding of wrongfulness? If not, what measures should the state undertake to remedy the breach and address the other state's grievances? This chapter addresses all six questions. The International Law Commission, which seeks to codify customary international law, updated its Draft Articles on Responsibility of States for internationally wrongful acts (hereinafter referred to as "Draft Articles" or "State Responsibility Draft Articles") in 2001. The State Responsibility Draft Articles are available on the web at <http://www.un.org/law/ilc/convents.htm>.

A. Attributing Acts to States [§116]

When a dispute arises between two or more states, they must determine which human beings caused the conflict and whether their acts (either individually or collectively) can be attributed to a state. Domestic law determines who is a representative or organ of a state. International law governs which activities of that individual or organ are attributable to the state.

155

States have several agents and organs that represent them, and they are held accountable for the acts of these individuals and entities. These agents may be *de jure*, or legal, representatives of the state. They may also be *de facto*, or factual, representatives of the state.

De jure agents and organs have this status under the state's internal or domestic law. They may be elected individuals in a democracy or members of the royal family in a monarchy. Heads of states and heads of governments, along with numerous elected and appointed officials, speak for their states. An organ may belong to the legislative, executive, or judicial branches of the state.

Even the conduct of territorial units within the states (i.e., the federated divisions that comprise the entire state) may be attributed to the state. For example, the United States is responsible to other nations for the acts of the states of Nevada, Nebraska, and New York. Similarly, Germany is responsible for acts of Bavaria, as is India for its state of Gujarat.

Another category of individuals, organs, and entities that legally act on behalf of the state are those who are not a part of the state's formal structure, but who have been empowered by internal law to exercise governmental authority. This empowerment may be temporary to perform specific duties.

De facto agents are those who act on behalf of the state, yet may lack roles under domestic law. As such, their conduct may be attributed to the state. States often employ individuals to carry out secret missions that they do not wish to have overtly linked to them. Nevertheless, covert operations are associated with the state. States cannot disclaim responsibility for clandestine activities once they become public by asserting the actor was *ultra virus*, or exceeded the scope of his legal authority.

State Responsibility Draft Article 7, for example, provides that the "conduct of an organ of a State or of a person or entity empowered to exercise elements of the governmental authority shall be considered an act of the State under international law if the organ, person or entity acts in that capacity, even if it exceeds its authority or contravenes instructions."

International law is concerned with whether the deeds can be linked to the state, and not whether they may be illegal under domestic law. In the Iran-Contra matter, for example, Richard Secord, a private citizen retained by the Reagan Administration to negotiate and assist with selling weapons to Iran to obtain money to support the Nicaraguan contras, became a *de facto* agent of the U.S. government. Because he acted on behalf of the U.S. government in carrying out his transactions, which may have been illegal under U.S. law, Secord's actions were attributable to the U.S. government, making the U.S. responsible under international law for his actions.

Article 6 of the State Responsibility Draft Articles indicates that states incur responsibility for those organs placed at their disposal by another state. When a state hires or borrows troops, such as the French foreign legion, it becomes responsible for the conduct of those troops while they are under its disposal. Draft Article 8 accords the borrowing state responsibility for directing and controlling the troops.

According to Draft Article 9, states may be held liable for conduct carried out in the absence or default of official authorities. This refers to people or groups who exercise elements of governmental authority when official authorities have failed to act either by their absence or by default. This may involve circumstances where governmental officials were required to act and failed to do so. Individuals who step into the vacuum create responsibility for the state.

157

Even insurrectional movements, which subsequently become the new government or the new state, will be held responsible for their conduct while they were insurrectional movements. The responsibility of insurrectional movements is set out in Draft Article 10. Further, the state may decide to acknowledge and adopt conduct as its own. If it decides to do so, then it becomes responsible for the conduct.

Moreover, states are not responsible for everything that occurs within their territory in general terms. They are not responsible for individuals who are not acting on behalf of the state. They are also not responsible for the conduct of other states or international organizations within their territory, unless those organs were placed at the disposal of the territorial state.

B. Breaching International Obligations [§117]

Once it becomes clear that an act can be attributed to a state, the next question is whether that act or series of acts constitute a breach of an international obligation. States breach their international obligations when they fail to act in conformity with international law. The breach occurs at the moment when the act is performed, even if its effects continue, according to State Responsibility Draft Article 14(1).

Draft Article 14(3) indicates that if a state was required to prevent a given event, and does not do so, the breach occurred when the event took place. The breach may also consist of a composite act, meaning the aggregate of many acts, under Draft Article 15. In these instances, the breach extends to the entire period starting with the first acts and omissions of the series and continuing for as long as the acts and omissions are repeated and fail to conform to the international obligation.

C. State Responsibility [§118]

States become responsible for their breaches of international obligations that they are bound to perform. This includes treaty and customary obligations. Lack of fault, caused by unintended consequences, does preclude a finding of responsibility.

For example, both customary law and Article 2(3) of the United Nations Charter require states to settle disputes peacefully. *See* U.N. Charter, *supra* §59, at art. 2(3). A state would breach its obligations if it unilaterally bombed its neighbor just because its head of government did not like the neighboring state's head of government. If the bombing state also occupied its neighbor's territory, the breach would begin with the first bomb blasts and continue until the bombing ceased and all foreign troops were removed.

States also become responsible if they aid or assist another state in the commission of an internationally wrongful act if the state does so with the knowledge that the act is illegal and if the act would be illegal if committed by that state, according to Draft Article 16. This is similar to domestic laws on aiding and abetting, which make the accomplice equally liable with the principal for the violation.

Further, under Draft Article 17, if the state directs and controls another state in the commission of an internationally wrongful act, it becomes responsible for the act. Thus, similar to domestic law, the leader of a group committing illegal acts cannot escape liability if he or she knew the group's actions were illegal.

Additionally, states are responsible if they coerce another state to commit an internationally wrongful act, according to Draft Article 18. By analogy, domestic law charges a person with a crime who forced another person at gunpoint to rob a bank.

States likewise owe duties to other states to prevent their territory from being used to commit significant harm to other states. Transboundary pollution, for example, can subject the polluting state to liability if the pollution escapes its territory and damages another. The U.S. brought an action against Canada after sulphur dioxide fumes drifted from a plant at Trail, British Columbia, to the state of Washington over a 12-year period between 1925 and 1937. A Special Arbitral Tribunal held Canada responsible, and ordered injunctive relief and payment of reparations. *See* Trail Smelter Case (*U.S. v. Canada*) 3 U.N. Rep. Int. Arb. Awards 1905 (1941). Some 40 years later, Canada would complain about acid rain caused by pollution emitting plants on its U.S. border.

Sometimes the acts of individuals cannot be attributed back to the state, which means the state is not responsible. However, the state remains responsible for a failure of its own duties under international law. In the *U.S. v. Iran* case, for example, the I.C.J. concluded that Iran could not be held responsible for the acts of students in seizing the U.S. embassy and taking personnel as hostages, as the students had no official or factual connection to the government. Nevertheless, it was accountable under the Vienna Convention on the Law of Treaties and customary law for its failure to protect the U.S. embassy and to take action to restore the premises and its personnel to its rightful owner, the United States government.

Other times an act may be declared legal internally, although it could create responsibility under international law. For examp le, in the *Alvarez-Machain* case, Chief Justice Rehnquist acknowledged that his decision, permitting U.S. courts to exercise jurisdiction over the kidnapped Mexican doctor, might violate international law. The U.S. courts had the imprimatur of the Supreme Court to proceed with the case, but doing so could give rise to an international violation for which the U.S. would owe remedies to Mexico, the country of Alvarez-Machain's nationality. Had Mexico taken the dispute to the I.C.J., it is possible that Court would have determined that the kidnapping of Dr. Alvarez-Machain, which was organized by U.S. nationals and carried out by U.S. agents, violated the Mexico-U.S. extradition treaty. This would make the U.S. legally responsible to Mexico.

D. Requirement of an Injury [§119]

Does the breach of an international obligation by a state towards another state infringe the right of that state irrespective of actual damage to it? The general rule is that only the party to whom an international obligation is due can bring a claim for a breach of that obligation. Some rules do not require an injury before a state can assert a claim. For example, a state may be held liable for violating a human rights convention or a *jus cogens* norm even when no harm was done to the state asserting the claim. This is because certain obligations are owed to the international community as a whole.

Other rules require injury to constitute a breach. Failing to protect an embassy, for example, may not give rise to a breach if no injury is suffered to the premises or its personnel. However, if the embassy and its personnel suffer damage, as was the case in the Iran hostage incident, then the receiving state has breached its international obligations.

In *Barcelona Traction, Light and Power Co.*, 1970 I.C.J. 3, the I.C.J. considered whether Belgium could sue on behalf of its nationals, who were shareholders of a Canadian corporation, which was injured by an organ of the Spanish Government. The company was incorporated in 1911 with the mission to create and develop electric power in Catalonia, Spain. The Canadian corporation was a holding company with wholly owned subsidiaries, several of which were incorporated in Spain. The Belgium citizens had purchased most of their stock in Barcelona Traction after World War I. They constituted 88% of the shareholders.

The problem arose after Barcelona Traction began issuing bonds, sometimes in pesetas (the Spanish currency at the time) or pounds sterling (the British legal tender). In 1936, the servicing of the bonds was suspended during the Spanish Civil War. In 1940, servicing resumed but the Spanish government prohibited

161

the transfer of the foreign currency necessary for the servicing of the pound sterling bonds.

In 1948, three Spaniards petitioned the Spanish court for a declaration that the company was bankrupt because it could not pay interest on its bonds. The petition was admitted and the company declared bankrupt three days later. Its assets were seized and liquidated. The national company protested the bankruptcy and seizure. The Canadian government protested, as did the British, United States, and Belgium governments.

The locus of the injury was in Spain. The I.C.J. had to consider whether there were *erga omnes* obligations at stake. *Erga omnes* obligations derive from the outlawing of acts of aggression and genocide, and also from the principles and rules concerning the basic rights of the human person, including protection from slavery and racial discrimination. These are obligations that all states have an interest in protecting, such as prosecuting international crimes. Any country can bring a claim for an *erga omnes* violation.

The Court opined, "When a State admits into its territory foreign investments or foreign nationals, whether natural or juristic persons [i.e., corporations], it is bound to extend to them the protection of the law and assumes obligations concerning the treatment to be afforded them." *Id.* at 32. While these obligations are important, the Court concluded that they were not of the same category as *erga omnes* obligations because not all states have an interest in protecting a particular foreign investment.

The I.C.J. rejected Belgium's claim to represent Barcelona Traction, ruling on behalf of Spain. The Court would not permit Belgium to pierce the corporate veil and thus it could not protect its shareholders. Only Canada, as the nationality state of the corporation, could offer diplomatic protection. The type of claim that Belgium asserted required a direct injury, like all claims

162

other than *erga omnes* obligations or *jus cogens* norms, before a state could claim a breach.

E. Circumstances Precluding a Finding of Wrongfulness [§120]

Certain circumstances will preclude a finding of wrongfulness and excuse a breach. These circumstances include consent, self-defense, countermeasures in response to a previous internationally wrongful act, *force majeure*, distress, necessity, and compliance with peremptory norms.

1. Consent [§121]

States may express consent to acts by other states through their conduct or by their words. Under State Responsibility Draft Article 20, "Valid consent by a state to the commission of a given act by another State precludes the wrongfulness of that act in relation to the former State to the extent that the act remains within the limits of that consent." For example, a state may consent to another state sending troops to assist its citizens following a natural disaster. The consent would excuse what would normally be a breach of the state's territorial independence. If, however, the troops proceeded to take over the state's territory, that action would exceed the limits of the initial consent.

Further, consent does not excuse the wrongfulness of any act obtained by coercion or in violation of a *jus cogens* norm. Coercion of any kind, like putting a gun to a leader's head or threatening to bomb the territory, precludes a finding of consent. Similarly, there can be no consent to a *jus cogens* norm violation. A state could not consent to the enslavement of part of its population, for example.

2. Self Defense [§122]

States have a moral obligation to defend their population and territory against harm. State Responsibility Draft Article 21 provides, "The wrongfulness of an act of a State is precluded if the act constitutes a lawful measure of self-defense taken in conformity with the Charter of the United Nations." The reference to lawful measure refers to the requirement that the act must be necessary to stop the original harm and a proportionate response so as to not create further breaches.

Thus, if one state invades the territory of another state, the victim state has a moral responsibility to defend its territory and its people. If it responds to the incursion with equal force, that would preclude any finding of wrongfulness under international law. However, if the response is disproportionate, such as dropping a nuclear bomb on the capital in response to a border raid, that would give rise to further breaches under international law.

3. Countermeasures [§123]

State Responsibility Draft Article 22 provides, "The wrongfulness of an act of a State not in conformity with an international obligation towards another State is precluded if and to the extent the act constitutes a countermeasure taken against the latter State...." Countermeasures may include reprisals and retorsion.

Reprisals respond to a preliminary act that the state views as contrary to the law of nations. Reprisals constitute forms of self-help that are necessary to terminate a violation, prevent further violation, or to remedy a violation. Before a state enacts a reprisal, however, it must demand a redress of grievance. In the preceding hypothetical on self-defense, the victim state must first demand the removal of troops involved in the border attack.

If no response is forthcoming, then the state may initiate reprisals. Any reprisal must also be proportionate to the harmful act so that it does not lead to an escalation of the conflict.

Retorsion is an equivalent act of retaliation to an unfriendly act. Examples include the rupture of diplomatic relations; trade embargos; and migration stoppage. The retaliation must be proportionate; otherwise, it gives rise to an abuse of right claim.

A state has the option to break off diplomatic relations with another state at any time. The sending state may recall its diplomat either to temporarily protest a particular action by the receiving state, or it may choose to permanently close its embassy. Similarly, a receiving state may break off relations with a sending state and request closure of its mission. Even when relations are ruptured, however, the premises of the sending state's embassy continue to be inviolable. The receiving state must protect it from harm.

Similarly, the state has four other obligations that cannot be affected by countermeasures. States must continue to refrain from the threat or use of force; protect fundamental human rights; and observe obligations of a humanitarian character prohibiting reprisals. Further, states cannot enact countermeasures that violate peremptory norms of general international law. For example, a state cannot torture or enslave another state's population as a countermeasure.

4. *Force Majeure* or Fortuitous Events [§124]

Force majeure refers to an irresistible force or an unforeseen external event beyond the state's control that makes it materially impossible to act in conformity with an international legal obligation. A common example occurs when another state's public vessel enters a state's territory without permission during bad weather. The unfortunate weather becomes the circumstance precluding a finding of wrongful trespass.

State Responsibility Draft Article 23 provides, "The wrongfulness of an act of a State not in conformity with an

165

international obligation of that State is precluded if the act is due to *force majeure*, that is the occurrence of an irresistible force or of an unforeseen event beyond the control of the State, making it materially impossible in the circumstances to perform the obligation." The *Rainbow Warrior* case between France and New Zealand, mentioned in the preceding chapter, tested this principle. France claimed that *force majeure* circumstances precluded a finding of wrongfulness for its transfer of two agents from an isolated French military base to France without notifying New Zealand. France asserted that the illness of one agent and the other agent's pregnancy and dying father constituted *force majeure*.

The France-New Zealand Arbitration Tribunal disagreed with France's claim. It noted that difficult and burdensome circumstances do not constitute a case of *force majeure*. It concluded that the excuse was of no relevance in the case. *See* 82 International Law Reports 500 (1990).

5. Distress [§125]

In *The Rainbow Warrior* case, France also claimed that distress excused its actions, citing the same facts. Under international law, a situation of extreme distress, such as to save a life, will excuse an act that might otherwise be unlawful. The France-New Zealand Tribunal decided that extreme urgency and humanitarian considerations did justify removing Major Mafart without obtaining New Zealand's consent, but did not excuse the failure to return him after his illness abated. Indeed, a New Zealand doctor arrived to examine Mafart the very day he landed in Paris. He confirmed that Mafart's condition required sophisticated tests not available on Hao. Later, he said that Mafart could be moved back to the island, but France refused to do so. Because there were no circumstances precluding wrongfulness, France was in breach of its obligations toward New Zealand.

To make a strong case for distress under the State Responsibility Draft Article 24(1), there must be "no other reasonable way … of saving the author's life or the lives of other persons entrusted to the author's care." Further under Article 24(2), this does not apply if the state contributed to the distress or if the act would create a comparable or greater peril. France should have permitted New Zealand doctors to examine Mrs. Prieur to verify that she needed special care for her pregnancy.

6. Necessity [§126]

State Responsibility Draft Article 25 permits a state to invoke necessity if it is "the only way for the State to safeguard an essential interest against a grave and imminent peril" and "[d]oes not seriously impair an essential interest of the State or States towards which the obligation exists, or of the international community as a whole." Further, states may not invoke necessity as a circumstance precluding wrongfulness if they contributed to the situation of necessity.

As discussed in §43 in the *Case Concerning the Gabcikovo-Nagymaros Project (Hungary v. Slovakia)*, 1997 I.C.J. 7, Hungary claimed necessity to excuse its suspension and abandonment of its 1977 treaty with Czechoslovakia. The I.C.J. concluded, however, that the perils invoked by Hungary were not sufficiently established in 1989, nor were they "imminent" to justify treaty termination. *Id.* at 42.

7. Compliance With a Peremptory Norm [§127]

State Responsibility Draft Article 26 provides, "Nothing in this chapter precludes the wrongfulness of any act of a State which is not in conformity with an obligation arising under a peremptory norm of general international law." States cannot claim necessity, duress, *force majeure*, or any other excuse to justify failure to comply with peremptory norms. For example, there is no excuse to justify a state committing genocide against another state's population.

167

F. Remedies [§128]

When states breach legal obligations, which cannot be excused by a circumstance precluding wrongfulness, they are required to remedy the situation. For example, they have a continuing duty to perform the obligation breached, according to State Responsibility Draft Article 29. Further, they must cease any illegal activities, offer assurances that the breach will not continue, and offer to repair the harm caused. Draft Article 32 makes clear that states cannot invoke domestic law to justify their failure to comply with these obligations.

In some instances, the most appropriate remedies are reparations, which aim to discharge the breach of the international obligation and to repair the harm. Draft Article 31 notes that the injury may include "any damage, whether material or moral, caused by the internationally wrongful act of a State." Reparations should wipe out all consequences of the illegal act and reestablish the situation that would have existed if the act had not been committed.

Draft Article 34 indicates that reparation can appear in "the form of restitution, compensation and satisfaction, either singly or in combination." With restitution in kind, the goal is to reestablish the situation that would have existed if the act had not been committed. Restitution may include performing the obligation that the state initially failed to discharge; returning property wrongfully removed; or abstaining from further wrongful conduct.

Monetary compensation should wipe out the consequences of the illegal act. Draft Article 36 indicates that money compensation should be given only for damage that cannot be made good by restitution. This compensation can include loss of profits.

Draft Article 37 notes that satisfaction may consist of "an acknowledgement of the breach, an expression of regret, a formal apology or another appropriate modality." It is to be given for injury that "cannot be made good by restitution or compensation."

States may also seek remedies in domestic courts. States must have standing to make claims, which are not barred by laches or an unreasonable delay that prejudices the other party. Some courts require negotiation of a claim as a prerequisite to settlement procedures. Other tribunals compel states to exhaust local remedies.

To enforce and execute awards from an international tribunal, the state may look to domestic courts of any state in which the funds of the judgment debtor are located. They may refer to enforcement provisions in multilateral or bilateral treaties. In some instances, the state may seek the establishment of a fund for payment of awards as was set up with the U.S.-Iran claims tribunal.

In other instances, some states have refused to enforce U.S. judgments for punitive damages. *See* Adam Liptak, *Foreign Courts Wary of U.S. Punitive Damages*, N.Y. Times (Mar. 26, 2008).

In conclusion, this chapter gives law students a framework for approaching an essay question on an exam and lawyers a structure for preparing an international legal claim before a court. Simply ask and answer the following six questions:

1. Were there acts that could be attributed to a state?
2. If so, did these attributable acts constitute a breach of an international obligation?
3. Did the breach give rise to state responsibility?
4. Was this the type of breach that required an injury to be actionable?
5. Were there circumstances that would preclude a finding of wrongfulness?
6. If not, what remedies are available to repair the wrong?

169

A well-written answer to these questions applying the facts at hand will earn students points on their essay tests and assist lawyers in presenting their best case before an international tribunal.

CHAPTER X

X. The Laws of War and Use of Force

A. Definitions of War [§129]

Militarist philosophers have debated the definition and purpose of war for centuries. Over a thousand years ago, Sun Tzu, the Chinese army general, wrote in the *Art Of War*, "War is a matter of vital importance to the state," and "victory is the main object of war." *See* Sun Tzu, *supra* §3, at 63, 73. In his book *On War*, Carl von Clausewitz, a Prussian army general, defined war as "an act of violence to compel our opponent to fulfill our will." He also opined, "War is merely a continuation of politics by other means." Carl von Clausewitz, *On War*, 2, 23, (Col. J.J. Graham trans., Barnes & Noble 1968) (1832). Mao Tse-Tung, who led the revolution that produced modern China and became its Chairman, viewed war as politics with bloodshed and politics as war without bloodshed. In his book *Problems of War and Strategy*, Mao wrote, "Politics grows out of the barrel of a gun." Mao Tse-Tung, *Selected Works of Mao Tse-Tung*, 170 (Bruno Shaw ed., Harper & Row 1970). These writers still resonate in the 21st Century because states have resorted to violence to resolve their most difficult disputes.

Founded in 1945 to "save succeeding generations from the scourge of war," the United Nations has yet to fulfill its promise. Well over a hundred wars within states or between two or more nations have taken place since World War II ended with a bang and not a whimper. Brothers continue to fight brothers, sisters against sisters, and ethnic groups against each other in civil wars. States invade their neighbors with their armies, navies, marines, or fly air force personnel thousands of miles to drop bombs on other countries.

Several centuries ago, war was viewed as a means of self-help by states. They deployed their military apparatus to effectuate claims based, or alleged to be based, upon international law. The term "just war" was cited to indicate that certain violence could be righteous, particularly when employed to increase the membership of religious organizations by expanding the number of adherents. Wars that were sanctioned by religious organizations, in the names of God, Allah, Buddha, and other religious deities, were considered legal.

As the influence of religion on state behavior declined, war became a secular transaction for increasing power and possessions of a state at the expense of other states. States played a zero sum game; what one state won, another lost.

Fear, greed, and a host of reasons as varied as the states themselves are asserted to justify external breaches of other states' boundaries. Wars have been triggered because one head of state insulted another and failed to apologize. Accidents have caused others. Then there are those caused by sheer greed where one leader sees something in another state that he wants and is willing to use military might to acquire it.

No matter the reason given, war harms all that it touches, creating slippery slopes of unintended consequences. The soldiers fighting on battlefields, in the air, and on ships risk their lives for the cause declared by their leaders. Those same leaders have sometimes been assassinated, jailed, and dethroned. Others have committed suicide as the end to the war approaches, and their countries have been reduced to ruin. Civilians have their lives disrupted and homes destroyed under harsh conditions.

This chapter outlines the efforts of states to limit the spread of, and harm from, wars, be they internal, within a given state, or external, involving two or more states. States have adopted international rules to lessen the harmful effects of war on soldiers, civilians, and their property. Perhaps the most important rule of war required combatants to distinguish civilians from soldiers.

172

B. Declarations of War [§130]

During the 19th Century, war had to be declared, which activated the rules of war. Declarations of war theoretically separated the belligerent states from the peaceful ones. Belligerent states were required to recognize the dichotomy between war and peace. They had a duty to observe the rules of war and to respect the neutrality of non-belligerent states. However, a problem developed as states stopped declaring war in order to refrain from complying with the rules of war. Instead of war, leaders spoke of police or enforcement action, or limited wars.

In the 20th Century, nations asked, "Is there large scale fighting?" If the answer is "yes," then the Hague Conventions and the Geneva Conventions apply to the conflict. Thus, whether or not they declared war, states became required to treat civilian populations and soldiers in a humane manner.

The Second World War, for example, was the last time Congress declared war according to U.S. Constitutional provisions. By a joint resolution dated December 8, 1941, Congress declared war on Japan following the bombing of Pearl Harbor. The resolution proclaimed that the Imperial Government of Japan had committed unprovoked acts of war against the government and the people of the United States of America. It authorized President Roosevelt to employ the entire naval and military forces of the United States and the resources of the government to carry on war against the Imperial Government of Japan. It also pledged all the country's resources to bring the conflict to successful termination.

As an ally of Japan, Germany declared war on the United States on December 11, 1941. Congress, noting that a war with Germany had been thrust upon the United States, responded the same day with a declaration of war against Germany. Congress again vowed all U.S. assets to bring the conflict to successful conclusion.

173

Since the close of World War II in 1945, the United States has been involved in sustained violent action in Korea, Vietnam, Grenada, Lebanon, Nicaragua, Afghanistan, and Iraq (twice). Not once has Congress issued a formal declaration of war.

Congress expressed its dismay that the executive branch launched the country into a sustained military campaign in Vietnam by passing the War Powers Resolution in 1973. In doing so, Congress sought to "fulfill the intent of the framers of the Constitution of the United States and insure that the collective judgement (sic) of both the Congress and the President will apply to the introduction of United States Armed Forces into hostilities." *See* War Powers Resolution, Public Law No. 93-148, 87 Stat. 555, 93rd Con., H. J. Res. 542 (Nov. 7, 1973). The Resolution observed that the Constitution limited the President's power, as Commander-in-Chief, to introduce United States Armed Forces into hostilities "pursuant to (1) a declaration of war, (2) specific statutory authorization, or (3) a national emergency created by attack upon the United States, its territories or possessions, or its armed forces." *Id.*

The War Powers Resolution requires a president to consult with Congress before introducing United States Armed Forces into hostilities, and report back to Congress after having done so. The President is supposed to terminate the use of armed forces within sixty calendar days "unless the Congress (1) has declared war or has enacted a specific authorization for such use of United States Armed Forces, (2) has extended by law such sixty-day period, or (3) is physically unable to meet as a result of an armed attack upon the United States." *Id.*

This Resolution has not stopped presidents from introducing U.S. troops and/or covert operatives into countries in Europe, the Middle East, Africa, Asia, and South America. In most instances, the President did not consult with Congress, as envisioned by the War Powers Resolution, before shipping U.S. troops to foreign soil. President George W. Bush, however, did consult with Congress before sending troops to Iraq in March 2003.

In response to President Bush's report on the dangers that Iraq posed to the United States, Congress passed "Joint Resolution on Iraq." It authorized Bush to use the Armed Forces of the United States as he determines to be necessary and appropriate in order to "(1) defend the national security of the United States against the continuing threat posed by Iraq; and (2) enforce all relevant United Nations Security Council resolutions regarding Iraq." *See* Joint Resolution on Iraq, Public Law No. 107-243, 116 Stat. 1498, 107th Congress (Oct. 16, 2002).

The U.S. involvement in Iraq illustrates why international law shifted its focus from whether or not a declaration of war exists to assessing the state of the fighting. President George W. Bush launched the second Iraq war on March 20, 2003. On May 1, 2003, he declared an end to major combat. At that time, 138 U.S. soldiers had lost their lives. On March 23, 2008, the U.S. death toll in Iraq surpassed 4,000 with approximately 30,000 wounded in action. Thus, over 96% of U.S. casualties came after President Bush declared that there had been an end to major combat.

Fighting against an organized state power or an insurgency seems to only vary the intensity of the conflict. Historically, insurgents unite to remove foreign troops from their soil and then battle each other to determine who will control the country. The consequences of all fighting in Iraq has been so severe that an estimated 1.2 million Iraqi citizens had lost their lives by September 2007, according to a poll from ORB, a British polling agency. *See* Los Angeles Times, *Survey: Civilian Death Toll Tops 1 Million* (Sept. 14, 2007). By launching a war, or large scale fighting, in Iraq, the U.S. became bound to follow the conduct of war rules, whether facing an organized army or an unstructured insurgency.

C. Conduct of War Rules [§131]

The shift away from requiring a declaration of war came about because nations avoided implementing conduct of war rules. Basing a state of war on the existence of large-scale fighting removes this option.

Conduct of war rules arise from humanitarian law. They focus on regulating uses and types of weapons; the treatment of prisoners and injured participants; the treatment of enemy nationals and their property; the treatment of the populations of occupied territory; the protection of non-military ships; and even the protection of art during times of war. Their goal is to make war more humane, if not tolerable, for the soldier who risks his life and for the civilians that he protects.

A state is said to violate conduct of war rules when it deviates from accepted law. These rules do not distinguish between a just and unjust war. This prohibits nations from avoiding the application of these rules by proclaiming something special, or unique, about their conflict.

1. Hague Conventions [§132]

The Hague Conventions of 1899 and 1907 regulate the conduct of war. The subsequent Annex to the 1907 Hague Convention Respecting the Laws and Customs of War on Land provides, "The laws, rights, and duties of war apply not only to armies, but also to militia and volunteer corps." *See* Hague Convention Respecting the Laws and Customs of War on Land, Arts. 4, 5, 7, 8, 17, 18, 56, Oct. 18, 1907, 36 Stat. 2277, T.S. 539. Thus, when groups act like an army—by carrying arms openly, wearing distinctive emblems, and being commanded by a person responsible for his subordinates—then the rules of war should apply to them.

An annex to Hague Convention Relative to the Treatment of Prisoners of War says it applies to all wars, whether they are declared wars, other armed conflicts, or internal wars. An important provision declares that prisoners of war are in the power of a hostile government, and not of the individuals or corps who capture them. Thus, the Detaining Power is responsible for its troops' treatment of prisoners. While a country may punish its soldiers who violate the rules of war, it remains responsible under international law to the other state for injuring its nationals.

This Hague Convention mandates that the Detaining Power treat prisoners humanely. All their personal property remains their property, although they may not keep arms or military papers. Prisoners of war may be interned in a town, fortress, camp or other place within fixed limits. The Detaining Power becomes responsible for their maintenance, and should treat prisoners of war on the same footing as the government troops who captured them. Officers should be treated differently from enlisted men, and must receive a rate of pay that corresponds to rank, to be refunded by their Government. POWs may exercise their religion, including attending church services. States may discipline escaped prisoners to keep order; however, they are not permitted to murder or torture them.

The Hague Conventions of 1899 and 1907 established guidelines for the protection of cultural property in the event of armed conflict. The Conventions require that the property of institutions dedicated to arts and sciences be treated as private property and cannot be confiscated. Art has been viewed as a prize of war by warring nations. The Romans, in approximately 400 B.C., first glorified the plunder of art, believing that collecting booty from vanquished nations was a legitimate by-product of war. The Romans had their art plundered around 455 A.D. *See* DuBoff, Burr, and Murray, *Art Law: Cases and Materials* 31-32 (William S. Hein & Co., 2004).

The problem of protecting art during times of war continues. Soon after the U.S.-led invasion of Iraq in March of 2003, the Baghdad Museum of Art was ransacked. Many items were eventually found, yet over 8,000 treasures have yet to be accounted for several years later.

2. The Geneva Conventions [§133]

The four Geneva Conventions of 1949 and two 1977 protocols similarly apply to all wars, whether they are declared or classified as armed conflicts or internal wars. The documents are:

Geneva Convention No. I: Geneva Convention for the Amelioration of the Condition of the Wounded and Sick in Armed Forces in the Field, Aug. 12, 1949, 6 U.S.T. 3114, 75 U.N.T.S. 31;

Geneva Convention No. II: Geneva Convention for the Amelioration of the Condition of the Wounded, Sick, and Shipwrecked Members of the Armed Forces at Sea, Aug. 12, 1949, 6 U.S.T. 3217, 75 U.N.T.S. 85;

Geneva Convention No. III: Geneva Convention Relative to the Treatment of Prisoners of War, Aug. 12, 1949, 6 U.S.T. 3316, 75 U.N.T.S. 85;

Geneva Convention No. IV: Geneva Convention Relative to the Protection of Civilian Persons in Time of War, Aug. 12, 1949, 6 U.S.T. 3516, 75 U.N.T.S. 287;

Protocol I: Additional Protocol Relating to the Protection of Victims of International Armed Conflicts, June 8, 1977, 1125 U.N.T.S. 3;

Protocol II: Additional Protocol Relating to the Protection of Victims of Non-International Armed Conflicts, June 8, 1977, 1125 U.N.T.S. 609.

178

Similar to The Hague Conventions, states cannot escape the application of these conventions and protocols by failing to declare war, or by declaring war against a concept, like poverty, drugs, or terrorism so long as there is sustained violence.

Under the Geneva Convention Relative to the Treatment of Prisoners of War, the Detaining Power has responsibility to treat prisoners humanely. Toward that end, for example, the Detaining Power must do the following: (1) permit POWs contact with their family; and (2) collect and care for the wounded and the sick. *See* Geneva Convention Relative to the Treatment of Prisoners of War, Arts. 3, 13, 16, 52, 70, Aug. 12, 1949, 6 U.S.T. 3316, 75 U.N.T.S. 135.

Further, the Detaining Power cannot do the following: (1) murder, mutilate, or torture POWs; (2) take hostages; (3) sentence and execute POWs without a previous judgment by a regularly constituted court with judicial guarantees; (4) conduct medical experiments on prisoners; (5) humiliate or degrade POWs; (6) discriminate against prisoners of wars on the basis of race, nationality, political beliefs, or political opinions; and (7) give them inherently dangerous work. *Id.*

The Geneva Convention Relative to the Protection of Civilian Persons in Time of War prohibits violence to life and person. Countries may not make distinctions based on race, religion, or political opinion. *See* Geneva Convention Relative to the Protection of Civilian Persons in Time of War, Art. 2, 3, 27, Aug. 12, 1949, 6 U.S.T. 3516, 75 U.N.T.S. 287. This Geneva Convention applies to belligerent occupation. Both belligerents and inhabitants have a common interest in law and order during this difficult time. The goal — the humane treatment of the population — upholds the value of human dignity. This is a precondition for administering the territory with minimal force. The occupying power should use the court structure of

179

the country to maintain the law. The occupying power must not discriminate on grounds of race, religion or political opinion.

Prior to and during the U.S. conflict in Afghanistan and Iraq, a debate took place between the U.S. State Department and the U.S. Justice Department on the application of the Geneva Conventions to prosecuting the war on terror in these countries. Two deputy assistant attorneys general, John Yoo and Robert Delahanty, argued that the Geneva Conventions did not apply to Al-Qaeda and Taliban detainees. These two individuals argued that the detainees were neither protected POWs nor civilians. They maintained that the Geneva Conventions did not protect them from "physical or mental torture [or] any other form of coercion ... to secure ... information of any kind whatsoever." *See* Steven Gillers, *The American Lawyer*, June 14, 2004. Further, the two men proclaimed that the detainees were not civilians protected "against all acts of violence or threats thereof," nor were the women protected from "rape ... or indecent assault." The memos redefined the detainees into a separate category as "enemy combatants," distinguishing them from soldiers and civilians. *Id.*

The State Department argued against this advice, stating that the United States was bound by the Geneva Conventions as a signatory and must apply them to the detainees. White House counsel Alberto Gonzales relied on the Justice Department's advice in his recommendations to the President, who adopted them. When soldiers commit torture based on policies issued by the state, the acts can be attributed to the state. All the individuals involved become responsible under international law for their actions, and the state becomes responsible for the harm caused to other states.

Defense Secretary Donald Rumsfeld and President Bush were subsequently sued by individuals challenging their detention as unlawful combatants. The U.S. Supreme Court issued rulings in three cases on June 28, 2004. In *Hamdi v. Rumsfeld*, 542 U.S. 507 (2004), Hamdi claimed he was captured in Afghanistan and turned over to U.S. military authorities during the U.S. invasion in 2001. The U.S. government alleged that he was there fighting for the Taliban, while Hamdi, through his father, claimed that he was merely there as a relief worker and was mistakenly captured. Hamdi was initially held at Guantanamo Bay, but subsequently transferred to a military prison in Charleston, South Carolina, where, after it was discovered that he was a U.S. citizen, he was detained as an unlawful combatant without access to an attorney or the court system.

In *Hamdi*, the Supreme Court considered whether the administration could detain Hamdi as an unlawful combatant, without oversight of presidential decision-making, or access to an attorney or the court system. The plurality opinion, written by Justice O'Connor, stated that although Congress had expressly authorized the detention of unlawful combatants in its Authorization for Use of Military Force, 107 P.L. 40, 115 Stat. 224 (2001), due process required that Hamdi be provided a meaningful occasion to challenge his detention before an impartial decision maker (although a judge may not be required). *Id.* at 509. Specifically, this called for notice of the charges and an opportunity to be heard. *Id.* at 510.

Rumsfeld v. Padilla, 542 U.S. 426 (2004), also concerned a U.S. citizen being held indefinitely as an unlawful combatant at a military prison in South Carolina. Padilla, who was initially apprehended as a material witness in connection with the September 11 terrorist attacks, brought a similar claim to Hamdi. Rather than reach the merits of his case, the Court held that this *habeas corpus* petition had been improperly filed. Because Padilla was being held in military prison in South Carolina, the Court concluded that the petition should have been filed in the United States District Court for the District of South Carolina and should have named the commander of the brig because he was Padilla's immediate custodian. *Id.* at 434. The Court remanded the case for dismissal without prejudice, allowing Padilla to refile the petition.

In *Rasul v. Bush*, 542 U.S. 466 (2004), the Supreme Court decided that the U.S. court system has authority to consider whether foreign nationals captured in connection with the war in Afghanistan and held in Guantanamo were rightfully imprisoned. These foreigners had also been classified as unlawful enemy combatants without access to counsel, the right to a trial, or being told of the charges against them. The Court held that detainees have access to U.S. courts to challenge their detention. *Id.* at 480.

Finally, in *Hamdan v. Rumsfeld*, 126 S. Ct. 622 (2005), the Supreme Court announced on November 7, 2005, that it would review the appeal of Salim Ahmed Hamdan, a Yemen citizen captured during fighting in Afghanistan. The U.S. government alleged that Hamdan served as a bodyguard and driver for Osama bin Laden. On July 15, 2005, the Court of Appeals for the D.C. Circuit had held that Hamdan could be tried by a military commission because the Geneva Conventions do not apply to the conflict between the U.S. and al-Qaeda, or to the individual members of al-Qaeda. *See Hamdan v. Rumsfeld*, 367 U.S. App. D.C. 265 (D.C. Cir. 2005). In 2006, the Supreme Court reversed the D.C. Circuit in *Hamdan v. Rumsfeld*, 548 U.S. 557, 126 S. Ct. 2749 (2006).

In 2008, the Supreme Court in *Boumediene v. Bush*, —S.Ct. —, 2008 WL 2369628, rejected the Bush administration's argument that Guantanamo detainees have no writ of habeas corpus rights because the United States lacks sovereignty over the naval station. The Supreme Court made clear that alien detainees possess the constitutional right to challenge the legality of their detention in federal courts.

182

3. Other Rules of War [§132]

With regard to regulating weapons, international law focuses on armaments to eliminate weapons that cause unnecessary suffering. *See* Damrosch, *supra* §29, at 1056. Some rules ban dum-dum bullets, for example, because they expand on impact, and tear a great wound in the soldier. Poisons and poisoned weapons can be particularly harmful to soldiers and civilians. Mustard gas burns flesh and internal organs. With biological warfare, microbial or biological agents or toxins are released into the air, causing sickness or death to all who breathe them. Chemical weapons, such as nerve and mustard gasses, have been known to injure and disfigure individuals and cause damage to children subsequently born to previously exposed victims.

One problem with aerial bombardment, which was first introduced by Germans in World War I and became accepted practice during World War II, is that it fails to distinguish between civilians and combatants. *Id.* Nuclear weapons are the ultimate form of aerial bombardment, as one weapon can wipe out part of or an entire country and the winds can carry the chemicals to neighbors and distant continents. MAD, or mutually assured destruction, was the acronym the U.S. and U.S.S.R. called their form of nuclear détente.

International law regulates the treatment of enemy property. Belligerents may confiscate the enemy's public property, but they may not seize private property belonging to individuals.

Enemy commercial ships may not be attacked unless they refuse to submit to visitation to determine that they are not armed. However, unlike fishing vessels, as discussed in §47, they are not immune from capture. After the visit, the ships can be taken to port and adjudicated as a prize of war. Thereafter, disposition is governed by municipal law. Immunity is granted to hospital ships, and vessels with religious, scientific, or philanthropic missions.

183

In conclusion, there are many treaty and customary rules that govern a state's conduct of war. Does the state gain or lose if it does not comply with the conduct of war rules? Not applying the rules may give a momentary advantage if mistreatment of prisoners leads to helpful information. But ultimately, non-application gives rise to reciprocity where the other state will mistreat its captured prisoners. Further, not applying the rules can give rise to war crimes, leading to charges against the soldiers, their immediate officers, and all the way up the chain of command to the leaders who authorized the war or the mistreatment policy. Since all states have universal jurisdiction over war crimes, soldiers, officers, and leaders who violate conduct of war rules may be tried in other countries that obtain personal jurisdiction after finding the individual in their country or through the extradition process.

D. Civil Wars [§135]

Civil wars, often referred to as internal wars, inflict the most damage upon countries as the people kill each other and destroy their own territory. Civil strife, such as Switzerland experienced in the 1840s and the United States endured in the 1860s, can be particularly devastating on a population when the country divides into opposing camps. The South seceded from the United States, leading to the Civil War with the North, although the conflict is still called "The War of Northern Aggression" by many Southerners. If asked to name the war that cost the most U.S. lives, many U.S. citizens would name the Civil War. Over 500,000 Americans in both the Union and Confederacy perished in the Civil War. This number can be contrasted to 58,000 soldiers who died in Vietnam, and the 386 who perished during the 1990-1991 Persian Gulf War. Every soldier or person who died in the Civil War was an American, with a few exceptions for the foreigners who fought on behalf of one side or the other.

In modern times, civil wars have sometimes become precursors to genocide when one ethnic group decides the only way to

184

win is to exterminate the other group. There may be several types of actors involved in civil wars: combatants, neutrals, and international intervenors.

1. The Combatants [§136]

Combatants may be members of the government's armed forces or they may be those fighting against the government such as rebels, guerillas, insurgents, or belligerents. Rebels, guerillas, or insurgents typically have no control over the state's territory. They may fight from another state or within the state but have yet to conquer enough territory to proclaim themselves as a government. Belligerents are forces contesting control over the country, and have acquired power over at least part of the territory. The government may be *de facto* or *de jure*, exercising factual or legal control, based on how much of the territory it actually controls.

2. Neutrals [§137]

Neutrals are not supposed to take part in a war between other states. As Dr. David Hawkins wrote in *Power v. Force*, "the Neutral condition allows for flexibility and nonjudgmental, realistic appraisal of problems. To be Neutral means to be relatively unattached to outcomes." David Hawkins, *Power v. Force* 85 (Hay House 2002).

If a state assumes an attitude of impartiality, their policies have to apply equally to all belligerents. Neutrals are guaranteed the inviolability of their territory and freedom from belligerent acts. There is no legal duty to remain neutral, but it prevents escalation of conflict.

Switzerland demonstrates the advantages of neutrality. Switzerland has been neutral for more than 160 years. It fought its last war as a civil war in 1847, and has been neutral since. After much controversy over whether joining the United

Nations would prejudice their valued principle of neutrality, the Swiss people voted 55% to 45% in favor of joining the United Nations as its 190th member on 10 September 2002.

3. International Intervenors [§138]

Certain rules prohibit intervention in civil wars. Under the classic rule, governments are entitled to assistance during the conflict, but rebels are not.

In the 1936-1939 Spanish Civil War, for example, the Allied powers (France, U.K., U.S., and U.S.S.R.) feigned a neutral policy and did not send assistance to the Spanish government. The Axis group (Germany and Italy), meanwhile, sent arms and ammunition to General Francisco Franco's forces, which were the rebels. Consequently, Franco's forces went directly from rebels to government, without going through the belligerency phase. Germany and Italy recognized his forces as a government in November 1936. Although the initial conflict involved an internal struggle for control of a national society, this intervention internationalized the conflict.

Civil conflict can also become a surrogate war for two powerful nations that refuse to fight each other openly. This happened often during the Cold War between the U.S. and the U.S.S.R. Given that both were nuclear powers, with the capacity to destroy each other, they aided separate sides in internal conflicts with covert military support.

4. Vietnam [§139]

The U.S. involvement in Vietnam began surreptitiously when President Truman began sending aid to assist the French who were fighting a war within their former colony. Each succeeding U.S. president increased involvement, with covert advisors and other aid to South Vietnam, until it became a full fledged conflict under President Johnson.

What type of civil war was Vietnam? Professor Louis Henkin identified three types of civil war models. *See* Louis Henkin et al., *International Law* 2nd ed. 764-765 (West Group 1987). Model A viewed the conflict as a civil war within an independent South Vietnam. North Vietnam, an outside state, helped one side; and the United States, another outside state, helped the other side. Neither violated the rules of international law as long as activities were just supporting one side or another. When the U.S. bombed North Vietnam, it switched the war into an international war. The world community perceived the U.S. as expanding an internal affair. *Id.*

Model B viewed the conflict as a civil war within a single state of Vietnam. United States' support of South Vietnam became a violation of traditional international law norms. When the U.S. bombed Laos or Cambodia, two countries that supported North Vietnam, this further internationalized the conflict. *Id.*

Model C viewed North Vietnam as launching an armed attack against South Vietnam, violating its territorial integrity and political independence. South Vietnam had a right to self-defense under Art. 51 of the U.N. Charter and could call for assistance. The U.S. then could provide collective self-defense under mutual defense treaties or policies between the two states. *Id.*

Whatever the view, the United States lost the Vietnam War. Secretary of State Henry Kissinger negotiated the Paris Peace Accords with Le Duc Tho to end the conflict. The treaty between the United States and Vietnam entered into force on January 17, 1973. In Articles 1 and 2 of the Accords, the United States agreed to an immediate cease-fire, and to respect "the independence, sovereignty, unity and territorial integrity of Viet-Nam as recognized by the 1954 Geneva Agreements on Viet-Nam." Both men were awarded the Nobel Peace Prize in 1973, although Le Duc Tho declined to accept the award.

On April 30, 1975, the last Americans evacuated Vietnam after over 58,000 had died. North and South Vietnam officially reunited in 1976.

This example illustrates how civil wars become a problem for the international community as they are easily internationalized with the intervention of another country. The United Nations may become involved in both civil and international wars.

E. International Wars [§140]

What is the dividing line between international and internal conflicts? Contained civil wars threaten international peace and security to the extent that one group commits genocide or otherwise violates the human rights of another group, or when the conflict spills over to neighboring states. Sometimes, for their own internal reasons, foreign nations intrude in an internal conflict. They may have a mutual defense treaty requiring them to come to the aid of a friendly state.

The United Nations has sought to implement security operations to contain wars, be they civil or international in scope. The U.N. Security operations can be divided into six phases. The first phase occurred immediately after World War II when the U.N. Charter conceptualized a Security Council with five permanent members who must act unanimously to send peacekeeping forces to combat aggression. *See* Damrosch, *supra* §29, at 1006. This phase was never implemented due to the almost immediate rise of the Cold War by 1946, when the former allies that comprised the Security Council split into two opposing East and West blocs.

This political reality brought the second phase, *Id.* at 1002, which meant that the goal of creating a permanent military force envisioned in Articles 43-47 of the United Nations Charter were never implemented. *See* U.N. Charter, *supra* §59, at arts. 43-47. Under Article 45, for example, members were required

188

to "hold immediately available national air-force contingents for combined international enforcement action." Article 47 called for the establishment of a "Military Staff Committee to advise and assist the Security Council on all questions relating to the Security Council's military requirements for the maintenance of international peace and security, the employment and command of forces placed at its disposal, the regulation of armaments, and possible disarmament." These articles envisioned a strong Security Council and an active General Assembly to endow the U.N. with watchdog functions over international conflicts. But such was not to be during the Cold War.

The third phase, Damrosch, *supra* §29, at 1008, coincided with the birth of dozens of new states after de-colonization led to massive political change around the world. The two opposing blocks brought paralysis in the Security Council, as one block would veto another's measure, preventing the U.N. from censoring particular actions or calling for peacekeeping troops.

The Security Council's paralyses during these phases should have led to an increase in the General Assembly's power. However, a measure to give the General Assembly the power to recommend collective action, when the Security Council cannot act, never passed.

In the fourth phase, the United Nations peacekeeping forces functioned more as a deterrent force. They operated best when invited by, or without resistance from, the parties who were seeking détente.

The fifth phase arguably coincided with the end of Cold War, the collapse of communist regimes in Europe and the U.S.S.R, and the ensuing first Gulf War when Saddam Hussein invaded Kuwait. *Id.* No longer uninhibited by the East-West conflict, Hussein proclaimed Kuwait as the 19th province of Iraq after he took it over. The Security Council acted as initially envisioned

189

when it sent substantial military troops to force Iraqis out of Kuwait and back to their country. It then imposed sanctions to keep Iraq contained. Hussein remained in power until 2003, when the U.S. and its accompanying coalition forces invaded Iraq and ousted him. He was convicted and hung in 2006.

This U.S. action gave rise to a sixth phase in the Security Council. President Bush of the United States and Prime Minister Blair of Britain initially sought approval from the United Nations for their planned action in Iraq to search out and destroy weapons of mass destruction, and expel Hussein from power. After vigorous debate on whether military action was the appropriate response for the former task, given that the International Atomic Energy Agency had thus far found no such weapons capability, the United States and Great Britain withdrew their request and invaded Iraq in March 20, 2003. As of April 2008, the United States and Great Britain remained in Iraq fighting an insurgency. On its website, <www.un.org>, the United Nations maintains a section monitoring the situation and urging a transition to an internal political process.

F. Nuclear War [§141]

Nuclear war is potentially the most harmful war to people and territory, as it potentially wipes out both. If the introduction of aerial bombing destroyed the distinction between civilians and combatants, as both are harmed with the dropping of bombs on a particular state, nuclear war threatens to wipe out part or all of the state's territory.

Sam Cohen, a U.S. national, invented the neutron bomb to kill people and leave the territory intact. This turned out to be useless for the state deploying such a weapon, as the enhanced radiation would make the territory uninhabitable for decades, if not hundreds of years. As such, the state would gain little by deploying such weapons, unless its intent was to wipe out an entire people from the face of the earth. If so, it would violate the *jus cogens* norm prohibiting genocide.

There are three policy goals that underlie nuclear weapons treaties: (1) avoid nuclear war; (2) minimize crisis instability and temptation; and (3) reduce the arms race. International law distinguishes between possession and use of weapons. Possession of them is not illegal, unless the state has signed a non-proliferation treaty to not acquire them. Using nuclear weapons against the territorial integrity and political independence of another state would be a crime.

Non-proliferation treaties seek to limit nuclear powers to the current possessors: the U.S., U.K., Russia, France, Germany, China, India, Pakistan, Israel, and South Africa. The policy behind the limitations is that expanding the users increases the chances that they will be used. Nevertheless, North Korea announced in 2003 that it possessed nuclear weapons capability. By 2005, it entered into negotiations to abandon weapons capability in return for support for its energy sector and food. The World Food Program determined that over 6 million North Koreans needed food and over a million could die if the situation wasn't addressed immediately. In 2005, the European Union negotiated with Iran to get it to abandon its nuclear program. When Iran was non-responsive the European Union submitted a motion to the International Atomic Energy Agency, which became the first step toward referring Iran to the Security Council if it fails to halt some of its nuclear activities. The Security Council could impose sanctions.

In 1961, the General Assembly declared the use of nuclear weapons a violation of the United Nations Charter and treaties outlawing particularly dangerous weapons. Resolution 1653, entitled "A Declaration on the Prohibition of the Use of Nuclear and Thermonuclear Weapons," came sixteen years after the end of World War II and the U.S. nuclear bombing of Hiroshima

191

and Nagasaki. *See* G.A. Res. 1653 (XVI), Art. 1, U.N. GAOR, 16th Sess., Supp. No. 17, U.N. Doc. A/5100 (Nov. 24, 1961). The General Assembly expressed concern that weapons of mass destruction may cause unnecessary human suffering. The Resolution declared that the use of nuclear weapons was contrary to the U.N. Charter, and would exceed the scope of war and cause indiscriminate suffering and destruction to civilization and mankind. Further, Resolution 1653 proclaimed that the use of nuclear weapons is a war directed not against a particular state's enemies, but against mankind in general. As such, the use of nuclear weapons is a crime against humanity, humankind and civilization.

Resolution 1653 was followed two years later by the 1963 Nuclear Test Ban Treaty, known officially as the Treaty Banning Nuclear Weapon Tests in the Atmosphere, in Outer Space and Underwater. *See* Treaty Banning Nuclear Tests in the Atmosphere, in Outer Space and Underwater, Art. 1, 4, Aug. 5, 1963, 14 U.S.T. 1313, 480 U.N.T.S. 43. The goal of this treaty was the discontinuance of all test explosions of nuclear weapons for all times. Article I requires parties to prohibit, prevent and refrain from nuclear weapon test explosions. Article IV provides states the right to withdraw if national sovereignty issues are at stake. A state must give three months advanced notice in order to withdraw. The problem with the treaty is that it failed to ban underground explosions and possessed a loophole for so-called "peaceful nuclear explosions." The U.S. and U.S.S.R. signed this treaty after the Cuban missile crisis brought them to the brink of launching a nuclear war.

By 1996, over 160 states had signed "Comprehensive Nuclear Test Ban Treaty," which closed some of the prior treaty's loopholes. *See* Comprehensive Nuclear Test Ban Treaty, UN Doc A/Res/46/29 (1991). Of the over 160 state signatories, 85 states ratified it. This treaty came into being after the relationship between the United States and U.S.S.R. improved significantly. It welcomes the treaties between the U.S. and U.S.S.R. that signal a reversal of the arms race. The treaty states that it is convinced that the end to nuclear testing by all states in all environments is essential to the eventual elimination of nuclear weapons.

Is the elimination of nuclear weapons a utopia or a realistic goal? In between the 1961 limited test ban treaty and the 1996 comprehensive test ban treaty, several other treaties were enacted, including the 1970 Treaty on the Non-Proliferation of Nuclear Weapons. *See* Treaty on the Non-Proliferation of Nuclear Weapons, arts. 1-3, 10, 21 U.S.T. 483, 729 U.N.T.S. 161 (March 5, 1970). It recognizes that the proliferation of nuclear weapons seriously enhances the dangers of nuclear war, and declares the intent to cease the nuclear arms race. Article 1 prohibits the transfer of nuclear weapons or explosive devices directly or indirectly to any non-nuclear weapon state. Article 2 prohibits non-nuclear states from receiving nuclear weapons. Article 3 requires the International Atomic Energy Agency to verify compliance with the treaty. Article 10 gives each party the right to withdraw from the treaty if it decides that extraordinary events have jeopardized the supreme interest of the country. The states that have not signed this treaty include Israel, India, Pakistan, Libya, and South Africa. They are known to possess or to have attempted to possess nuclear weapons.

In 1972, the United States and the U.S.S.R. signed a bilateral treaty on the Limitation of Anti-Ballistic Missile Systems. *See* Treaty Between the United States of America and the Union of Soviet Socialist Republics on the Limitation of Anti-Ballistic Missile Systems, U.S.-U.S.S.R., arts. 1, 2, 4, 5, 9, 12, March 26, 1972, 944 U.N.T.S. 13. Its Preamble declares that it seeks an end to the nuclear arms race. Under Article 1, "Each Party undertakes to limit anti-ballistic missile (ABM) systems and to not deploy ABM systems for a defense of its country." Article 2 defines an ABM System to include counter strategic ballistic missiles, interceptor missiles,

193

launchers, and radars. Article 3 permits deployment of one ABM system having a radius of 150 kilometers centered on the capital. Article 4 permits testing of ABM systems or components within currently agreed test ranges. Article 5 prohibits testing of ABM systems or components that are sea-based, air-based, space-based, or mobile land-based. Article 9 bans the parties from transferring to other states or deploying outside their territory ABM systems or their components. Article 12 permits the parties to use national technical means to verify compliance with treaty, but they may not use deliberate concealment measures that impede verification. The irony of this treaty was that the states lacked the technology to deploy such a system, which was considered astronomically expensive.

The United States and Soviet Union would sign several more treaties before the Soviet Union endured another state transformation. After it became Russia again, its economic circumstances limited its ability to continue to engage in an arms race with the United States.

When the Cold War ended in 1989, this lessened the threat of nuclear war from the superpowers. Nevertheless, the world community remained concerned about the possible use of nuclear weapons from burgeoning proliferation among states with avowed hatred towards each other, such as India and Pakistan. This increased the danger that someday these weapons may be used.

In 1994, the General Assembly asked the International Court of Justice to ascertain the international legality of the threat or use of nuclear weapons. *See* Legality of the Threat or Use of Nuclear Weapons (1994-1996), Advisory Opinion of 8 July 1996. The Court determined that there was neither customary nor conventional international law that authorized the threat or use of nuclear weapons. Further, it found that a threat or use of force by means of nuclear weapons would be contrary to Article

194

2(4) of the United Nations Charter. Finally, in a tie vote, with the President of the Court casting the deciding vote, the Court said it could not conclude definitively whether the threat or use of nuclear weapons would be lawful or unlawful in an extreme circumstance of self-defense, in which the very survival of a State would be at stake.

While it would appear that war is likely to remain part of the international community for time immemorial, the hope is that no state will threaten or use nuclear weapons.

CHAPTER X

MULTIPLE CHOICE QUESTIONS AND ANSWERS

PRACTICE MULTIPLE CHOICE QUESTIONS

Question 1

Who is considered the father of International Law?
(A) No one.
(B) Francisco de Vitoria.
(C) Hugo Grotius.
(D) Both b and c, depending on whom you ask the question.

Question 2

What is the international legal status of the Vatican?
(A) It is not a state, because it is too small at only 0.15 square miles.
(B) It is not a state, because too few people live there.
(C) It is not a state, because it lacks the capacity to interact on the international plane.
(D) It is a state, because it meets the four criteria.

Question 3

The Zuni Nation would be considered which one of these various categories of states?
(A) A State in Training.
(B) A Failed State.
(C) A Domestic Dependent Nation.
(D) A Micro-State.

Question 4

A stateless person is one who:
(A) Lacks a community willing and able to guarantee rights.
(B) Likes living on ships.
(C) Loves being confined to airports.
(D) Lost his or her passport.

Question 5

Karl Running Gun was born in Srebrenica to Greek nationals on October 10, 1942 who were residing in the former Yugoslavia. Bosnia and Herzegovina is the current name of the country and it accords nationality similar to the former Yugoslavia. Two days after Running Gun's birth, his family moved to Greece, where they continued to live. When Karl turned 18 on October 10, 1960, the Greek Government sent him a notice commanding him to report for national service required of all Greek nationals. If Karl successfully challenges the legality of the order and does not have to report, it will be because:

(A) Both Greece and Bosnia and Herzegovina only accord nationality based on *jus soli*.

(B) Both Greece and Bosnia and Herzegovina only accord nationality based on *jus sanguinis*.

(C) Either a or b.

(D) Neither a or b.

Question 6

Same facts as Question 5, except assume for this question only that Karl Running Gun moved to Australia when he turned 25. He incorporated the company Ex-Gun in Australia. The Greek government sent Karl a bill representing taxes on all the worldwide sales of Ex-Gun. If Karl successfully challenges the legality of the bill, it will be because:

(A) Ex-Gun is a Greek company since its principal owner used to live in Greece.

(B) Ex-Gun is an Australian company since it was incorporated in Australia.

(C) Ex-Gun is a Yugoslavian company since its owner was born there.

(D) Neither a, b, nor c.

198

Question 7

Same facts as Question 5, except assume for this question only that while living in Australia, Karl Running Gun, who was born in the former Yugoslavia (now Bosnia and Herzegovina) of Greek parents, married an Australian national who gave birth to three children born in Australia. If Australia, Bosnia and Herzegovina and Greece accord nationality based only on *jus sanguinis*, then Karl's children would be:

(A) Nationals only of Australia.
(B) Nationals only of Greece.
(C) Dual nationals of Australia and Greece.
(D) Dual nationals of Australia and Yugoslavia.

Question 8

Which of the following does not exist as a *jus cogens* norm?

(A) A *jus cogens* norm prohibiting states and individuals from engaging in the slave trade.
(B) A *jus cogens* norm banning states from engaging in war, for whatever reason.
(C) A *jus cogens* norm prohibiting states from engaging in genocide.
(D) A *jus cogens* norm banning states and individuals from engaging in torture.

Question 9

The International Court of Justice is permitted to apply all the following sources of law to resolve the disputes between parties in contentious cases, except one. Which one?

(A) I.C.J. decisions as precedent.
(B) Treaties between the parties.
(C) Customary law.
(D) General principles of law common throughout legal systems in the world.

199

Question 10

Following a hurricane, Purpleville requested that Aspen state assist in providing aid to the citizens of Purpleville. Aspen state sent in its troops, who assisted and then proceeded to occupy the state. After Purpleville protested, Aspen state claimed that Purpleville had consented to the occupation. Was Purpleville's consent a circumstance that precluded a finding of wrongfulness on the part of Aspen state?

(A) Yes, because Purpleville did invite Aspen state troops to come into its state.

(B) No, because Aspen state exceeded the scope of its initial invitation.

(C) Yes, because Purpleville did need the help when it invited in Aspen state.

(D) No, because Aspen state came of its own accord.

Question 11

Which of the following is not a circumstance that would preclude a finding of wrongfulness?

(A) Green state abrogated its mutual defense treaty with White state after White state attacked Green state.

(B) Green state crossed White state's borders without permission to save the lives of several Green state citizens caught in an earthquake.

(C) Green state abrogated a trade treaty with White state because it could get a better deal with Yellow state.

(D) Green state invaded White state with its armed forces to separate two warring factions in White state after one ethnic group killed 800,000 of another ethnic group.

200

Question 12

In May 1991, French Prime Minister Michel Rocard said he was sorry to New Zealand for the suffering caused by France's sinking the Rainbow Warrior vessel while it was docked in Auckland harbor. This apology came after France paid $2 million into a fund to encourage better relations between the parties. Rocard then honored French Major Mafart who had been adjudicated responsible for sinking the Rainbow Warrior. New Zealand may view his apology as ineffective for which of the following primary reason(s)?

(A) Rocard did not acknowledge the harm France caused New Zealand.

(B) France did not do anything to repair the harm.

(C) By the honoring of Mafart, New Zealand received no reassurance from France that the harm would not be repeated.

(D) All of the above.

Question 13

The independent territorial state was ushered in by the Peace of Westphalia. Which of the following international legal concepts cannot be attributed to the Peace of Westphalia?

(A) Individuals have rights and duties under international law.

(B) States possess a right to territorial integrity.

(C) States possess exclusive jurisdiction within their territory.

(D) States may not intervene in the domestic jurisdiction of other states.

Question 14

If the General Assembly assesses Saudi Arabia 7% of the U.N. budget and 7% of the cost associated with peacekeeping operations, that means Saudi Arabia:

(A) Controls 7% of the world's oil reserves.

(B) Controls 7% of the world's land.

(C) Controls 7% of the world's population.

(D) Controls 7% of the world's gross national product.

201

Question 15

In the *Case Concerning the S.S. Lotus*, **Turkey asserted jurisdiction over Lt. Demons under what principle?**

(A) The Nationality Principle, because Lt. Demons was a Turkish citizen.

(B) The Passive Personality (Nationality) Principle, because Lt. Demons caused harm to Turkish nationals.

(C) The Protective Principle, because it was seeking to protect its economy from Lt. Demons because he damaged a Turkish ship.

(D) The Universal Principle, because causing a ship to collide with another ship is an international crime.

Question 16

If Nigeria had asserted that the Act of State Doctrine instead of Foreign Sovereign Immunity justified its actions in the *Texas Trading Co. v. Nigeria* **case, the court would have:**

(A) Still possessed jurisdiction because the Act of State doctrine is a choice of law principle, and there was no Nigerian legal principle at stake in the case.

(B) Still possessed jurisdiction because U.S. courts can sit in judgment of another state's laws.

(C) Lacked jurisdiction because Nigeria acted as a sovereign when it canceled the contracts.

(D) None of the above.

Question 17

While the United Nations was engaged in a peacekeeping operation in Green state, five officials from Green state shot into a group of U.N. Peacekeepers and killed ten, five of whom were nationals of Green state and the other five were nationals of Yellow state. If the United Nations brings an action against Green state on behalf of its ten agents in the International Court of Justice, the I.C.J. will:

(A) Take jurisdiction only over the lawsuit for the nationals of Green state because the U.N. can only sue on behalf of agents who are not nationals of the injuring state.

(B) Take jurisdiction over the entire lawsuit because the U.N. can sue on behalf of both agents who are nationals of the injuring state and agents who are not members of the injuring state.

(C) Decline jurisdiction over the entire lawsuit because the U.N. possesses no international legal personality.

(D) Decline jurisdiction over the entire lawsuit because U.N. personnel assumed the risk associated with death by becoming peacekeepers trying to separate warring factions.

Question 18

Under which of the following circumstances can Orange state void a treaty with Purple state?

(A) When Purple state falsely misrepresented its economic circumstances causing Orange state to enter into a treaty it would otherwise not have.

(B) When Purple state pays Orange State's Ambassador U.S. $100,000 into a secret Swiss bank account if he will sign a treaty that benefits Purple state but not Orange state.

(C) Neither (A) nor (B).

(D) Both (A) and (B).

Question 19

Fishing vessels are exempt from seizure as prizes of war because
(A) States have agreed to do so under customary law.
(B) States have agreed to do so because they felt it was in their best interest.
(C) States have agreed to do so because they object to not doing so.
(D) States have agreed to do so because of scholarly writing.

Question 20

Which of the following does not constitute international lawful means for a state to acquire new territory?
(A) Brown state purchased territory from Red state.
(B) Brown state discovered a territory that was unoccupied, put up its flag to claim the territory, and brought in Brown people to occupy the territory.
(C) Brown state discovered a territory that was unoccupied when it arrived, but unbeknownst to it the territory contained nomadic Blue people who roamed from water hole to water hole depending on the season.
(D) Brown state entered into a treaty with Grey state to merge into the BrownGrey Nation.

Question 21

Erga Omnes **obligations are similar to which type of international norms?**
(A) *Jus cogens* norms, because they are owed to the international community of states as a whole.
(B) Treaty norms, because they only apply between the states that enshrine them in a treaty document.
(C) Customary norms, because they don't apply to states who persistently objected.
(D) General principles of law, because they are general obligations.

Question 22

In the *Case Concerning the Barcelona Traction, Light and Power Co., Ltd.*, which state possessed the right to offer diplomatic protection over the company in the International Court of Justice?
(A) Belgium, because 88% of the shareholders were Belgium citizens.
(B) The United Kingdom, because the company's bonds were to be serviced in pound sterling.
(C) Canada, because it was the country of incorporation.
(D) Spain, because it was the country that injured the company.

Question 23

If Blue state breached its international legal obligations to Green state, which of the following options can Blue state undertake to repair the harm?
(A) Blue state could offer restitution in kind, by issuing a statement that it planned to honor its initial obligations and then doing so.
(B) Blue state could nuke Green state so that it stopped complaining.
(C) Blue state could invade Green state, and annex it so that it is now part of Blue state.
(D) None of the above.

Question 24

Laurence Fishter, an independent contractor, was secretly hired by Yellow state to train assassins in Maroon state. Maroon state captured Fishter. Both Yellow and Maroon state are parties to the I.C.J. statute and have accepted the compulsory jurisdiction of the Court. If Maroon state sues Yellow state in the I.C.J., how will the Court most likely resolve the merits of the dispute?

(A) The I.C.J. will hold that the acts of Fishter cannot be attributed to Yellow state because Fishter's acts were illegal in Yellow state.

(B) The I.C.J. will hold that the acts of Fishter can be attributed to Yellow state because he was a *de jure* agent of Yellow state.

(C) The I.C.J. will hold that the acts of Fishter cannot be attributed to Yellow state because Fishter's acts were illegal in Maroon state.

(D) The I.C.J. will hold that the acts of Fishter can be attributed to Yellow state because he was a *de facto* agent of Yellow state.

Question 25

The Dalai Lama is the head of the state of Tibet, but he lives in India. What does this mean?

(A) The Dalai Lama represents a neutral state.

(B) Tibet is a failed state because its government does not control its territory.

(C) Tibet is a rogue nation because it does not follow international law.

(D) The Dalai Lama represents a government-in-exile because the Tibetan people still accord him allegiance.

ANSWERS TO THE MULTIPLE CHOICE QUESTIONS

Answer to Question 1.
(D) is the correct choice.
Francisco de Vitoria is considered the Spanish father of International Law and Hugo Grotius is considered the Dutch father of International Law. Depending on whom you ask the question and in what part of the world, they may name one or the other.

Answer to Question 2.
(D) is the correct choice.
The Vatican meets the four criteria to be considered a state. It has a defined territory of 0.15 square miles, a permanent population of 950 (as of 2008), a government led by the Pope, and the government is capable of interacting on the international plane.

Answer to Question 3.
(C) is the correct choice.
The Zuni Nation cannot be considered a state-in-training because it is not an insurgent community or movement for national liberation. Nor can it be considered a failed state because its government has not lost control over its people or territory. Furthermore, the Zuni Nation cannot be considered a micro-state, such as Monaco or the Vatican, because its government does not function as a full member of the international community. Instead, the Zuni Nation can only be considered a domestic dependent nation because, similar to the Cherokee Nation in *Cherokee Nation v. State of Georgia*, it lacks the fourth criteria, or the capacity to interact on the international plane.

Answer to Question 4.

(A) is the correct choice.

A 1974 article in the *Yale Law Journal* defines a stateless person as one who lacks "a community willing and able to guarantee any rights whatsoever." Stateless individuals experience limits on their freedom of movement. They are unable to enter and leave foreign nations because of their inability to obtain a passport.

Answer to Question 5.

(A) is the correct choice.

Jus soli grants nationality status based on birth within the territory. *Jus sanguinis* grants nationality status based on birth to nationals. In order to successfully challenge the order, Karl will have to argue that he is not a Greek national. If Karl argues that both Greece and Yugoslavia only accord nationality status based on *jus soli*, then he would be a national only of Yugoslavia and not of Greece. This prevents the Greek government from drafting him into military service.

Answer to Question 6.

(B) is the correct choice.

The nationality of juristic persons (i.e., corporations) is determined according to the state of incorporation and not the nationality of the individual that owns the corporation. Since the corporation was incorporated in Australia, it is a national of Australia. Greece cannot tax the Ex-Gun Corporation.

Answer to Question 7.

(C) is the correct choice.

Because *jus sanguinis* accords nationality status based on birth to nationals, for this question Karl would be considered a Greek national. Furthermore, because his children were born to Greek and Australian nationals, they would be dual nationals of both Greece and Australia.

Answer to Question 8.

(B) is the correct choice.

Jus cogens norms are peremptory norms that can preempt and invalidate a treaty. In order to be considered a *jus cogens* norm, a principle must be a norm of general international law, which permits no derogation and is accepted and recognized by the international community as a whole. Finally, these norms can only be modified by new peremptory norms. The bans on slavery, genocide and torture have been long considered *jus cogens* norms by the international community of states. There is no *jus cogens* norm banning states from engaging in war for whatever reason because states have retained the right to wage war in self-defense.

Answer to Question 9.

(A) is the correct choice.

Because the I.C.J. cannot create international law, its duty is only to determine the law that applies to the states as evidenced by their treaties, customary practice, and other documents and practices indicating state consent, such as general principles of law common throughout legal systems. As a result, the I.C.J. is not bound by the principle of *stare decisis* and does not have to follow its prior decisions and opinions.

Answer to Question 10.

(B) is the correct choice.

State Responsibility Draft Article 20 provides that valid consent will preclude a finding of wrongfulness "to the extent that the act remains within the limits of that consent." Thus, because Aspen state exceeded the initial invitation to enter in order to assist and provide aid to Purpleville, the consent of Purpleville will not preclude a finding of wrongfulness on the part of Aspen state.

Answer to Question 11.

(C) is the correct choice.

There are several circumstances that will preclude a finding of wrongfulness. They are consent, self-defense, countermeasures, *force majeure*, distress, necessity, and compliance with a peremptory norm. A state cannot arbitrarily decide to abrogate a treaty; instead, it must do so according to terms in the treaty or upon the consent of all parties. In answer C, Green state abrogated a treaty because it could get a better deal with a different state. This is not a circumstance that would preclude a finding of wrongfulness on the part of Green state.

Answer to Question 12.

(C) is the correct choice.

To be effective, an apology must do three things: (1) acknowledge the harm that was caused to the injured state; (2) offer to repair the harm; and (3) offer reassurances that the damage will not be repeated. In the *Rainbow Warrior* case, the apology by the French Prime Minister was ineffective because, although it acknowledged the harm that was caused to New Zealand and offered reparations to repair the harm, it offered no reassurances that the harm would not be repeated because France honored Major Mafart, one of the individuals who bombed the ship.

Answer to Question 13.

(A) is the correct choice.

The international community evolved the concept that individuals have rights and responsibilities under international law following the defeat of the Nazis in World War II. The 1648 Peace of Westphalia, which is also known as the Peace of Exhaustion, ended the 30-year war between the Holy Roman Empire and several European states and ushered in the era of the independent territorial state. Under the Peace of Westphalia, an independent territorial state is founded on three concepts: (1) territorial integrity; (2) exclusive jurisdiction; and (3) non-intervention in the domestic affairs of other states.

Answer to Question 14.

(D) is the correct choice.

The United Nations calculates the percentage that each member contributes to its budget based upon the percentage of the world's total gross national product controlled by each member state. This amount may be adjusted to take into consideration factors such as per capita income.

Answer to Question 15.

(B) is the correct choice.

There are several principles for the assertion of jurisdiction, including nationality, territorial, effects, protective, passive personality, and universal. In the *Case Concerning the S.S. Lotus*, the Turkish government asserted jurisdiction over Lt. Demons under the passive personality principle because the victims of the accident were Turkish citizens. Turkey could not assert jurisdiction under the nationality principle because Lt. Demons was not a Turkish citizen. Also, it could not assert jurisdiction under the protective principle because the actions of Lt. Demons did not threaten the existence of the Turkish state. Finally, Turkey could not have asserted jurisdiction under the universal principle because the actions of Lt. Demons did not violate a *jus cogens* norm.

Answer to Question 16.

(A) is the correct choice.

Under the Act of State doctrine, which is a choice of law rule, national courts show special deference to the public acts of foreign states done within their own country. Furthermore, the Supreme Court in the *Underhill* case stated that, "the courts of one country will not sit in judgment on the acts of the government of another done within its own territory." Additionally, in the *W.S. Kirkpatrick & Co.* case, the Court held that where the validity of the act of the foreign state is not at issue, the Act of State doctrine has no applicability. Therefore, because the Nigerian government in the *Texas Trading Co. v. Nigeria* case was acting in its commercial capacity rather than its sovereign capacity and there was no Nigerian legal principle at stake, the court would have still possessed jurisdiction.

211

Answer to Question 17.

(B) is the correct choice.

The U.N. is an international legal entity possessing international rights and duties, including the capacity to maintain its rights by bringing claims. In the *Case Concerning Reparations for Injuries Suffered in the Service of the United Nations*, the I.C.J. stated in an advisory opinion that the U.N. could bring an action on behalf of its agents injured by a state's breach of its international obligations regardless of whether the agents are nationals of the injuring state or not.

Answer to Question 18.

(D) is the correct choice.

Treaties can be voided where there are allegations of error, fraud, and corruption. Answer A is correct because treaties are voidable when false statements, misrepresentations, or deception gives rise to fraud. Answer B is correct because treaties are absolutely void if a state or its representatives have been coerced or corrupted into signing the treaty. Thus, since both A and B are correct, then D is the most correct choice.

Answer to Question 19.

(A) is the correct choice.

In the *Paquette Habana* case, which involved the U.S. Navy's seizure of Spanish fishing vessels as prizes of war during the Spanish (Cuban) American war, the U.S. Supreme Court determined that states, including the U.S., had created by their practice a customary rule of international law exempting fishing vessels from capture as prizes of war.

Answer to Question 20.

(C) is the correct choice.

Brown state would not be considered *terra nullius*, or unoccupied, if there are nomadic Blue people with social and political organization inhabiting the territory. The other answers present lawful means of acquiring territory, such as through purchase, discovery and occupation of *terra nullius* territory, or treaty.

212

Answer to Question 21.

(A) is the correct choice.

Erga omnes obligations, which originate from the principles concerning the basic human rights of all individuals as well as the outlawing of acts of aggression and genocide, are obligations that all states have an interest in protecting. Furthermore, any state can bring a claim for the breach of an *erga omnes* obligation. As such, *erga omnes* obligations are similar in nature to *jus cogens* norms because the obligations are owed to the international community as a whole.

Answer to Question 22.

(C) is the correct choice.

In the *Case Concerning the Barcelona Traction, Light, and Power Co., Ltd.,* the court determined that only Canada possessed the right to offer diplomatic protection over the company because it was the nationality state of the corporation. That the majority of the shareholders were Belgium, the locus of the injury was in Spain, and the shares were to be serviced in pounds sterling did not give the other three countries the right to sue on behalf of the corporation.

Answer to Question 23.

(A) is the correct choice.

Because Blue state breached its international obligations to Green state, Blue state became obligated to offer reparations aimed at discharging the breach of the international obligation and repairing the harm. Under State Responsibility Draft Article 34 reparations can take the form of restitution in kind, aimed at reestablishing the situation as it existed before the breach. Thus issuing a statement that it planned to honor its initial obligations and then doing so would be appropriate reparations.

Answer to Question 24.

(D) is the correct choice.

To attribute acts to a state, an organ or individual must act as a *de jure* or *de facto* agent of the state. A *de facto* agent is an individual who may lack a legal role under domestic law, but in fact acts on behalf of the state. The acts of individuals, such as Fishter who are employed to carry out clandestine activities, can be attributed to the state. International law is not concerned with whether the acts are illegal under domestic law, but only whether those acts can be linked to the state.

Answer to Question 25.

(D) is the correct choice.

A government-in-exile is one that has lost effective control over the state's territory, but whose population still accords it allegiance. Even though the Dalai Lama lives in India, he is still considered the head of the state of Tibet.

PRACTICE ESSAY QUESTIONS

Question No. 1

The United Cantons of January (UCJ) sent Cumina Jackson to be its ambassador to the Republic of Blink (ROB). ROB rejected Jackson because she had been involved in a prior international incident that caused a great deal of public shame to ROB. UCJ then sent Dorman Fink, and ROB accepted him. Two months after his arrival, Ambassador Fink became involved with a ROB citizen. In the course of a scuffle at a public park, he stabbed to death the ROB citizen. Fink ran to the embassy. A passerby called the ROB police from her cell phone to report the incident and where she saw Fink enter. The ROB police went into the embassy without permission, and arrested Ambassador Fink. Ambassador Fink has been detained in a ROB jail. The UCJ has signed the Vienna Convention on Diplomatic Immunity, but ROB has not.

Write an essay analyzing the rights and duties of the various parties under international law.

Question No. 2

Sowbenia is an oil rich Persian Gulf state located on the northwest coast of Africa. In January of this year, Sowbenia entered into a treaty with Costa Marrónita. In this treaty, Sowbenia agreed to ship Costa Marrónita a high grade of crude oil for $80 a barrel for the next three years. On January 31, earthquakes damaged the refineries of two other crude oil producing nations, causing an international shortage of high-grade crude oil. After the price of high-grade crude oil jumped to $120 a barrel, Sowbenia began shipping low-grade crude oil for $80 a barrel to Costa Marrónita.

Because Costa Marrónita planned to use the oil to improve infrastructure projects, the low-grade crude oil was less effective for its needs. Costa Marrónita retained the oil, but refused to pay the

215

contracted price. It ordered its banks not to pay on the letters of credit. It issued a demand that Sowbenia immediately ship the appropriate high-grade crude oil and it would pay on its letters of credit and return the low-grade crude oil.

Sowbenia refused. Instead, Sowbenia sent five supertankers to the shores of Costa Marrónita. The supertankers sit 190 miles off the shores of Costa Marrónita in a menacing posture. Sowbenia has stated that if the $80 a barrel is not paid by 31 October, it will have the supertankers begin laying mines in the harbor of Costa Marrónita.

Write an essay analyzing the rights and duties of the various parties under international law.

Question No. 3

On 4 July 2004, two spaceships, flying the separate flags of the National Democratic Republic (NDR) and the State of Treetop (Treetop), collided on the moon. The collision resulted in decimation of Treetop's spaceship and the loss of two of its crewmembers.

The NDR spaceship decided that under the circumstances they should offer to give Treetop's spaceship's remaining crewmembers a ride home. When the NDR spaceship reached Treetop, that state impounded the NDR spaceship. Treetop also arrested and charged the six NDR crewmembers with murder.

NDR protested to Treetop, claiming that the collision was an accident and that the astronauts were operating in a governmental capacity. NDR requested that its astronauts be extradited to the NDR under their bilateral extradition treaty. Treetop refused to extradite the NDR citizens, stating it would try them. The NDR-Treetop extradition treaty contains a clause that a party can deny an extradition request if the person would be charged with an offense that subjects them to the death penalty. NDR imposes the death penalty for murder and Treetop does not.

216

On 4 September 2005, the NDR President ordered a mission to retrieve the NDR astronauts. NDR paid Treetop citizens to surreptitiously retrieve the NDR astronauts from jail and to sneak them to its border with Treetop. NDR operatives were waiting at the border to receive the NDR astronauts. The operatives whisked the astronauts to a nearby helicopter and flew them to the NDR capital. The next day, a ticker tape parade was held on the streets of the NDR capital to honor the returning astronauts.

When the Treetop Prime Minister heard about the escape, he was furious. He has called you in as his principal international legal advisor. He wants you to write him a memo advising him as to his options under international law. What are the various states' rights and remedies under international law?

Question No. 4

Alexi Mashoggi was born to a wealthy family in Excel Nation, an oil rich state located on the Asian Subcontinent. In 1995, when Mashoggi was 25, he established residence and a subsidiary of his family's business in Costa Pobre, a state located on the Atlantic coast of South America. In 1997, he married a Costa Pobre woman. They had three children in rapid order.

In March of this year, Mashoggi spent a month visiting his brother and an oil refinery subsidiary of his family's business in Lari, a neighboring state of Excel Nation. While there, Mashoggi applied for and received naturalization. Mashoggi sought and received dispensation from residency requirements, paid his fees, gave a U.S. $1,000,000 security deposit for the payment of taxes, and completed the naturalization process by taking an oath of allegiance within two weeks of his arrival. Mashoggi obtained a Lari passport and had it visaed by the Costa Pobre Consul General in Lari.

In April, Mashoggi returned to Costa Pobre and immediately had its Register of Aliens photocopy his Lari nationality papers. Mashoggi continued with his life and business affairs until July, when he was arrested by the Costa Pobre officials and extradited, pursuant to their bilateral extradition treaty, to The Freedom State (TFS). TFS suspects that Mashoggi may be using his oil wealth to sponsor terrorism in its country. TFS has detained Mashoggi in a special naval base in a small island off its coast. To obtain information from him, TFS has implemented harsh stress techniques approved by its Defense Minister and President. The techniques include stripping Mashoggi naked and having attack dogs bark at him as he is questioned. TFS agents have also placed him in a pool of cold water up to his ears where he can barely breathe from his nose. When he was returned to his windowless cell, TFS left the lights off for 23 hours. As a consequence, he is slowly going blind.

While Mashoggi was gone, Costa Pobre nationalized all of his property except his homestead, which continues to be occupied by his family.

Write an essay analyzing the rights and duties of the various parties under international law.

Question No. 5

The Novemberdom Democratic Republic (NDR) is a landlocked state situated on the South American subcontinent. NDR has a history of friendly relations with one of its neighbors, the October States (OS). Throughout decades of their friendly relations, OS constantly granted NDR access to the sea by way of OS territory. In 1960, NDR and OS entered into a Treaty of Friendship, Commerce, and Navigation (FCN). This 1960 FCN treaty contained, *inter alia*, the following provisions:

Art. II. Nationals of either Party shall be permitted to enter the territories of the other Party, to travel therein freely and to reside at places of their choice.

Art. XXII. Disputes arising under this treaty shall be referred to the International Court of Justice.

218

In 1970, both NDR and OS acceded to the United Nations Charter and to the Vienna Convention on the Law of Treaties. While both OS and NDR became parties to the Statute of the International Court of Justice in 1970, the OS's declaration provided that its acceptance of the compulsory jurisdiction of the court "shall remain in force for a period of five years and thereafter until the expiration of six months after notice may be given to terminate the declaration."

Following the ratification and entry into force of the FCN treaty, NDR began shipping its people to work in the State of Septdrom by way of OS territory. In 2001, several NDR citizens decided to take up residence in the OS. When the OS President protested, the NDR Prime Minister said that he would take care of the matter. Instead, the NDR Prime Minister encouraged the continued exodus.

Last month, the OS President sent a notice to the I.C.J that OS was immediately withdrawing its acceptance of the I.C.J's compulsory jurisdiction. The OS President ordered the closure of the border with NDR and of their diplomatic mission, and that all NDR citizens be rounded up and put in concentration camps to await their return to NDR.

Write an essay analyzing the rights and duties of the various parties under international law.

SUGGESTED ANALYSIS TO THE ESSAY QUESTIONS

Answer to Question No. 1.
United Cantons of January (UCJ) v. Republic of Blink (ROB)
(1) Can the acts be attributed to the state? UCJ can sue ROB for violating its embassy premises when ROB police entered to retrieve Fink. The acts of the ROB police, as officials of ROB, can be attributed to ROB.

(2) Did the state breach an international obligation? ROB arguably breached an international obligation to protect and not invade the UCJ embassy premises without permission. Although ROB did not sign the Vienna Convention on Diplomatic Immunity, it is still bound by its underlying provisions that codify customary law. Under both the Vienna Convention and customary law, the embassy premises shall be inviolable. Also, ROB breached an international obligation not to harm the personhood of the ambassador. Its options were to either request a waiver of immunity, or declare Fink *persona non grata* and give him a certain number of days to leave the country.

(3) Was ROB responsible for the act? Yes, the state can be held responsible for the actions of its *de jure* officials.

(4) Was UCJ injured? Yes, it was directly harmed when the ROB police entered its embassy and removed its ambassador. UCJ was not harmed when ROB rejected Cumina Jackson because ROB had a right to reject her.

(5) Were there circumstances precluding a finding of wrongfulness? ROB might argue distress, to save the other lives of ROB citizens from being harmed by Fink or necessity because it believed it had to safeguard an essential interest against a grave or imminent peril. However, by the time the ROB police went inside the premises, Fink posed no further threat to ROB citizens.

220

(6) What are the remedies available? The two parties can negotiate this dispute or request a mediator, such as the Secretary-General. ROB can offer reparations that aim to discharge the breach. ROB can ask UCJ to waive diplomatic immunity so they can try Fink. ROB can offer to release Fink to UCJ, with the understanding that he will be removed immediately from their territory. ROB could request that UCJ and/or Fink pay money compensation to the victim's family and issue an apology. UCJ could seek extradition of Fink for trial in UCJ, and request that ROB pay compensation for invading its premises and arresting its diplomat.

Answer to Question No. 2.
(1) Can the acts be attributed to the state? Here, all acts can be attributed to the states which are responsible for all of them.

(2) Did the state breach an international obligation? Both states acted as commercial actors when they entered into contracts to purchase and supply high-grade crude oil for $80 a barrel. As such, neither is immune from the jurisdiction of the other's courts for breaches of obligations. Sowbenia (S) breached first when it sent non-conforming low-grade oil. Costa Marrónita (CM) breached second when it kept the oil and ordered its banks not to pay on the letters of credit.

(3) Did the state have responsibility for the act? Both states are responsible for their acts.

(4) Was a state injured by the act? CM can argue that it was injured by S's breach of shipping the wrong oil. S can argue that it was injured by CM's refusal to pay because it did not get paid. Both would be able to sue directly in the I.C.J. for this kind of harm, as it is direct to them.

(5) Were there circumstances precluding a finding of wrongfulness? S could argue that *rebus sic stantibus* (fundamental change of circumstances) or *force majeure* (irresistible force) excused its sending the low grade crude oil as a substitute. The fundamental change of circumstances argument

fails because the earthquakes did not damage S's refineries. *Force majeure* must be an irresistible force or an unforeseen external event beyond the state's control. Because earthquakes constitute unforeseen events, S may have an argument for its non-performance of the treaty. However, S should have negotiated and explained the circumstances to CM.

CM could argue it was bound to pay the $80 a barrel price, even if the price dropped. Thus S has to ship the high-grade crude oil, even though the price rose. CM will argue that its response was a counter measure to S's non-performance. Because S breached first, it could keep the low-grade crude oil and not pay. Before a state can institute a reprisal, it must demand a redress of grievance. CM did not issue such a demand. Further, reprisals must be necessary to terminate, prevent, or remedy a violation, and they must be proportionate to the original harm. S could argue that CM should either return the low-grade crude oil and not pay, or keep the oil and pay. It can't both keep the oil and not pay, as that is unjust enrichment.

S may argue that sending five supertankers to CM and threatening to lay mines constitutes a countermeasure. However, this may be viewed as an act of coercion that exceeds the scope of the original CM act. CM can also argue that S's actions violate Art. 2(4) of the U.N. Charter and customary law because they threaten the peace of the region and violate CP's territorial sovereignty.

(6) If not, what measures should the state undertake to remedy and address the other state's grievances? Both parties should try to resolve their disputes peacefully through negotiation, mediation, arbitration, or dispute settlement. Both parties should try to repair the harm. CM could offer to send back the low-grade crude oil in exchange for high-grade crude oil, and the appropriate payment. S should remove its supertankers and withdraw the threat.

Answer to Question No. 3.
(1) Can the acts be attributed to the state? The astronauts' actions can be attributed to their respective states as they were officially hired to

fly the spaceships of their respective countries. They were thus legal representatives of the state. Further, the actions of Treetop citizens who were hired by NDR to retrieve the NDR astronauts from jail can be attributed to NDR, as can the acts of the NDR operatives who whisked the astronauts to the NDR capital.

(2) Did either state breach an international obligation by exercising jurisdiction? Both countries can exercise jurisdiction over the accident. Treetop has jurisdiction based on the nationality principle (the spaceship flew its flag) and based on the passive personality principle since NDR astronauts are legally responsible to Treetop nationals for the deaths. NDR has jurisdiction based on the nationality principle (a NDR flag ship was involved in the collision). Did Treetop breach an international obligation in refusing to extradite the astronauts? This is a difficult question because a party can deny an extradition request if the retained individual would be subject to the death penalty in the other state. Since NDR imposes the death penalty for murder and Treetop does not, it can argue that it legitimately denied the extradition request. NDR may object by stating that it could have issued a statement of reassurance that the astronauts would not be subject to the death penalty in NDR. Treetop will claim that NDR breached an international obligation not to invade the territorial boundaries or political independence of other states by kidnapping astronauts from Treetop.

(3) Did the state have responsibility for the act? NDR is responsible to Treetop for its breaches of international obligations. The acts of the Treetop citizens it hired can be attributed to NDR.

(4) Was a state injured by the act? Treetop can argue that it was injured by the breach of its territorial sovereignty, which deprived it of jurisdiction to try the astronauts for their crimes.

(5) Were there circumstances precluding a finding of wrongfulness? NDR may argue that it acted under distress to save the lives of the astronauts; however, they were not subject to the death penalty in Treetop.

(6) If not, what measures should the state undertake to remedy and address the other state's grievances? Both parties should try to resolve their disputes peacefully through negotiation, mediation, arbitration, or dispute settlement. Both parties should try to repair the harm. Thus, Treetop could sue NDR directly, instead of holding the individual astronauts responsible. NDR will argue that is more appropriate since the astronauts were agents of the state of NDR when they flew the mission. They should not have been retained and prosecuted in their personal capacities as they were flying public spaceships.

Answer to Question No. 4.
(1) Can the acts be attributed to the state? The acts of the Defense Minister and the President, as officials of The Freedom State (TFS) can be attributed to the state as they are officials of the government. Similarly, the acts of Costa Pobre in nationalizing Mashoggi's property can be attributed to Costa Pobre.

(2) Did the state breach an international obligation? The state of Lari may claim that both Costa Pobre and TFS breached international obligations to its citizens. International human rights law protects the rights of individuals to own property, and international law requires that property cannot be nationalized without just compensation. A *jus cogens* norm prohibits states from engaging in torture, such as the harsh stress techniques. Thus, while the facts do not indicate whether the states have signed the conventions prohibiting torture, it does not matter as both customary law and *jus cogens* norms prohibit torture. TFS is in breach of its international obligations. Any state can bring a claim for a *jus cogens* norm violation.

(3) Did the state have responsibility for the act? Both Costa Pobre and TFS have responsibilities for their acts.

(4) Was a state injured by the act? Costa Pobre and TFS may argue that Lari was not injured since it does not possess a genuine link with Mashoggi and thus cannot protect him. This is similar to the *Nottebohm* case where the I.C.J. said that without a genuine connection between the

224

individual and the state of naturalization, the state could not protect the individual. Here, Mashoggi's only connection to Lari is his brother and an oil refinery subsidiary of his family business. Lari waived residency requirements before permitting Mashoggi to pledge allegiance to its flag. Without a genuine connection, Costa Pobre and TFS do not have to recognize the Lari citizenship. Since Mashoggi was born in Excel Nation (EN), EN may have the genuine connection sufficient to maintain an action on behalf of Mashoggi. EN must choose to bring such an action, as there is no duty to sue another state on behalf of nationals.

(5) Were there circumstances precluding a finding of wrongfulness? TFS can argue that a state of necessity, whereby it acted to avoid grave and imminent threat to its citizens, justified the harsh stress techniques. It wanted Mashoggi to own up to sponsoring terrorism. TFS can also argue that it was acting to defend its territory. However, self-defense measures must be necessary and proportionate to the original act.

(6) If not, what measures should the state undertake to remedy and address the other state's grievances? If Lari is unable to negotiate a return of Mashoggi, or to protect him in an international forum, Mashoggi can pursue claims in his individual capacity against both CP and TFS in either their respective national courts or in international human rights courts that permit individuals to sue a government.

Answer to Question No. 5.
(1) Can the acts be attributed to the state? The acts of both the OS President and the NDR Prime Minister can be attributed to their respective states. Similarly, the state is responsible for all direct acts.

(2) Did the state breach an international obligation? Initially, OS granted NDR access to the sea out of friendship. The FCN treaty went further and permitted citizens of both countries the rights of travel and of residence. OS will argue that NDR violated the FCN treaty, by its spirit if not its letter, by encouraging its nationals to establish residence in OS. The treaty contemplated some citizens residing in the territory of the other, but not an encouraged exodus.

NDR will claim that OS violated the FCN treaty when it closed its border and rounded up and put NDR citizens in concentration camps. The FCN treaty permitted NDR citizens to take up residence in OS. NDR may also claim that OS breached the FCN treaty by withdrawing from the acceptance of the I.C.J.'s compulsory jurisdiction. However, the I.C.J still has jurisdiction based on both parties' acceptance of the compulsory clause, and based on the FCN treaty provision that specifically refers disputes under the treaty to the I.C.J. The OS declaration required six months' notice before OS can withdraw. Once the I.C.J has possession of a case, it cannot be deprived of jurisdiction by a subsequent withdrawal.

(3) Did the state have responsibility for the act? Both parties clearly had responsibilities under the treaties they signed.

(4) Was any state injured by the act? OS will claim that it was injured by the mass immigration. NDR will claim that it was injured by the placing of its citizens in concentration camps, by the closing of the border, and by the closure of its diplomatic mission. Septdom may argue that it was injured when OS cut off of its steady labor supply.

(5) Were there circumstances precluding a finding of wrongfulness? OS could argue that *force majeure* excused its rounding up the NDR citizens and placing them into concentration camps. *Force majeure* must be an irresistible force or an unforeseen external event beyond the state's control. OS could argue that the massive immigration created an unforeseen problem that taxed its resources. OS could also argue that its actions were necessary to protect its citizens from imminent harm caused by the massive migration.

(6) If not, what measures should the state undertake to remedy and address the other state's grievances? Both parties should try to resolve their disputes peacefully through negotiation, mediation, arbitration, or dispute settlement. OS could remedy the situation by releasing NDR

citizens, and reopening the NDR mission. NDR could agree to stop encouraging its citizens to migrate to OS and take up residence there. NDR could offer to pay money compensation to address the harm caused.

CASE SQUIBS

STATES

Cherokee Nation v. State of Georgia, 30 U.S. 1 (1831)

This case addresses whether the Cherokee Nation, an Indian tribe, constituted a foreign state as defined by the U.S. Constitution. The Cherokee Nation sought an injunction to restrain Georgia from executing certain laws, which the Cherokees believed would annihilate them as a political society and seize lands protected by treaties with the United States government. If judged a foreign nation, the Cherokees could avail themselves of the original jurisdiction of the Supreme Court and sue the state of Georgia.

Justice Marshall acknowledged that the Cherokees have been uniformly considered a state from the settlement of the country. The U.S. government recognized them as a state in treaties. In those same treaties, the Cherokees acknowledged themselves to be under the protection of the United States. Marshall concluded that the Cherokees should be denominated domestic dependent nations. They were in a state of pupilage, resembling that of a ward to a guardian. As such, they are completely under the sovereignty and dominion of the United States. For support, he cites the eighth section of the Constitution's third article, which empowers Congress to "regulate commerce with foreign nations, and among the several states, and with the Indian tribes." This clause means Indian tribes were separated by name from foreign nations and the states comprising the union. Otherwise, Congress would have been empowered "to regulate commerce with foreign nations, including Indian tribes, and among the several states."

Thus, because the Cherokees are not a foreign nation, they cannot sue the state of Georgia in the Supreme Court and obtain an injunction prohibiting Georgia from seizing their lands.

The Legal Status of Eastern Greenland, 1939 P.C.I.J., Ser. A/B., No. 53, 3 Hudson, World Ct. Rep. 148

The Permanent Court of International Justice, the predecessor court to the International Court of Justice, analyzed the claims of Denmark and Norway to exercise sovereignty over Eastern Greenland. Norway issued a proclamation on July 10, 1931, placing portions of Eastern Greenland under Norwegian control on the theory that Eastern Greenland was *terra nullius*, not occupied by anyone. The court said that Norway had to base its claim on (1) discovery; and (2) continued display of authority. To satisfy the latter, Norway could demonstrate (a) intention and will to act as a sovereign; and (b) some actual exercise or display of authority.

Denmark asserted that its claim to title over Eastern Greenland was "founded on the peaceful and continuous display of state authority over the island." Denmark showed that it had established colonies on Greenland after its initial discovery as early as the 10th century, although these colonies subsequently vanished. It also put forth Danish treaties with other countries that mentioned Greenland, and recognized Denmark's rights over Greenland. Norway became a party to various bilateral and multilateral agreements in which Greenland was described as Danish or in which Denmark excluded Greenland from the operation of the agreement, an indication of sovereign control. Norway had also promised not to contest Danish sovereignty over the whole of Greenland.

The court ruled that Norway's proclamation of July 10, 1931 was invalid and stated that Denmark possessed a valid title to the sovereignty over Greenland because Denmark had both discovered Greenland and displayed continuous authority over the island. Greenland is the largest island in the world at 856,160 square miles.

Recognition Of Governments

Autocephalous v. Goldberg, 917 F.2d 278 (7th Cir. 1990)

The Turkish military government, which came into being after the Turkish invasion of Cyprus, issued decrees providing that all abandoned property now belonged to the Turkish government. After the Turkish invasion of Cyprus forced Greeks to flee and abandon their churches, the Church was vandalized and everything of value was removed. This included four Byzantine Mosaics that belonged to the Kanakaria Church.

The U.S. court refused to give legal effect to the nationalization decrees of an unrecognized government. Turkey was the only state that recognized the military government's legitimacy. Most other states considered its actions of invading and issuing the divestment decrees to be illegal.

Salimoff v. Standard Oil of New York, 262 N.Y. 220 (1933)

At issue was the legal effect of the decrees of the Soviet Government, which succeeded the Russian government. Russian nationals sought the return of oil lands confiscated in Russia by the successor Soviet Government. The court declared that the Soviets were a government, and "its decrees have force within its borders and over its nationals."

Rather than create the state, the court said, "Recognition … simply gives to a *de facto* state international status." While a court could not recognize a state, it could say that the Soviets are "a government, maintaining internal peace and order, providing for national defense and the general welfare, carrying on relations with our government and others."

The court maintained that to refuse to recognize Soviet Russia as a government is to give fictions an air of reality that they do not deserve. The court was, in effect, taking the declaratory view of recognition, i.e., that recognition would merely declare what already exists.

231

SOURCES

Treaty Law

The Case Concerning the Gabcikovo-Nagymaros Project (Hungary v. Slovakia), 1997 I.C.J. 7

Hungary and Czechoslovakia entered into a treaty on 16 September 1977, to provide for diversion of the Danube River, which formed the countries' common boundary for approximately 85 miles, and to build structures. The Danube was to be diverted into a by-pass canal in Czechoslovak territory. A structure downstream at Nagymaros was to generate additional power and moderate the flow of waters released. If not moderated, this flow could adversely affect water management and navigation further down the Danube.

In May 1989, Hungary suspended its work on the project in response to public protests about the potential environmental impact. In the 1980s, Czechoslovakia made provisional plans under the name "Variant C" in anticipation that Hungary would abandon the project. Variant C called for a dam at Cunovo, on Czech territory.

The I.C.J. considered whether Hungary's suspension and later abandonment of the project could be justified by the defense of necessity. The court answered negatively because environmental concerns did not amount to a necessity when Hungary could show no grave and imminent peril. Slovakia's "Variant C," on the other hand, was also an intentionally wrongful act. Slovakia became the successor state of Czechoslovakia.

Hungary also claimed that both impossibility of performance and fundamental changes of circumstances justified its May 19, 1992, termination of its treaty with Slovakia. The I.C.J. determined that the parties had rejected amendment to allow impossibility of performance based on serious financial difficulties.

232

Hungary cited profound political changes, the project's diminishing economic value, the progress of environmental knowledge, and the development of new norms and prescriptions of international environmental law as examples of fundamental changes that justified its terminating the treaty. The I.C.J. did not find Hungary's changed circumstances argument to be compelling. It noted that the prevalent political conditions were not closely linked to the object and purpose of the treaty. While the environmental knowledge and growth of environmental law was unforeseen, the treaty's articles 15, 19 and 20 were designed to accommodate change so the parties could take into account such developments. For this to work, the existence of the circumstances at the time of the treaty's conclusion must have constituted an essential basis of the consent of the parties to be bound by the treaty. In this case, the treaty remained in force and Hungary remained obligated to Slovakia for fulfilling the terms.

Customary Law

The Paquette Habana, 175 U.S. 677, 20 S.Ct. 290, 44 L.Ed. 320 (1900)

This case discusses the creation of customary international law. The plaintiffs were two Spanish nationals of Cuban birth who lived in Havana and owned separate fishing vessels that flew the Spanish flag. The vessels' cargo consisted of fresh fish, when they were seized and condemned as prizes of war. The crew had no knowledge of the Spanish (Cuban) American War or the blockade. The ship carried no arms or ammunition on board and made no attempt to run the blockade or resist capture.

The U.S. Supreme Court considered whether the armed vessels of the U.S. could legally capture these fishing smacks during the war with Spain. The answer depended on whether a customary law exempting fishing boats from seizure would bind the United States.

The Court declared that states by their practice had created the following customary rule, "Coastal fishing vessels, pursuing their vocation of catching and bringing in fresh fish have been recognized as exempt with their cargoes and crews, from capture as prize of war." The Court asserted that this ancient usage among civilized nations began centuries ago and gradually ripened into a rule of international law.

Haya De La Torre (Colombia v. Peru), 1950 I.C.J. 266

This case addresses whether a regional customary principle existed that would bind Peru even though it had not signed particular conventions that contained the rule. On October 3, 1948, Victor Raul Haya de la Torre was the leader of the American Peoples Revolutionary Alliance when, on January 3, 1949, he sought asylum in the Colombian embassy in Lima. On January 4, 1949, Colombia requested safe passage for him out of Lima, which Peru refused.

Colombia claimed the right as the state granting the asylum to Haya de la Torre to qualify his offence as political for asylum purposes. Colombia proclaimed this right as a principle of American international law, a regional custom local to American states. Colombia cited three treaties to support its claim, but Peru had not signed them.

The I.C.J. required Colombia to prove that the custom was established in such a manner as to bind Peru by showing consistent and uniform usage and an acceptance of the practice as law. The I.C.J. found the cases Colombia cited to be contradictory, and full of uncertainty, inconsistency, fluctuations, discrepancies, and political expediency. The I.C.J. did not find a customary practice giving one state the right to unilaterally characterize an offence as political for asylum purposes. Further, the I.C.J. found that even if there were such an established custom, it could not be invoked against Peru, which had persistently objected to such a claim at every term and had not ratified the Montevideo convention.

234

Case Concerning Right of Passage Over Indian Territory (Portugal v. India), 1960 I.C.J. 6

The I.C.J. adjudicated whether Portugal or India established a local custom between them. Portugal had two enclaves (Dadra and Nagar-Aveli) on the Indian peninsula surrounded by India. A rebellion broke out in the enclaves (reportedly sponsored by India with the blessings of Prime Minister Nehru) to overthrow Portuguese rule. Portugal attempted to send military weapons to help the government maintain its sovereignty over the enclaves. India objected, claiming that Portugal did not have a right of passage through India to get to its colonies.

Portugal claimed that it had a right of passage through Indian territory to maintain sovereignty over its enclaves. After reviewing the history between Portugal and India, the I.C.J. concluded that Portugal did not have a right of passage to bring armed forces, armed police, arms, and ammunition through India to its territories. In its prior relations with Britain, which had colonial authority over India when the colonies were established, Portugal only received a right to transport private persons, civil officials, and goods through India to its enclaves.

The Diversion of Water from the Meuse (The Netherlands v. Belgium), 1937 P.C.I.J. Ser. A/B, No. 70, 76-78

The Permanent Court of International Justice considered a dispute between the Netherlands and Belgium over construction of locks and canals to alter the water level and rate of flow of the Meuse River. The P.C.I.J. rejected the Netherlands' claim against Belgium because the Netherlands had been the first to put a lock on the Meuse River. Judge Hudson said in his individual concurring opinion, "It would seem to be an important principle of equity that where two parties have assumed an identical or a reciprocal obligation, one party which is engaged in a continuing non-performance of that obligation should not be permitted to take advantage of a similar non-performance of that obligation by the other party." He also repeated maxims such as "Equality is equity," and "He who seeks equity must do equity."

The Corfu Channel Case (United Kingdom v. Albania), 1949 I.C.J. 4

The United Kingdom sued Albania after it placed mines in the Corfu Channel that damaged British warships and took British lives. In the Corfu Channel case, the Court maintained that Albania had a duty to warn Britain of the imminent danger of the minefields based on "elementary consideration of humanity, even more exacting in peace than in war."

The Cayuga Indians Case, 6 R.I.A.A. 173, Nielsen Reports 203, 307 (1926)

The Cayuga Indians were a tribe split between the U.S. and Canadian borders. The Canadian Cayugas claimed they had not received their fair share of revenue payments for land ceded to the U.S. The arbitration tribunal determined that the claim of the Cayugas was founded "in the elementary principle of justice that requires us to look at the substance and not stick in the bark of the legal form."

The Tribunal determined that special circumstances made the equitable claim of the Canadian Cayugas especially strong, particularly their lack of international status, their dependent legal position, and that the 1926 treaty between the U.S. and Canada required that decisions be made on principles of law and equity. The tribunal held that the Canadian Cayugas were entitled to money damages because they had not received their fair share of the revenues.

INTERNATIONAL ORGANIZATIONS

Case Concerning Reparations for Injuries Suffered in the Service of the United Nations, Advisory Opinion of 11 April 1949

The first issue concerned whether the U.N. has international legal capacity to bring claims against a *de facto* or *de jure* government for injuries to itself or its agents. The I.C.J. answered affirmatively, as the U.N. is an international legal person. As a subject of international law, the U.N. possesses international rights and duties, including the capacity to maintain its rights by bringing claims. Members have clothed the United Nations with the international legal personality necessary to carry out its duties.

The second issue concerned whether the U.N. had the right to bring a claim against a state to obtain reparation for injuries suffered by a U.N. agent while on duty. The Court again answered affirmatively, as its members have endowed it with the capacity to bring international claims when necessitated by the discharge of functions. Such a claim would result from a breach by a member of its international obligations. The measure of reparations should depend upon the amount of damage that the organization suffered.

A third issue considered whether the United Nations could bring a claim for damage to the victim. The court found this to be an implied right under the principle of functional necessity. The traditional rule that diplomatic protection is exercised by the national state does not involve the giving of a negative answer to the question. The rule rests on two bases. First, the defendant has breached an obligation toward the national state in respect of its nationals. Second, only the party to whom an international obligation is due can bring a claim in respect of its breach. Here, the question presupposes that the injury from which the reparation is demanded arises from a breach of an obligation designed to help the agent in performance of his duties.

A fourth issue asked who has superior right of diplomatic protection: the U.N., or the State. The court said that both could bring an action. The U.N. could bring an action against the state even if the defendant state is also the state of nationality.

INDIVIDUALS

Nottebohm (Liechtenstein v. Guatemala), 1955 I.C.J. 4

Liechtenstein claimed that Guatemala violated international law by arresting, detaining, expelling and refusing to readmit Frederich Nottebohm, and in seizing and retaining his property. Liechtenstein requested that Guatemala pay compensation for the harm it caused him. Guatemala asserted that Liechtenstein could not defend Nottebohm, as it was not the proper state of nationality and there was no genuine link between the two.

Under international law, nationality is a legal bond having as its basis a social fact of attachment, a genuine connection of existence, interests and sentiments, together with the existence of reciprocal rights and duties. States can only exercise juridical protection over a claimed national if the naturalization was based on juridical facts.

The I.C.J. determined there were not genuine links between Nottebohm and Liechtenstein. Nottebohm and Liechtenstein had tenuous connections. Nottebohm had no settled abode there. He had no continuous residence. The only reason he went to Liechtenstein in 1946 was because Guatemala refused to readmit him. His only real link to Liechtenstein was his brother who had lived there since 1931.

United States ex rel. Schwarzkopf v. Uhl, 137 F.2d 898 (2d Cir. 1943)

After the German Reich annexed Austria, it conferred German citizenship on all Austrian citizens by a decree dated July 3, 1938. By a subsequent German executive order on November 25, 1938, the Reich deprived Jews residing abroad of German citizenship and subjected their property to confiscation.

The United States government considered the German takeover of Austria to be illegal. The Second Circuit noted, "under generally accepted principles of international law Germany could impose citizenship by

238

annexation (collective naturalization) only on those who were inhabitants of Austria in 1938." The new nationality could only be conferred on or made eligible for election to those inhabitants who remained in the territory. The court concluded that the new allegiance was not transferred to inhabitants who voluntarily departed before the annexation and never elected to accept the sovereignty of the new government.

The court observed former nationals of an invaded country had the right to flee and establish a residence abroad. They could elect a new nationality and remain stateless until they had acquired it. While Paul Schwarzkopf may no longer be Austrian, since his country did not exist during the German takeover, he was not German either. Thus, he could not be retained as an enemy alien in the United States.

U.S. v. Smith, 18 U.S. 153, 158 (1820)

The Court noted the general practice of all states was to punish "all persons, whether natives or foreigners, who have committed this offence against any persons whatsoever." Article 1, section 8, clause 10 of the United States Constitution grants Congress the power to "define and punish Piracies and Felonies committed on the high Seas, and Offences against the Law of Nations." In the eighth section of the act of Congress of 1790, ch. 9, Congress subsequently deemed piracy as "robbery and murder committed on the high seas." Thomas Smith was convicted of committing piracy on the high seas against a Spanish vessel.

Filartiga v. Pena-Irala, 630 F.2d 876 (2d Cir. 1980)

The Second Circuit held that it possessed jurisdiction over Americo Norberto Pena-Irala, who was accused of kidnapping and torturing to death Joelito Filartiga. Dr. Joel Filartiga, Joelito's father, brought the action in New York, after his daughter discovered Pena living in Brooklyn. The Immigration and Naturalization Service arrested Pena and the Filartigas served him with a summons. All parties were citizens of Paraguay and the action took place in Paraguay. The U.S. Alien Tort Statute provides original jurisdiction over an alien for a tort committed in violation of the law of nations or a treaty of the United States. The Second Circuit said, "[F]or purposes of civil liability, the torturer has become like the pirate and slave trader before him *hostis humani generis*, an enemy of all mankind."

U.S. v. Calley, U.S. Court of Military Appeals, No. 28,875 (Dec. 21, 1973)

During the Vietnam War, First Lieutenant Calley, a U.S. national, claimed that his troops were ordered "to kill every living thing-men, women, children, and animals-and under no circumstances were they to leave any Vietnamese behind them as they passed through the villages en route to their final objective." Calley and another soldier opened fire on unarmed old men, women, and children in My Lai. When a few children remained standing, Calley personally shot them. He then came upon a group of 75 to 100 Vietnamese civilians and killed them as well. While there was contradictory testimony as to whether such an order was ever issued, the court found that an order to kill unarmed civilians would be illegal. The court stated, "For 100 years, it has been a settled rule of American law that even in war the summary killing of an enemy, who has submitted to, and is under, effective physical control, is murder." The court affirmed Calley's conviction of the premeditated murder of not less than 22 Vietnamese civilians and of assault with intent to murder a Vietnamese child.

U.S. v. Alvarez-Machain, 504 U.S. 655 (1992)

U.S. Drug Enforcement Administration (D.E.A.) agents arranged the kidnapping of Dr. Humberto Alvarez-Machain from his office in Guadalajara, Mexico. The D.E.A. agents hired Mexican nationals to transport him to El Paso, Texas, where he was transferred to Los Angeles to stand trial for participating in the alleged torture and killing of D.E.A. agent Enrique Camareno-Salazar. Dr. Alvarez-Machain challenged the jurisdiction of U.S. courts, claiming that he was brought to the United States in violation of the U.S.-Mexico extradition treaty.

The U.S. Supreme Court declared that the U.S.-Mexico extradition treaty did not deprive U.S. courts of jurisdiction because the treaty was silent on the issue of kidnapping. Since the treaty did not forbid kidnapping, it was permissible. The Court acknowledged that while the kidnapping may violate international law, it did not deprive U.S. courts of jurisdiction to try Dr. Alvarez-Machain.

Sosa v. Alvarez-Machain, 124 S.Ct. 2739 (2004)

Dr. Alvarez-Machain sued José Francisco Sosa, Antonio Garate-Bustamante, five unnamed Mexican citizens, the United States government, and four D.E.A. agents, seeking damages against the United States for false arrest under the Federal Tort Claims Act (F.T.C.A). He sued Sosa and other individuals for participating in his kidnapping under the Alien Tort Statute (A.T.S.)

The F.T.C.A. permits individuals to sue the U.S. government for personal injury caused by the negligent or wrongful act or omission of any government employee while acting within the scope of his office or employment. Pursuant to the A.T.S., U.S. district courts are given original jurisdiction over any civil action by an alien for a tort committed in violation of the law of nations or a treaty of the United States.

The U.S. Supreme Court ruled that Dr. Alvarez-Machain was not entitled to a remedy under either the F.T.C.A. or the A.T.S. The Supreme Court determined that the U.S. had not waived immunity from suit, and that the A.T.S. did not apply to this type of violation.

The Mavrommatis Palestine Concessions case, 1924 P.C.I.J., Ser. A, No. 2

The Permanent Court of International Justice declared that an injury to a national becomes an injury to the state. The state is protecting its own rights. According to the P.C.I.J., the dispute enters the domain of international law as "a dispute between two States." The P.C.I.J. also said

241

in this case, "It is an elementary principle of international law that a State is entitled to protect its subjects, when injured by acts contrary to international law by another State, from whom they have been unable to obtain satisfaction through the ordinary channels."

INTERNATIONAL JURISDICTION, CONFLICTS, AND IMMUNITIES

International Jurisdiction

The Nuclear Tests Cases (Australia v. France), 1974 I.C.J. 253, and **(New Zealand v. France)**, 1974 I.C.J. 45

In both these cases, France failed to appear to discuss their atmospheric testing near Australia and New Zealand. After the cases were filed, the French Minister said, "We have now reached a stage in our nuclear technology that makes it possible for us to continue our program by underground testing, and we have taken steps to do so as early as next year."

While the Australian Attorney-General believed this statement fell short of a commitment to no longer conduct atmospheric testing, the I.C.J. disagreed. The Court stated, "It is well recognized that declarations made by way of unilateral acts, concerning legal or factual situations, may have the effect of creating legal obligations." In this instance, the I.C.J. found that France had created a legal obligation of a binding character that it had a good faith obligation to observe. Thus, the I.C.J. found that the dispute had disappeared as France had already given Australia what it sought. The I.C.J. reached the same conclusion in Nuclear Test Case (New Zealand v. France), 1974 I.C.J. 457. Since the I.C.J. viewed that the objective of Australia and New Zealand was to terminate all tests, it found no reason to continue the cases as the objective had been accomplished.

Blackmer v. U.S, 284 U.S. 421, 52 S.Ct. 252, 76 L.Ed. 375 (1932)

The U.S. Supreme Court determined that the U.S. had jurisdiction over a citizen while he lived in France. Although residing in a foreign country, the court found that Mr. Blackmer remained "personally bound to take notice of the laws that are applicable to him and to obey them." This included a subpoena requiring him to appear as a witness on behalf of the United States in a criminal trial.

American Banana Co. v. United Fruit Co., 213 U.S. 347, 29 S.Ct. 511, 53 L.Ed. 826 (1909)

Writing for the Supreme Court, Justice Holmes stated, "[T]he general and almost universal rule is that the character of an act as lawful or unlawful must be determined wholly by the law of the country where the act is done." Here, the acts took place in Panama and Costa Rica, and Justice Holmes concluded that the U.S. lacked jurisdiction to criminalize acts within those countries.

U.S. v. Aluminum Co. of America, 148 F.2d 416 (2d Cir. 1945)

The Second Circuit considered whether two agreements between foreign companies violated U.S. laws. The 1931 agreement created an alliance between a French corporation, two German corporations, a Swiss corporation, a British corporation, and Aluminum Ltd., a Canadian corporation. The agreement called for the formation of a Swiss corporation to issue shares and fix quota on production. In 1936, the parties agreed to include imports into the United States.

The Second Circuit held that the 1936 agreement violated Sec. 1 of the Sherman Act, which prohibits contracts in restraint of trade. Congress can attach liability to conduct of aliens because states may impose liabilities for conduct outside their borders that has consequences within their borders. This liability is only for conduct that produces consequences within the states, regardless of intent.

243

Case Concerning the S.S. Lotus (Turkey v. France), 1927 P.C.I.J. Ser. A., No. 9

In this case, a collision took place on the high seas between a French steamer, the S.S. Lotus, and a Turkish steamer, the Boz-Kourt. The Turkish boat sunk, taking with it eight Turkish citizens. When the French ship reached Constantinople, the Turkish authorities instituted criminal proceedings against Lt. Demons.

France argued that international law recognizes the exclusive jurisdiction of the state whose flag is flown as regarding everything which occurs on board a ship on the high seas. The I.C.J. rejected this argument, finding that the state receiving effects from an offense can regard the offense as having been committed within its territory and it can prosecute the delinquent individual. Here, there were two ships, flying different flags, and consequently two different states had jurisdiction.

Turkey possessed passive personality jurisdiction over Lt. Demons, a French citizen, because his actions caused death to Turkish citizens and harm to a Turkish flag vessel. Turkey's passive personality jurisdiction arose because Demons was legally responsible to Turkey's nationals.

Conflicts

In re Union Carbide Corp. Gas Plant Disaster, 809 F.2d 195 (2d Cir. 1987)

This case arose after a gas plant disaster in India caused the deaths of over 2,000 Indian citizens and injuries to over 200,000 after exposure to a lethal gas known as methyl isocyanate. The government of India sought to keep the case in the U.S. where the law was more favorable to its position and would yield higher damages. However, the Second Circuit concluded that the district court's finding that Indian courts provided an adequate alternative forum could not be labeled as clearly erroneous or an abuse of discretion. The district court had determined India to be the proper forum because, among other things, the relevant evidence was there; the Indian judiciary was developed, independent, and progressive; and the Indian tort law was suitable to resolve legal issues involving complex technology.

London Films Productions Ltd. v. Intercontinental Communications, Inc., 580 F.Supp. 47 (S.D.N.Y. 1984)

A British corporation sued a New York corporation in the United States for infringement of British copyrights that occurred in Chile and other South American countries. London Films alleged that Intercontinental was showing its motion pictures on television in South America. Intercontinental sought to dismiss the suit, claiming the court lacked jurisdiction. The wrongdoings did not violate U.S. law. The court determined that it possessed jurisdiction over whether an American corporation had acted in violation of a foreign copyright. The court noted that it was the only forum in which the defendant is the subject of personal jurisdiction. The court concluded that where "the balance does not tip strongly in favor of an alternative forum it is well-established that the plaintiff's choice of forum should not be disturbed."

Absolute Theory of Sovereign Immunity

The Schooner Exchange v. McFaddon, 11 U.S. (7 Cranch) 116, 3 LEd. 287 (1812)

While peacefully sailing to Spain, the Schooner Exchange ship was seized on December 30, 1810 by Napoleon, Emperor of France and Italy. When the Schooner Exchange subsequently became distressed during bad weather on the high seas, it entered U.S. ports seeking refreshment and repairs. The original owners sought the return of their ship in court, claiming that the ship was their private vessel and not the public vessel of Napoleon. The district court dismissed the case with cost, finding the ship immune and not subject to U.S. jurisdiction. The circuit court reversed.

245

The U.S. Supreme Court reversed the circuit court and affirmed the district court opinion's that a public armed ship, in the service of a friendly foreign sovereign, was exempt from U.S. jurisdiction. The Court proclaimed that national ships of friendly nations enjoy the same immunity from arrest and detention as does the sovereign and foreign ministers.

Restrictive Theory of Sovereign Immunity

Texas Trading & Mill Corp. v. Nigeria, 647 F.2d 200 (2d Cir. 1981)
This case illustrates the restrictive theory of sovereign immunity. Nigeria entered into 109 contracts with 68 suppliers to purchase 16 million metric tons of Portland cement, worth approximately a billion dollars. Nigeria planned to use the cement for infrastructure construction. When Nigeria's docks and harbors became clogged with ships waiting to unload cement, Nigeria unilaterally changed the terms of its letter of credit contracts requiring ships to convey to the Port Authority information concerning time of arrival two months ahead of time. It subsequently repudiated numerous contracts, and asked suppliers to settle. Many did; however, four American suppliers chose to sue Nigeria in federal district court. In three of the cases, the district judge found jurisdiction and in one case the district court found jurisdiction lacking. The four cases were consolidated on appeal to determine whether Nigeria could invoke sovereign immunity to escape liability for breaching its contracts.

The Second Circuit found that Nigeria engaged in commercial activity when it entered into contracts and acquired letters of credit to purchase the cement. The Foreign Sovereign Immunities Act defines commercial activity as "a regular course of commercial conduct or a particular commercial transaction or act. The commercial character of an activity shall be determined by reference to the nature of the course of conduct or particular transaction or act, rather than by references to its purpose." Under this section, Nigeria could not use its intent to construct public infrastructure to escape liability. The restrictive theory of sovereign

246

immunity permitted U.S. courts to exercise jurisdiction over Nigeria and the cases could proceed.

Act of State Doctrine

Underhill v. Hernandez, 168 U.S. 250, 252 (1897)

The Supreme Court stated, "Every sovereign state is bound to respect the independence of every other sovereign state, and the courts of one country will not sit in judgment on the acts of the government of another done within its own territory." The Court concluded that it could not adjudicate the acts of the defendant, which were imputable to the government of Venezuela, even if those acts harmed the American citizen who brought the lawsuit.

Banco Nacional De Cuba v. Sabbatino, 376 U.S. 398 (1964)

An American commodity broker complained about Cuban Law No. 851, which gave the Cuban President and Prime Minister discretionary power to nationalize, by forced expropriation, property or enterprises in which American nationals had an interest. The Cuban President and Prime Minister proceeded to nationalize the rights and interests of American companies, including those of the plaintiffs. Even if the U.S. State Department proclaimed the action a violation of international law, the Court said, "However offensive to the public policy of this country and its constituent States an expropriation of this kind may be, we concluded that both the national interest and progress toward the goal of establishing the rule of law among nations are best served by maintaining intact the act of state doctrine in this realm of its application."

W.S. Kirkpatrick & Co. v. Environmental Tectonics Corp. International, 493 U.S. 400, 410 (1990)

In this case, foreign officials possessed an unlawful motivation in the performance of their official acts. The officials sought to obtain bribes or commissions equal to 20% of the contract price. The U.S. Supreme Court noted, "All parties agreed that Nigerian law prohibits both the payment and the receipt of bribes in connection with the award of a government contract." Thus, U.S. courts could exercise jurisdiction over the dispute because the Act of State Doctrine has no application where "the validity of no foreign sovereign act is at issue."

Diplomatic and Consular Immunity

Case Concerning the United States Diplomatic and Consular Staff in Tehran (United States v. Iran), 1980 I.C.J. 3

This case arose from the 1979 Iranian Hostage crisis when Iranian students took over the U.S. embassy on November 4, 1979. For over three hours, embassy personnel called Iranian authorities seeking help. Iran did not send security forces to protect the embassy, nor did it rescue the hostages or persuade the students to terminate their actions. Twenty-eight hostages were diplomats, and four were members of the Consular Section of the Embassy.

After the U.S. sued Iran in the I.C.J., Iran contested jurisdiction. The Court found that the optional protocols to the Vienna Conventions on Diplomatic Relations and Consular Relations provided jurisdiction. Both countries were signatories of the treaties and their optional protocols concerning dispute resolution.

Once jurisdictional issues were resolved, Iran elected not to appear in the merits phase. While the Court noted the difficulty of discerning facts when there is a missing party, it observed that much about the dispute between the two parties was public information. The Court then used information in the news to determine Iran's concerns.

The Court considered whether Iran violated the two Vienna Conventions. The initiation of the embassy attacks could not be imputed to Iran. These were private acts by students. However, Iran was responsible for its own conduct. As the receiving state, it had a responsibility to ensure the protection of the U.S. Embassy and Consulates, their staffs, the archives, their means of communication, and the staff's freedom of movement. As the receiving state, Iran failed to protect the inviolability of the diplomats, archives, and documents. Iran was also held to have violated the Vienna Convention on Consular Relations and ordered to restore the Consulates at Tabriz and Shiraz to the U.S. government.

Case Concerning Avena and Other Mexican Nationals (Mexico v. United States), 2004 I.C.J. 1

On January 9, 2003, Mexico sued the United States for violating the Vienna Convention on Consular Relations. It based jurisdiction on the same optional protocol the U.S. used to sue Iran. Mexico charged that the U.S. had arrested, detained, tried, convicted and sentenced 54 Mexican nationals to death in violation of its international obligations to Mexico. Specifically, Mexico claimed that the U.S. had violated Articles 5 and 36 of the Convention. Article 5 indicates the sending state shall have right to protect its nationals, both individuals and corporate bodies. Article 36 addresses communication and contact with nationals of the sending state. This article gives the sending state the right to be informed when its nationals are arrested, committed to prison, or detained in any manner. The U.S. government denied that it owed such obligations to dual nationals.

The I.C.J. ruled that the U.S. had to prove which individuals were also dual nationals with the United States to support its claim. Mexico presented birth certificates and declarations from 42 individuals stating that they never acquired U.S. nationality to prove the individuals were solely Mexican.

The I.C.J. found three separate rights under Article 36. First, the Mexican nationals should have been informed, without delay, of their right under Article 36 to contact their Consulate. This duty arose once the U.S. authorities knew the person was a foreign national or had reason to think so. The Court recommended that the U.S. routinely inquire about nationality at the time of arrest, as when reading suspects their "Miranda" rights. Second, the Mexican consular post should have been notified, without delay, of the Mexican citizens' detention if they requested such notification. Third, as the receiving state, the U.S. was obliged to forward, without delay, any communication addressed to the consular post by the detained person. The I.C.J. concluded that the U.S. was in breach of its obligations to Mexico.

INTERNATIONAL DISPUTE SETTLEMENT

The Rainbow Warrior (France v. New Zealand), 26 I.L.M. 1346 (U.N. Secretary General Ruling: 1987)

France and New Zealand asked Secretary-General Javier de Perez de Cuellar from Peru to mediate their dispute that arose after two French agents sank the Rainbow Warrior, a vessel belonging to Greenpeace International, while in the Auckland, New Zealand harbor on 10 July 1985. The explosion caused the death of crewmember Fernando Pereira, a Netherlands citizen. New Zealand interviewed, arrested, and charged Major Alain Mafart and Captain Dominique Prieur with manslaughter and willful damage to a ship. After they plead guilty to manslaughter, the New Zealand Chief Justice sentenced them to 10 years in prison.

France and New Zealand attempted to negotiate their differences, but failed to reach a solution. They both formally approached the Secretary-General in June 1986 for a ruling. In his ruling, the Secretary-General set forth the facts, the violation of international law by France, and the international legal responsibility of the French government. He then ordered France to apologize to New Zealand for violating its sovereignty and its rights under international law, to pay no less than $7 million U.S. to New Zealand for the harm caused, and to release the two French agents to France to be immediately transferred to a French military facility in the isolated island of Hao in French Polynesia to serve three years. The Secretary-General's ruling further required France to give New Zealand reports on their situation every three months. Should any other differences arise, the Secretary-General ruled that either government could request binding arbitration.

The Western Sahara Case, Advisory Opinion of 16 October 1975, 1975 I.C.J. 12

The Western Sahara case came to the International Court of Justice as a request for an advisory opinion by the General Assembly. To resolve a dispute over legal ties to the Western Sahara, the General Assembly requested answers to two questions. First, was the Western Sahara (Río de Oro and Sakiet El Hamra) at the time of colonization by Spain a territory belonging to no one (*terra nullius*)? And, second, if the answer to the first question was in the negative, what were the legal ties between the territory and the Kingdom of Morocco and the Mauritanian entity?

After reviewing the history of the Western Sahara, the I.C.J. concluded that it was not *terra nullius* when colonized by Spain. In 1884, a country through "occupation" could legally acquire sovereignty over territory if the territory belonged to no one. However, if tribes and peoples having a social and political organization inhabited the territory, then it was considered occupied. Nomadic peoples organized into tribes occupied the Western Sahara. The territory, which forms part of the Saharan desert, is characterized by low and spasmodic rainfall. The nomads grazed their animals or grew crops where they found favorable conditions. They traversed the desert on more or less regular routes dictated by the seasons and the wells and water holes available to them. These nomadic routes passed through some of southern Morocco, present day Mauritania, Algeria, and other states.

As to the second question on the legal ties between this territory and the Kingdom of Morocco and the Mauritanian entity, the I.C.J. concluded that there were legal ties between the Western Sahara and both the Kingdom of Morocco and the Mauritanian entity. The court stressed the need for a referendum to let the peoples of the Western Sahara decide their fate.

251

INTERNATIONAL RIGHTS AND RESPONSIBILITIES

Case Concerning the Barcelona Traction, Light and Power Co., Ltd., (Belgium v. Spain) 1970 I.C.J. 3

The I.C.J. considered whether Belgium could sue on behalf of its nationals, who were shareholders of a Canadian corporation, which was injured by an organ of the Spanish Government. The company was incorporated in 1911 with the mission to create and develop electric power in Catalonia, Spain. The Canadian corporation was a holding company with wholly owned subsidiaries, several of which were incorporated in Spain. The Belgium citizens had purchased most of their stock in Barcelona Traction after World War I. They constituted 88% of the shareholders.

The problem arose after Barcelona Traction suspended the servicing of its corporate bonds during the Spanish Civil War. When servicing resumed after the war, the Spanish government prohibited the transfer of the foreign currency necessary for the servicing of the pound sterling bonds. A Spanish court subsequently declared the company bankrupt because it could not pay interest on its bonds. Its assets were seized and liquidated. The company protested the bankruptcy and seizure, as did the Canadian, British, United States, and Belgium governments.

The I.C.J. rejected Belgium's claim to represent Barcelona Traction. Because Belgium could not pierce the corporate veil, it could not protect its shareholders. Only Canada, as the nationality state of the corporation, could offer diplomatic protection. The type of claim that Belgium asserted required an injury, like all claims other than *erga omnes* obligations or *jus cogens* norms, before a state could claim a breach of an international obligation.

252

THE LAWS OF WAR AND USE OF FORCE

Legality of the Threat or Use of Nuclear Weapons (1994-1996), Advisory Opinion of 8 July 1996, 1996 I.C.J. 226

The General Assembly asked the Court to ascertain the international legality of the threat or use of nuclear weapons. The Court determined that there was neither customary nor conventional international law that authorized the threat or use of nuclear weapons. Further, it found that a threat or use of force by means of nuclear weapons would be contrary to Article 2(4) of the United Nations Charter. Finally, in a tie vote, with the President of the Court casting the deciding vote, the Court said it could not conclude definitively whether the threat or use of nuclear weapons would be lawful or unlawful in an extreme circumstance of self-defense, in which the very survival of a State would be at stake.

TABLE OF CASES

References are to section numbers

INDEX

References are to section numbers

Z